The Life of Fiction

JEROME KLINKOWITZ

THE LIFE OF FICTION

with graphics by
ROY R BEHRENS

University of Illinois Press
Urbana Chicago London

Library of Congress Cataloging in Publication Data

Klinkowitz, Jerome.
  The life of fiction.

    1. American fiction — 20th century — History and
criticism. I. Behrens, Roy R., 1946-   II. Title.
PS379.K549   813   77-22271
ISBN 0-252-00643-7

For Jonathan and Nina,
and to Bob Dorr and Michael Johnson,
for the music

I could sing you a song about the happier days
   but the happier days ain't here
String you along in a million ways
   but only the lies would be clear
You need something to believe in right or wrong
You would sell your soul tomorrow for a song

—Michael Johnson

What else is sacred? Oh, Romeo and Juliet,
for instance.
   And all music is.

—Kurt Vonnegut, Jr.

CONTENTS

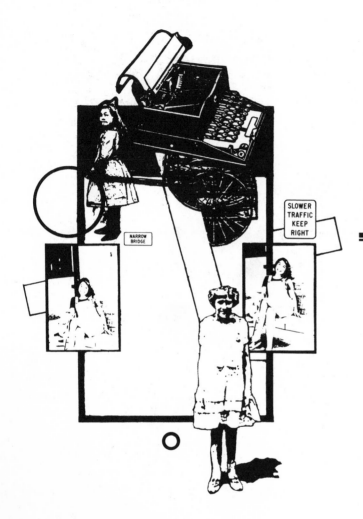

PROLOGUE: THE LIFE OF FICTION

Literary critics name things, as if the act of naming makes something one's own:

THE REVOLUTION AND EARLY REPUBLIC	NEOCLASSIC
THE TRANSCENDENTALISTS	ROMANTIC
THE REALISTS & NATURALISTS	VICTORIAN
THE MODERNS	MODERN

Therefore:

If Pound and Eliot and Joyce are the Moderns . . . . .Hugh Kenner
And if Beckett and those who follow are the Post-Moderns . . . . .Ihab Hassan
Then what are we to do with the writers who are as distant from Beckett as Beckett is from Joyce?

*

There are many good writers who are found to accept the Post-Modern avant-garde.
Critics have little trouble finding places for John Barth
                            Thomas Pynchon
                            John Hawkes and
                            Vladimir Nabokov
                                      in the continuum.

But for the fiction of William Carlos Williams ⎫
                   Kenneth Patchen   ⎪
                   Anaïs Nin   } **for example**
                   Douglas Woolf   ⎪
                   Paul Metcalf   ⎭
              and Gil Orlovitz a critical continuum seems not to exist.

Their fiction has, at best, been called the counterpart to the distinctly American strain of poetry running from Whitman through Williams to Charles Olson and Allen Ginsberg and Frank O'Hara. But Williams's own fiction never had the same hearing, while during the Forties and Fifties and Sixties the novels of Patchen, Nin, Woolf, Metcalf, and Orlovitz remained on the periphery, if not completely underground.

The fiction of Williams & Co. may have bypassed the Post-Modern revolt entirely.

Can one play a critical shell-game in which the poetry of Williams and Patchen becomes the analog for an unrecognized new fiction? The result would be relative at best and casuistic at worst.

But there is a style of fiction very much above ground which defies the Post-Modernist label. Its well known writers are
Kurt Vonnegut, Jr.
Donald Barthelme
Ishmael Reed and
Hunter S. Thompson.
Its emerging figures include: Ronald Sukenick
        Gilbert Sorrentino
        Michael Stephens
        Clarence Major
        Walter Abish
        Russell Banks
        Steve Katz
        Jonathan Baumbach and many others.

   Vonnegut & Co. are living writers. The substance of their writing is widely available not only in their fiction, but also in their commentary, reviews, interviews, letters, phone calls, and personal adventures. If the critic lives their lives of fiction, he may play their music as his own. He may improvise on their melodies, add his own new tunes to the chordal structure of their works, and even make admiring quotations, the way a jazzman wailing on the changes of Nat Adderley's "Work Song" might drop a coy reference to Bobby Timmon's "Moanin."
   As Frank O'Hara might say (think of his "Personism: A Manifesto"), there is no room here for abstraction. Living the life of fiction puts the work squarely between the critic and the reader. One faces the act of fiction itself. And as Frank O'Hara might say (modestly), it could be the death of criticism as we've known it. But such a highly personal response seems to be what this new fiction calls for. There are several reasons why:

1. To the newer fictionists, Beckett is as traditional as Joyce.

Michael Roloff, in his postscript to Peter Handke's *The Innerworld of the Outerworld of the Inner World* (New York: Seabury Press, 1974), talks about these very same conditions in which Handke grew. It is possible that the Austrian Handke shares with his American contemporaries what Roloff calls the "by now traditional animadversion to the dominant literary tradition of the time. Which meant that this aversion, this ennui with the once used, this compulsion to find ever new personally and historically appropriate ways of expression would eventually result, as indeed it has in Handke's case, in a turning against these avant-garde origins and traditions too, without—and this should perhaps be self-evident—a reversion to the dominant tradition against which he had initially revolted."

2

How, then, does one begin a critique? By talking of the Post-Post-Modern? By considering the Death of the Death of the Novel? Or the Death of the Death of the Death of the Novel, exponentially to infinity? By replacing that useless term "Contemporary" with the pranksterish "Post-Contemporary"?

2. The fiction we're discussing bypasses the Post-Modern "gnosis" in favor of an imaginative confrontation with the outside world.

It does not bypass life, as lived in the world's historical construct, in favor of pure "mind." It does not fit the description which Ihab Hassan in *Paracriticisms* (Urbana: University of Illinois Press, 1975) finds appropriate for the Post-Modern: "There is a new gnosticism taking hold of our age, a new insistence of mind to apprehend reality immediately and gather more and more mind in itself, a new suspicion of matter, of culture, and even of language insofar as it derives not from the pure *logos* but from historical circumstance." Alain Arias-Misson, who coined the term "SuperFiction" to describe his own work, writes from Belgium: "We are branching onto a current anyway, wherever the source of the real is. I have read one remarkable thing in all these magazines [picked up on a visit to New York's Gotham Book Mart]: Walter Abish's 'model' account of a visit to Austria and your real interview of him [*Fiction International* #4/5, 1975]—not another posturing interview. This is SuperFiction: the language-model. I also read an essay by Ihab Hassan which draws I think exactly the wrong conclusion: the new fiction as gnosis. Mentalism: that was the starting point as fiction was released from its moorings. And it is no doubt true of much of the new [Post-Modern] fiction. But like any dialectical movement (a new 'real') the new fiction must anchor itself—or be imbedded—in its medium, in a fresh fluent reality-relation. A new language/reality ratio; the dialectical shift takes place within the relation to the left of course. . . . I would like to get in touch with Walter Abish—could you give me his address?"

And so the life of fiction proceeds, with writers of similar interests drawn to one another regardless of the critical names. Arias-Misson meets Walter Abish, who a year before was introduced to Raymond Federman. Federman, who in turn had sought a meeting with Ronald Sukenick even earlier. Sukenick, who in 1962 had described (in his Brandeis doctoral dissertation) just how the artist uses his writing to establish the fresh language/reality ratio that Arias-Misson seeks. "When, through the imagination, the ego manages to reconcile reality with its own needs," Sukenick wrote, "the formerly insipid landscape is infused with the ego's emotion; and reality, since it now seems intensely relevant to the ego, suddenly seems more real." Mind is involved, but in the manner of the human imagination enriching matter, culture, and the language of historical circumstance. Sukenick's novels contain healthy doses of all three, as we shall see. The result is fiction at its full power energizing a world which by that very act becomes more interesting, relevant, and real. That's why the term "SuperFiction" is appropriate. To make a distinctly anti-Post-Modern, indigenously American metaphor, drawn right from historical circumstance: it's like what a supercharger does to a hot Chevy engine. Or what a phase shifter does to a Fender guitar. Or what twelve ounces of Miller beer does when it chases your shot of brandy, while the jukebox belts out Eric Clapton and the parking lot fills up with Formula Firebirds and turbo-charged Camaros.

3. The fiction we're discussing is peculiarly American.

It defies the academic influence which has favored fiction echoing older European models. To paraphrase a casual conversation with Steve Katz: it is as if John Barth and Thomas Pynchon, good writers who are easily accepted within the Post-Modern model, are forever apologizing for not being Europeans. For Pynchon especially, it's as if he were a young American composer who chooses for his instrument the Wagnerian grand opera rather than the Fender guitars and Moog synthesizers of his colleagues.

Other references to note:
—Kurt Vonnegut, Jr., describing his major influences as American comedians of the Thirties and Forties, and American jazz music.

—Donald Barthelme's allegiance to American comedy, rock music, and jazz.
—Ishmael Reed's argument that innovative black writing (the Neo Hoo Doo aesthetic) joins jazz and rock music, the Westerns, comic books, and detective novels as indigenous American art.
—Raymond Federman's immersion in the American Experience, as his fictional style and even as his very mode of life.

Hence: the life of fiction, a distinctly American life which chooses to ignore the European-based critical distinctions, but which forms an allegiance with younger Europeans such as Peter Handke and Alain Arias-Misson who revolt against their own academy: the academy of the Post-Modern avant-garde.

4. The writers we're discussing are out to create a good time.

Larry McCaffery sends his comments on "A Masque: In Praise of SuperFiction," as presented at the Center for Twentieth Century Studies, University of Wisconsin-Milwaukee, in their November 1973 conference, which also included Raymond Federman, Ronald Sukenick, Gilbert Sorrentino, and William H. Gass: "One specific comment you make which I like a lot is on page eight: 'The real issue is having aesthetic freedom for fiction, which is what makes it SuperFiction; the only test is to see what the SuperFictionist does with it.' "

The freedom that McCaffery mentions is used to exploit as many features of books and words and print as possible. Behind it all is the power of the imagination: McCaffery adds the reminder that "The writer shares with God the unique ability to make his imagination substantial."

Why is Post-Modernist criticism of writers like Federman inappropriate? Because the Post-Modernist critics inevitably spend more time with abstractions than with the writing itself. "Federman," McCaffery insists, "seems out to create a GOOD TIME for his readers—and I'm not sure that an imitation of an essay by Barth is the best way to deal with Federman."

In the Fall 1976 issue of *Boundary 2,* McCaffery formalizes these thoughts. "In most cases critics will only deal with writers whose formal and thematic concerns can be easily assimilated and explained in terms of the already existing literary systems of values." Hence the easy identifications for Barth and Pynchon. But McCaffery continues: "American writers such as Barthelme, Coover, Sukenick, Federman, Katz, Brautigan . . . and Ishmael Reed seem to share a playful, often highly sexual exuberance which sharply contrasts with the drier, more technical and serious (let's admit it: more boring) experiment of the European Post-Modernists (Sartre and Camus, the French New Novelists, the new-New novels of Sollers, LeClezio, Pinget, and so on)."

5. There are too many salient features which collectively set this fiction a world apart from what has gone before:

—it is expressive and not descriptive (as opposed to the Post-Modern *Nouveau Roman*), and sometimes generative (Sukenick)
—it uses the reader's imagination as a part of the action; just as jazz demands participatory listening, this writing asks for participatory reading (see especially Clarence Major's *Reflex and Bone Structure,* which has the reader participate in the ratiocination of the detective novel)
—it is both self-reflective and self-reflexive, respectively making the conditions under which one writes the subject of one's writing (a Post-Modern technique), but also using the writer's own self-created personalist mythology (see especially Kurt Vonnegut, Jr., and Hunter S. Thompson) as the very substance of one's approach to the world. We have, then, the life of fiction as invention, as artifact (again, Sukenick)
—it restores the act of reading to its original pleasure status: not as an academic exercise, but as a valid equivalent for the films and television and art and music which come into our lives
And that is as abstract as one dares get. One must thank:
—the writers who wrote these works and lived these lives of fiction

—the editors who first published some of these critical pieces, and who have granted permission to rewrite the material into book form:

Thomas Joyce and Timothy Erwin/*Chicago Review*
Charles Newman and Elliott Anderson/*TriQuarterly*
Joe David Bellamy/*Fiction International*
William Lawson/*Yardbird Reader #4*
Civia Cohen and Al Walavich/*Oyez Review*
James Dean Young/*Critique*
Robley C. Wilson, Jr./*North American Review*
Richard Kostelanetz and Henry James Korn/*Assembling*
André Le Vot/*Revue Française d'Etudes Americaines*

—Thomas Joyce, formerly of *Chicago Review,* for evaluating and critiquing the entire manuscript
—the hundred-odd writers and critics who offered suggestions on the abbreviated version of this book which circulated in *samisdat* fashion
—the University of Northern Iowa, its students, and its Committee on Research and Curriculum Development, who supported this work in all phases of its development
—the Miller Brewing Company of Milwaukee, Wisconsin, and the Paul Butterfield Blues Band, for assistance too comprehensive to list.

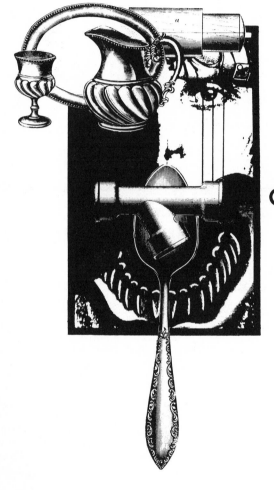

Chapter One

Jack O'Brien had been in New York, winding up the field work for his dissertation, *Interviews with Black Writers* (eventually published as such by Liveright in 1973). His initial reading of LeRoi Jones/Imamu Amiri Baraka had led him to younger writers whom we were both discovering: Charles Wright, Alice Walker, Clarence Major, and others who eventually filled his book. From DeKalb, Illinois, we hustled publishers for review copies, spent our pocket money on rare editions saved only by the specialty book dealers, and finished out the summer of 1971 as an assistant professor and a graduate teaching assistant who'd convinced ourselves that we were more on top of new fiction than anyone else between Bayonne, New Jersey, and Modesto, California.

The last thing likely to hold our interest would be a middle-aged, late-phase beatnik poet dating from Baraka's early days in New York. But all these hip young black writers kept telling Jack, "You've got to get in touch with Gilbert Sorrentino." Nothing in our past or present graduate school training had prepared us for this self-taught, raging, authoritative New York "figure": holding forth from his apartment in the subsidized-for-artists Westbeth, just a block and a half down from the famous White Horse Tavern on Hudson Street (which, we had all been told, Dylan Thomas made his home in America). O'Brien came back from his November meeting with Sorrentino highly enthusiastic but slightly unnerved. "He looks like a disciplinarian in a Catholic boys' high school," Jack reported. Though only forty-some years old, Sorrentino had taken on the role of an Angry Old Man, having spent his youth in the rapture of lower New York, when groups centered around Allen Ginsberg and LeRoi Jones and Joel Oppenheimer and Frank O'Hara and the Abstract Expressionists reigned supreme; when Sorrentino's group was given its own magazine, *Kulchur;* when the East Village was still a place where ethnic minorities and true artists—not panhandling WASP flower children—lived lives as yet uncomplicated by the distractions of the New Politics, Pop Art, and the commercialization of the youth/underground.

Sorrentino established his reputation in the late Fifties and early Sixties as a poet, and was nominally linked with the Black Mountain Group. As a fiction writer (since 1966) he sees himself as extending the tradition of William Carlos Williams, William Burroughs, Robert Creeley, Douglas Woolf, Hubert Selby, LeRoi Jones, Irving Rosenthal, and Russell Edson. An equally long list of younger writers views Sorrentino as a model, among them Michael Stephens, Clarence

Major, and Steve Katz. Sorrentino's own major influence is the lyric change in the language of poets who followed Williams; among these, Sorrentino's favorite seems to be Jack Spicer.

For most of a decade Sorrentino lived at the center of a literary and artistic group which has long since disbanded, its collective and sometimes even personal identities lost to time. His third novel, *Imaginative Qualities of Actual Things,* playfully satirizes these figures, but beneath the fun is a deep dissatisfaction with coterie life. Since writing the novel Sorrentino has kept pretty much to himself, despite his "rediscovery" in the mid-Seventies by such literary journals as *Chicago Review, Partisan Review, TriQuarterly,* and *New Directions.* His admonition for those who hear writers and painters beginning to talk: "Walk the other way."

GILBERT SORRENTINO

I. THE DEATH OF THE DEATH OF THE NOVEL

Tape

A suspiciously simple sense of life it is that is, in any one man, conclusive. Oh, for him—*of course; but for this world I wonder, or rather think it is only in the relationships men manage, that they live at all. People try with an increasing despair to live, and to come to something, some place, or some person. They want an island in which the world will be at last a place circumscribed by visible horizons. This island is, finally, not real, however tangible it once seemed to me. I have found that time, even if it will not offer much more than a place to die in, nonetheless carries one on, away from this or any other island. The people, too, are gone.*

[splice]

So there is left this other area, still the short story or really the tale, and all that can be made of it. Whereas the novel is a continuum, of necessity, chapter to chapter, the story can escape some of that obligation, and function exactly in terms of whatever emotion best can serve it.

The story has no time finally. Or it hasn't here. Its shape, if form can be so thought of, is a sphere, an egg of obdurate kind. The only possible reason for its existence is that it has, in itself, the fact of reality and the

pressure. There, in short, is its form—no matter how random and broken that will seem. The old assumptions of beginning and end—those very neat assertions—have fallen away completely in a place where the only actuality is life, the only end (never realized) death, and the only value, what love can manage.

Tape ends

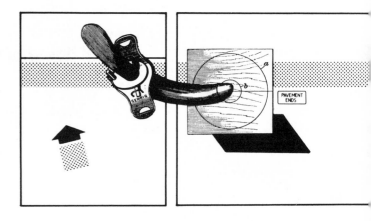

"The Death of the Death of the Novel" sounds poetic. Ronald Sukenick tried to stop all this idiocy when he titled his fiction collection *The Death of the Novel and Other Stories.* And other stories. What's your story? So maybe the poets can get us out of this: nobody has expected a "story" from poetry since the nineteenth century. Those guys have the marvelous freedom, granted every artist except the novelist, to tell something else besides real life stories. So Robert Creeley takes time off and writes fiction—the first tapes were the prefaces from his novel, *The Island,* and his collection of shorter pieces, *The Gold Diggers.* And now Gilbert Sorrentino is writing fiction, too. Does he think the two forms spill over into one another?

Tape

They're married. They're absolutely married. The whole sense of language, the conception, the syntax, my attempt to destroy metaphor, simile, and allegory. American poetry is one of the most elegant and formal arts in the world. Perhaps only painting and music can compare to it.

[splice]

The concept that language must convey information is a concept that poets long ago abandoned. Novelists continually grapple with that; they have to hold your attention by fleshing out an idea. Poems don't have ideas. Poems are artifacts, like sculpture.

Tape ends

Sorrentino is a veteran poet (b. 1929, five books of poetry from Jonathan Williams, Totem, Norton, and Black Sparrow) who began publishing fiction at just about the time when critics were announcing its demise. *The Sky Changes* (New York: Hill & Wang, 1966), *Steelwork* (New York: Pantheon, 1970), *Imaginative Qualities of Actual Things* (New York: Pantheon, 1971), *Splendide-Hôtel* (New York: New Directions, 1973), and his massive work in progress—sections of which have appeared in issues of *Chicago Review* (Winter 1973 and Winter 1975), *Partisan Review* (Winter and Spring 1975), *TriQuarterly* (Fall 1975), *New Directions* (#30, 1975), *Vort* (#6, 1974), and *Seems* (#6/7, 1975), plus the volume *Flawless Play Restored: Or, the Masque of Fungo* (Los Angeles: Black Sparrow, 1974)—are examples of the novel's renaissance, as it turns from an attempt to capture life through belief-suspending conventions back toward the truths which those conventions slight. In this respect his fiction bears resemblances to Creeley's theory, just as their poetry showed mutual influences for a while when the two writers emerged in the Fifties.

Tape

The one thing that bothers me a little is that it took me ten years before I was able to shed my "connection," if you will, with Creeley's work, and there are many people who thought and still think that my work is an imitation of Creeley's. Not to go into a great song and dance about it, but in the late Fifties I saw in Creeley's forms a way into poetry that seemed useful to me, and I utilized them until the early Sixties, when they no longer seemed relevant to the directions in which my own poetry was going. Since that time my work in both prose and poetry has had very little to do with Creeley's work. We are now *very different writers and hold, on the published evidence, dissimilar views of writing. Creeley is an analytic writer, although it may not always seem so: taking a whole and breaking it down into parts; while I proceed by means of synthesis: putting pieces together. Anyway, though Creeley was present in my earlier poetry, he is no longer, and he has never been apparent in my prose.*

Tape ends

The major affinity is that Sorrentino sees time as the enemy too, and seeks the same actuality beyond it, but one significant way in which he departs from Creeley is that he won't abandon the novel (for the short fiction) to do it. Revealing images are well expressed in shorter forms, but life is large, its truths are larger still, and it would be a shame to sacrifice the novel's great scope simply because its methods have been abused. "In the mind there is a continual play of obscure images which coming between the eyes and their prey seem pictures on the screen at the movies," Sorrentino quotes from William Carlos Williams as the epigraph to *Imaginative Qualities*. "The wish would be to see not floating visions of unknown purport but the imaginative qualities of actual things." To keep hold of these qualities within the novel's broad expanse is Sorrentino's aim.

II. THE MAN WHO HATES HIS STORY

"The shape of the gesture, the form of it"—that is what Gilbert Sorrentino announced he was after in his last collection of poems, Black & White. *The responsibility of forms continues to be his preoccupation in fiction, the way in which an art becomes accountable for a life which is otherwise merely lived or eluded (journalism or fantasy). And though every writer, as Robbe-Grillet has recently pointed out, believes he is a realist, there is, for all the accurate reporting here—"the Midwest is made up of police and drive-ins"; or, in a more intimate mode, "he locked the door of his roomette, took a slug of the bourbon, lit a cigarette, and began to read the* New Yorker*"—an austere dedication, on this novelist's part, to all the devices of art he can get his hands on, all the methods which will allow him by imagery, rhythm and narrative distortion to conjugate an observed physical environment with an inner weather felt by the characters.*

[splice]

The achievement of this novel [The Sky Changes] *is that it accounts for process; it tells us by a cunningly administered dose of images, in an intermittent but containing rhythm, how the mind gets from one place to another, and literally in what* space of time *the transformation occurs. Think of Donne's words, "This minute I was well, and am ill, this minute. I am surprised with a sodaine change, and alteration to worse, and can impute it to no cause, nor call it by any name." That is how most of us account—or fail to account—for the disasters of our lives, while it has been Sorrentino's peculiar care to embody, to articulate, to make metaphors which will accommodate chaos.*

Tape ends

His best reviews have come from poets, in this case Richard Howard. Sorrentino mystifies the conventional novelists and short-sighted critics of same: his work has characters who refuse to be drawn, action which will not be resolved, and a theme which resists statement—instead, his novels are rich in the materials of life which will not let themselves be perverted into the mistruths of conventional signals, those instructions to the reader which lead to a presupposed meaning and hence obscure the writer's truth. Sorrentino tells us constantly that it is all made up, that his truth resides not in some moral we draw from the life he has imitated but in his invention before us on the page.

Tape

Bunny Lewis, Christian name Joanne, née Joanne Ward. This is going to be a tough one, because there is something of the archetypal about her. Which is to say, what I have in my hands here is a cliché—before I start. This will not relieve me of the necessity of presenting this woman to you, of course. I could leave her out of the book, but there is much of interest here, she at least will illuminate something of our friend Guy . . .

She was born in a little town in New Jersey named Boonton. I know this town, it's very grim. It will be better to have her born in a Long Island town, for our purposes, which will soon become dazzlingly clear. Frightfully clear. So, she's in Long Island, you can pick your town, let's put her on the North Shore. Her mother was the kind of woman who served all her meals off unmatched tableware. "Each piece chosen separately, and with love." You know what I mean. . . .

Tape ends

Throughout *Imaginative Qualities* the author comes at us, raging at the restraints of his art yet breaking them hilariously at will. God save the character he comes to dislike. *It's only a story,* he keeps reminding us, to counter fiction's congenital defect of its illusion becoming real.

No art can succeed when it is willingly mistaken for reality. In the *New American Review* #13 Sorrentino's story, "The Moon in Its Flight," becomes in formal terms a carefully plotted exercise in literary hysteria, as the author tries to guide his characters through a romance in the historically lost year of 1948, all the time knowing how conventional fiction invites itself to be misread. "Isn't there anyone," he pleads, "any magazine writer or avant-garde filmmaker, any lover of life or dedicated optimist out there who will move them toward a cottage, already closed for the season, in whose split log exterior they will find an unlocked door? Inside there will be a bed, whiskey, and electric heater. Or better, a fireplace, white lamps, soft lights. Sweet music." Or, "All you modern lovers, freed by Mick Jagger and the orgasm, give them, for Christ's sake, for an hour, the use of your really terrific little apartment. They won't smoke your marijuana nor disturb your Indiana graphics. They won't borrow your Fanon or Cleaver or Barthelme or Vonnegut. They'll make the bed before they leave. They whisper good night and dance in the dark." But all that is impossible, for on the page "This was in America, in 1948. Not even fake art or the wearisome tricks of movies can assist them." Even worse, fears the narrator, how can the contemporary reader of his paperback magazine piece appreciate the meaning of this constructed world? "Who remembers the clarity of Claude Thornhill and Sarah Vaughan, their exquisite irrelevance? They are gone where the useless chrome doughnuts on the Buick's hood have gone." The value of the popular song, Sorrentino argues, is that it deals in superficialities that release the emotions. Scratch the veneer of those pedestrian lyrics, he goes on, and you look into a crystal ball of the past. "She was crying and stroking his hair. Ah God, the leaves of brown came tumbling down, remember?"

Tape

To discover, after 7 years, that he doesn't know her, his wife. And money available, to leave with, to go to Mexico? And why not, to face her there, break out of that cocoon that he has carefully wrapped himself in, the mummy. To look at his children, free, images of them brown and the sun hard-edged on them, chiseled out of sunlight.

Perhaps again to find her, have her come to him again, once, in the night, turn quietly toward him in the bed, and not in desperation, nor out of pity, God. To be able to say again "I love you" and not with his tongue full of dust, filth of the words, the lie, and her lie returned. . . .

Tape ends

The protagonist of Sorrentino's first novel, *The Sky Changes,* would "hide from the time that crushes him," taking the cross-country trip "to repair an event, a congeries of events, with the useless aid of space." But there is no change; "He had left a stable misery, a possible misery, to find the same misery on the road," mistaking the occasional peace and joy he finds from time to time "with a peace that he could only have made solid through his own manufacture, his own mind." He assumes that "the future would be a constant spiral upward, upward, until, in Mexico, they would all find themselves perfectly happy, perfectly reconciled. . . . And how he wanted to salvage his life." But they never reach Mexico, and there is no reconciliation.

Time would thwart him, the conquerer, but instead space oppresses them. The Midwest is made up of police and drive-ins, the South of stone Confederate soldiers who stare with the same eyes as the Mississippi state troopers. Las Vegas is still more appalling, for there is "at each end of the town, blackness, death, the howling wind off the Mojave bringing tons of red dust into the streets." Even the Southwest threatens with "a treacherous sort of cold, flat and primeval as the earth, a being of enormous power and one which held sway along with the space it filled." And nowhere is there an answer. "Wherever they drive, in whatever direction (now toward the south), they seem to head into clouds, into rain, as if even the weather is trying to tell him that the whole thing is stupid. The one thing he did not really know is that it would be stupid. He expected nothing in particular to change on the road, but he did not expect it to be stupid."

The protagonist's answer, and Sorrentino's meaning, will not be found in the linear structure. Such familiar signals of fiction obscure the writer's truth, or, as Sorrentino says in his essay on William Carlos Williams's fiction (*NAR #15*), "allow the writer to slip out from under the problems that only confrontation with his materials can solve." That the separation comes at the end of the line does not imply that the truth resides there; although *The Sky Changes* establishes a chronology, it does not hesitate to jump ahead and back in "the story" if that is where meaning leads, and the last section (all of which are set up in travel-note form) comes not in the separation at the end of the road, in San Francisco, but back several weeks and several hundred miles.

Tape

Albuquerque, New Mexico

Before making the move to Taos, he and the driver and M drove to Albuquerque to get a used refrigerator from a man well set up in business there. He was a heroin addict, but wealthy, and so his habit interfered with nothing, his wife was an alcoholic, spending her life in bed, propped up on pillows reading mystery novels and drinking a couple of fifths of brandy a day. They got the refrigerator on the trailer and went back in to have a drink before they started the long trip back to Santa Fe. The man sat in the living-room, his eyes clouded, smiling secretly. His wife weaved around the room unsteadily, making a pitcher of Martinis, getting ice and whisky, laying out cheeses and crackers. They sat in the *twilight, fast moving into the room, great rhomboid of crimson sunlight fixed on the wall behind the man and his wife, who now sat together, hand in hand. He was eating eclairs and drinking coffee and she gulped at her Martini, then poured another. There was a momentary lull in the conversation, and he gazed at the couple. They were looking at the three guests, smiling, their eyes calm and blank, their fingers intertwined. They sat, decorous and serene, staring into the gentle sunlight, blunted, secure from each other, and from everything else.*

Tape ends

From GHOST SHIPS (Steelwork)

They were to be destroyed as targets by the Navy. They were to be repaired and used as ferry boats. They were to be sunk as breakwaters up at Hell Gate. They were to rot forever.

The rats were bigger than dogs and could chew your arm off. They'd killed at least two kids who went swimming years ago. They spoke in tongues. The gypsies caught them and ate them. They were what they made bubble gum from, and glue. They came on shore all together once every ten years. Don't go near the water's edge at night. At full moon.

. . . .

There were men, alive, in the neighborhood, married, with children, who had been scheduled to sail into death on these ships. They didn't know who they were. At sunset they would glow red in the last pink rays from Jersey. Ghosts and rats.

End of imaginative possibilities

For the imaginative qualities in *Steelwork,* his second novel, Sorrentino draws upon the imaginative substance of childhood and adolescence. The book is a spatial portrait of a South Brooklyn neighborhood during 1935–51. The subject is change, and the book's form comes to terms with this fact, grasped imaginatively. But foremost is the sense of loss, the feeling of missing an empty lot or of seeing one where something used to be: "They walked slowly to Triangle Park, past the new extension on the Cities Service lot, the holy coalbox gone, past the new A & P on the old tennis court, past the new Baptist church, the doorway right where they used to roast mickeys." Although they are dated, the sections are not arranged in chronological order, for, as in *The Sky Changes,* true emotion follows space more accurately than time. Hence the book ends not in 1951, when the neighborhood has been destroyed, but on a cold night back in 1939, when the protagonist, roasting mickeys in the park eroded by highway construction, has a sense of what is to happen.

Tape

"They are all gone into the world of light."

Tape ends

Imaginative Qualities of Actual Things is Sorrentino's most fully realized expression of the novelist's proper role. Throughout he fights against the poor writing and misguided aesthetic that characterizes so much of recent conventional fiction. "These people aren't real. I'm making them up as I go along, any section that threatens to flesh them out, or make them 'walk off the page,' will be excised. They should, rather, walk into the page, and break up, disappear: the subtlest tone or aroma (no cracks, please) is all that should be left of them. I want you to remember this book the way you remember a drawing." Most of all, he tells the reader, "you don't need to know anything—see a movie," or "If you're interested in the kind of bag Dick would carry, check it in O'Hara—he'll tell you unerringly." As for what happens to his characters in time, "it is all mixed up, how can I tell you what I don't really know?" Sorrentino's aesthetic for fiction is different: "In this book, I'll muddle around, flashes, glints, are what I want. It's when one is not staring that art works. In the middle of all the lists and facts, all the lies and borrowings, there will sometimes be a perfect revelation. These curious essences. The shape and weight of a sentence that lances you." These are the heart of Sorrentino's fiction, "because these things themselves are the plot. They carry all the meaning. Isolate flecks."

People, real life characters, will not obey the author. But his prose will, and that's where Sorrentino rivets his meaning. As for anything else—hair color, luggage style, who's really sleeping with whom—Sorrentino could care less. "In other words, the reader is asked to write the book that I have no interest in writing."

The irony, and success, of Sorrentino's method is that in the process of his anti-illusionistic, self-consciously artistic writing, brilliantly conceived persons, places, and things are brought before the reader's eyes. Especially when he dislikes a character, Sorrentino's prose is superb. "I've got some stories to tell you about this lame," he begins a chapter on Anton Harley, "they'll make you throw tacks and broken glass in front of his bike." Sorrentino hates him so much that "I'll do my best to make him totally unbelievable," and therefore he will be one of Sorrentino's best-drawn people. "Greed was Anton's problem," we learn, and what's interesting is not how he got that way, but how he looks now, "let's say with three cheeseburgers in each hand." He visits friends in the evening, and soon "becomes distracted, passes his hand through his hair. Anton hungry is like a heroin addict who is just feeling the beginnings of junk need. He must eat. He *must* eat! HE MUST EAT! Eat, eat, eat, eat!! His eyes glaze over just a little. If you're a woman, close your legs. Or open them, if that's your pleasure. Anton eats anything. But there was nothing to give him. And, you will recall that I said his host had not cashed his paycheck. An interesting situation. Let's observe Anton in action here." His friends will not play baseball with him for fear "that he might eat the bats." Later, at a party, we see Anton in the corner, eating paper napkins. Sparked by his hate for this purely literary character, Sorrentino runs him through scene after scene to his detriment, and the result is wonderful, unexhausted fiction.

Tape

With one hand, Anton is reading Serenade, *with the other, he is pushing three slices of pizza into his mouth, there is pizza all over the floor, and from the looks of things, it seems as if Anton has been—fucking—some of the pizza. There is a banging from the bathroom, and muffled shouts. That is his latest girl, whom he has locked in so that she can't share any of the pie. He'll let her out soon and let her eat the pizza that he came over, if she wants it.*

Tape ends

A CAPSULE REVIEW

SPLENDIDE-HÔTEL by Gilbert Sorrentino. New Directions, 61 pp., $3.25; limited signed specially bound edition, $25.

Every picture tells a story. So can pieces of music, sculpture, practically anything made by the imagination. But only fiction must tell a story, and be critically exhausted by an explication of its narrative facts. Of all the arts the novel alone is subjected to so close a comparison with the serial aspects of life, which is patently unfair.

Gilbert Sorrentino's Splendide-Hôtel shows that the novel can transcend the story, that it may exist outside the world it pretends to deal with. Passing life, the easiest structure for fiction, can become a form so self-effacing that the sense of art may disappear entirely. So that a day in the life—or a slice of it—may not become the work itself, Sorrentino chooses a fully artificial structure, the twenty-six letters of the alphabet. Like baseball, his novel seeks play and virtuosity within defined limits: "The excellent pitcher mixes up his deliveries, all of which, however, travel sixty feet, six inches." And again like baseball, "It does not stand for anything else. It exists outside of metaphor and symbol" (Malamud, Coover, and Roth to the contrary). For Sorrentino it remains a "Shaped and polished artifact, a game of—nouns and verbs."

Although he has three other novels to his credit, Sorrentino remains best known as a poet, impressed and influenced by William Carlos Williams and, in our own day, Jack Spicer. "The poet is not an interpreter but a revealer," he has written of Spicer; things do not connect, they "correspond," and he shows in Splendide-Hôtel that "that minuscule flash, that occasion, has more value than the most staggering evasion by explanation of the real. Who will believe it?" Sorrentino's aesthetic is built around language itself, "divorced from the image" and disavowing objective connections as well as subjective, since he will not allow his egoism to impose a lie on what is "true chaos." Beware those who do. Motion exists to be frozen, time to be stopped. "One would almost think that in this peace there is some sort of truth."

The proper artist: through the employment of the imagination he lays bare the mundane. "The writer," we learn, "wishes to make this sense exact, or why bother? Precise registrations are beautiful, indeed. The popular novelist deals with feathery edges, one gets a 'tone.' One gets a 'feeling,' " but at worst it degenerates into a "story." "I know a writer," Sorrentino continues, "who wished his prose to be transparent so that only the growth of his story would be in evidence. What I mean by 'story' I leave up to you. Perhaps it is the story the unemployed auto worker tells his friend over red beer. The juke box is playing 'Your Cheating Heart,' another story. . . . The story ends with a quiet grace and one of the men gets up, spits phlegm on the floor, and plays Hank Williams again. They are totally unaware that they are in fashion." What these guys tell are real-life stories, the kind that prompt reviewers to say the paranovelist "has created a character who can stand alongside Raskolnikov, Flem Snopes, and Yossarian. He lives, he breathes, he walks off the pages!" Sorrentino keeps us on the pages, as a painter keeps us on the canvas, to have us sense "Movement of the line, its quantity, the shifting of the vowels, the A's breeding in decay." There are phrases that will change your life: by Lester Young, and by novelists like Gilbert Sorrentino.

14

Splendide-Hôtel will not retell in second-order terms a story about another reality. It is, as the author once wrote of Hubert Selby's work, something made—"it won't go away, a new thing has been made and placed in the world." Sorrentino's work stands for itself, and is also rich in the materials of life which will not allow themselves to be perverted into the mistruths of conventional "novelistic" signals, those instructions to the reader which lead to a presupposed meaning and thus obscure the writer's truth. Gilbert Sorrentino's fiction succeeds because its method controls its substance (instead of the other way around), which for all the forms of art is surprising only in the novel. A study not of things that happen but of how things happen to happen, his work avoids the bland business of parahistorical recording and is instead representational of the imaginative qualities of actual things, of the totally artificial place where meanings reside.

End of capsule review

Tape

The novel must exist outside of the life it deals with; it is not an imitation. The novel is an invention, something that is made; it is not the expression of "self"; it does not mirror reality. If it is any good at all it mirrors the process of the real, but, being selective, makes a form that allows us to see these processes with clarity. Signals in novels obscure the actual—these signals are disguised as conversation, physiognomy, clothing, accoutrements, possessions, social graces—they satisfy the desire that we be told what we already know, they enable the writer to manipulate the book so that it seems as if life has form and meaning, while it is, of course, the writer who has given it these qualities.

It is the novel, of itself, that must have form, and if it be honestly made we find, not the meaning of life, but a revelation of its actuality. We are not told what to think, but are instead directed to an essence, the observation of which leads to the freeing of our own imagination and to our arrival at the only "truth" fiction possesses. The flash, the instant or cluster of meaning must be extrapolated from "the pageless actual" and presented in its imaginative qualities. The achievement of this makes a novel which is art: the rest is pastime.

End of tape

The time of life and the time of art are two distinct realities: only when imitation is governed by imagination, and not vice versa, does fiction have the relevancy of art. Sorrentino's work is in this sense progressive. Within the letters of the alphabet used as forms of pure invention are situations, narrative explorations more ambitious than the solitary perception, fictions which in their cumulative effect address the scope of life. And again, the meanings are found in the imaginative qualities of actual things. For the letter P, the revealing memory of a photograph is contrasted with a piece of bad art on the same subject. "Seeing the painting again after locating the snapshot, I find it poorer than ever. The spurious function that it originally served has been wiped out, having been replaced by the absolute vector of the past." Which has been invented, of course, by the imagination, the better artist in this case and usually for all times.

Tape

Art cannot rescue anybody from anything.

End of Tape.

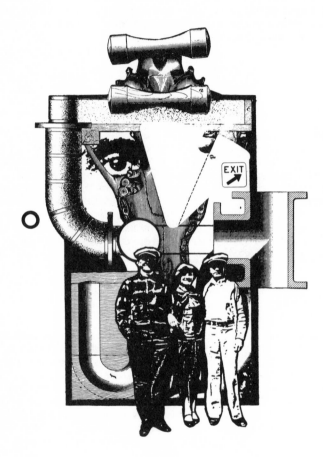

Chapter Two

Ronald Sukenick's first novel, *Up*, appeared in 1968, a year after his doctoral dissertation, ***Wallace Stevens: Musing the Obscure***, was published by the New York University Press. By 1970, when *Up* came out in an attractive Delta paperback edition, Sukenick was well known as an academic figure. Or rather as an anti-academic, since his Stevens book had been trounced by the more staid scholarly journals and his novel had found a loyal readership among the ranks of disaffected instructors and assistant professors who saw it as the ***Bildungsroman*** of their young professional lives.

Sukenick is the ultimately self-reflective and self-reflexive novelist, since his books are largely about themselves and he's the major character in each. But this self-created self confronts a very recognizable world, and a survey of Sukenick's works, beginning even with the Stevens dissertation, shows the experience of a human imagination within a definite historical construct: America of the Sixties and Seventies.

With his high critical profile and familiar, comfortable subject matter, Sukenick became the bridge to the new fiction for young scholars trained in the rigors of Modernism but confused by Post-Modern abstractions. His fiction boasts a sexual exuberance reflected in the times, and a comic approach to life quite welcome after the seriousness of his predecessors. His books parody themselves not with the heavy irony of Barth and Pynchon, but with a playfulness which indicates a strong self-confidence as well as self-consciousness; Sukenick's literature believes in its own reality. With his talk of the procreative powers of the imagination and the generative (as opposed to imitative, expressive, or illuminative) role of fiction, he seems to be formulating fiction's complement to Frank O'Hara's Personism in poetry. "William Gass talks about fiction as an addition to reality, and Gilbert Sorrentino talks about fiction as invention," Sukenick wrote in the Winter 1976 issue of ***Partisan Review***. "Both of these terms I would characterize as having to do with art as generation," but to them Sukenick adds the idea of fiction being neither a model of the world (Gass) nor a mirror of the process of the real (Sorrentino), but the incorporation of present experience (and one's imaginative reaction to it) "at the same level of other data."

In the Seventies Sukenick has emerged as the major critical spokesman for the style of fiction he shares with such writers as Barthelme, Major, and Katz. He was one of the founding members of the Fiction Collective, whose aim has been to print the innovative fiction which commercial publishers have come to shun; after several years on committees of the Coordinating Council of Literary Magazines, he assumed its chairmanship in 1975. His seemingly constant travels have brought him into contact with virtually every writer of this style in America today, and led him to speculate that under these conditions a portable salon was being created in the form of hotel-lobby conversations, barroom discussions, and hurried exchanges at airport ticket counters. From such meetings and dialogues have resulted his commentaries on Federman, Gass, and Sorrentino. As with so many of the newer writers, Sukenick's life seems indistinguishable from his fiction—except that his writing is an obvious imaginative refinement. Yet his historical life is ever present: from the young Dr. Sukenick of *Up*, whose contract will probably be renewed if registration doesn't drop second semester, to the drop-out California dreamer of *98.6*, thinking up the perfect life and making it his latest book.

RONALD SUKENICK

I. FICTION STRANGER THAN FACT

Tape

Fiction constitutes a way of looking at the world. Therefore I will begin by considering how the world looks in what I think we may now begin to call the contemporary post-realistic novel. Realistic fiction presupposed chronological time as the medium of a plotted narrative, an irreducible individual psyche as the subject of its characterization, and, above all, the ultimate, concrete reality of things as the object and rationale of its description. In the world of post-realism, however, all of these absolutes have become absolutely problematic.

The contemporary writer—the writer who is acutely in touch with the life of which he is a part—is forced to start from scratch: Reality doesn't exist, time doesn't exist, personality doesn't exist. God was the omniscient author, but he died; now no one knows the plot, and since our reality lacks the sanction of a creator, there's no guarantee as to the authenticity of the received version. Time is reduced to presence, the content of a series of discontinuous moments. Time is no longer purposive, and so there is no destiny, only chance. Reality is, simply, our experience, and objectivity is, of course, an illusion. Personality, after passing through a phase of awkward self-consciousness, has become, quite minimally, a mere locus for our experience. In view of these annihilations, it should be no surprise that literature, also, does not exist—how could it? There is only reading and writing, which are things we do, like eating and making love, to pass the time, ways of maintaining a considered boredom in the face of the abyss.

Not to mention a series of overwhelming social dislocations.

Tape ends

Ronald Sukenick: b., Brooklyn, 1932; B.A., Cornell; Ph.D., Brandeis [dissertation: "A Wallace Stevens Handbook," 1962]. Nonfiction: *Wallace Stevens: Musing the Obscure* (New York: New York University Press, 1967). Fiction: *Up* (New York: Dial Press, 1968); *The Death of the Novel and Other Stories* (New York: Dial Press, 1969); *Out* (Chicago: Swallow Press, 1973); *98.6* (New York: Fiction Collective, 1975); "The Endless Short Story," continuing parts of which have appeared in the *Village Voice* for 9/6/73, 9/13/73, and 2/21/74, in *Lillabulero* #14 (Spring 1974), and in the Fiction Collective's anthology, *Statements* (1975). Commentary: in the *Village Voice, New York Times Book Review, New York Review of Books, Chicago Review, Partisan Review, Fiction International,* and *New Literary History*.

Instruction A: Guess (or check it out) whether the above tape of Sukenick comes from his
1. Nonfiction
2. Fiction
3. Commentary
4. Doctoral dissertation

Instruction B: Why?

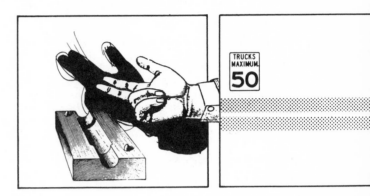

Tape

Leave it here.
Not my stuff says Trixie.
Throw it in the U-Haul says Harrold. Cover me while I go downstairs says Trixie. He opens the door steps into the hall flattens himself against the wall the bulb is out on the landing go on he says I'm watching. She runs for it down the stairs past the plasterpeeled walls around large cracks in the floor past the sign that says this hall is a bomb shelter to the super's apartment she knocks at the door.
Who.
Trixie quick.
The door opens a crack then wider. I can't let anybody in here you know that shid they take everything you got says Jojo.
Jojo can you help us take our things down to the U-Haul.

Whatsa matter you movin.
No we're just taking our things down to the U-Haul.
Shid man you smart man they take everything you got man. You know that man up in 4A they even take his bed they clean him out. An he's a junkie too man you know what him and his friends done man they steal all the copper pipes in the place next door then they go down an take all the brass fittings off the furnace so they ain't got no

heat or hot water in the whole building man somebody oughta call the cops on that guy.
Did you.
Nah he's a friend of mine come in for a beer.
I can't Harrold is upstairs we've got to get the things down.
I say come in for a beer split a joint you got time what the hell. He your boyfriend.

I can't he's waiting we have to move the things.
Okay look what I'll do I watch the U-Haul you don't have to worry about it okay.
Trixie and Harrold start moving the stuff down. When Trixie goes down the stairs Harrold covers her when Harrold goes down the stairs Trixie covers him Jojo takes the stuff from the stoop to the U-Haul they work hard and steady then Harrold comes down to lock the U-Haul.

Hey somebody rob your U-Haul says Jojo.
What do you mean.
There's nothin in there man them guys are smart I don know how they done it I was watchin alla time.
Where's Trixie I thought she was down here.
She your girlfriend man she's a terrific piece of ass.
Where is she in your place.
She ain't in my place come on back an take a look they

go back to Jojo's apartment.
See what I mean I tell you man.
Where is she.
Don ask me she aint my girlfriend. I bet she's a terrific lay.
Don't get smart let's check the street they go back outside the U-Haul is gone. So is the car hauling it. What the fuck says Harrold.

Maybe the girl took it says Jojo she can't drive says Harrold.
Maybe she found a driver what a you care man them U-Haul people got insurance.
How am I going to move says Harrold.
Where you movin to.
Brooklyn.
So it's simple you catch the BMT at Union Square now

you got nothin to carry you're all set.

Tape ends

More about that, and some more of that, later.

Tape

One of the reasons people have lost faith in the novel is that they don't believe it tells the truth anymore, which is another way of saying that they don't believe in the convention of the novel. They pick up a novel and they know it's make-believe. So, who needs it—go listen to the television news, right? Or read a biography.

Tape ends

Those are the three voices of Ronald Sukenick. The last is commentary (with Joe David Bellamy in the *Chicago Review*), the middle was part of his novel *Out*, and the first was—not his dissertation, not his criticism, not even his class notes from Brandeis, CCNY, Sarah Lawrence, California-Irvine, or a few other places he's taught, but the opening words of his *story*, "The Death of the Novel," from his *The Death of the Novel and Other Stories*.

His criticism actually reads much easier, although it's addressed to the same point. We find the *solution* stated near the beginning of *Wallace Stevens: Musing the Obscure*.

Tape

With what tenable attitude may one confront the difficult circumstances of contemporary American secular life [splice: "Reality doesn't exist . . . Time is reduced to presence . . . Reality is, simply, our experience. . . ."] and avail oneself of the good possible in it? How, in short, does one get along? Writing poetry was for Stevens a way of getting along. He must be taken seriously when he says that he writes poetry because he needs to (Opus Posthumous, p. xxxvii). The act of composition was for him a way of discovering and crystallizing what he called in one of his last poems, "Local Objects," the "objects of insight, the integrations/Of feeling. . . ."

Tape ends

Sukenick's work argues for the life of fiction; he's so good at it that the publishers should give him a medal or something. And he's right when he notes that the public despairs of the old novel, that shabby document which pretended to tell real-life stories about real-life people, but always with tight little beginnings, middles, and ends, offering morals, lessons for conduct, and an eminently ordered universe. Maybe that's why people kill each other so often, Kurt Vonnegut, Jr., has suggested—they are imitating story books, and homicide is a convenient device for ending a story. It misses the whole idea for the existence of fiction at all:

Tape

The great advantage of fiction over history, journalism, or any other supposedly "factual" kind of writing is that it is an expressive medium. It transmits feeling, energy, excitement. Television can give us the news, fiction can best express our response to the news. No other medium—especially not film—can so well deal with our strongest and often most intimate responses to the large and small facts of our daily lives. No other medium, in other words, can so well keep track of the reality of our experience. [splice to Bellamy's interview] Okay, if you could forget that business about illusion, you'd be more honest. Nobody is willing to suspend disbelief in that particular way, including me. So once you get to the point where you admit that you are writing a book and it is a book, there really is no difference between fantasy and realistic action. It's completely continuous—it's all made up.

Tape ends

II. MAKING IT UP

Two-thirds of the way though his novel *Up*, Sukenick (who is a character of the same name in the book) takes his manuscript so far and shows it to one of his characters. No tape here, this is old-fashioned explication:

"Seriously, it doesn't go anywhere. I mean I'm not so antediluvian to require that a novel have a plot, but this is just a collection of disjointed fragments. You don't get anywhere at all. Where's the control, where's the tension? You can do a lot better than this Ronnie."

"Thanks," I said.

"For one thing, the chronology is completely screwed up. First you start going out with Nancy again. Then you tell Slim you've broken up with her. Then you tell Slade you're living with her. Then you tell Otis she's moved out. Then the next time she appears she's living with you. I mean what the hell is going on? When are you going with her and when did you break up?"

"Well you know maybe we broke up and reconciled several times. It's a very stormy relationship after all."

"But this is just the thing you see. The reader doesn't know this. You can't do that sort of thing."

"Why not? In books one isn't obliged to pursue the banality of chronological order. What the fuck I'm not writing a timetable."

"You could at the very least indicate an underlying chronology."

"What for? It's just a sequence of words. The only thing that matters is the order of revelation in print."

"Sure. If you want to forego verisimilitude, which unfortunately happens to be the essence of fictive writing."

"Nuts. Why should we have to suspend disbelief? It's all words and nothing but words. Are we children reading fairy tales or men trying to work out the essentials of our fate?"

"All right, look, it's one thing to be honest with the reader and another to play tricks on him. What about the Cloisters for example? You're driving up to the Cloisters with Finch to meet Slade and his girl, and that's the last we hear about it."

"Well I lost that scene actually."

"How do you mean?"

"I wrote a long elaborate Cloisters scene and then I left it in a book I returned to the library. I tried lost and found, everything, but I couldn't get it back."

For two centuries schools of novelists and critics have debated where "reality," the proper realm for the novel, lies: in the panoramic, objective exterior, or in the introspective, subjective inside. Realism versus Romanticism, Accuracy versus the Deeper Truth. Sukenick would resolve this battle by settling for the realest thing at hand: the book itself, so much print on so many pages, put there by a self-responsible artist. His characters are not so real that they "walk off the pages." Instead they stay right there, on the pages, as figures remain on the canvas, so it might be appreciated as art and not life. What the reader reads is an honest account of the artist's work, and what the artist presents is a piece of genuine fabrication and craftsmanship, his *imaginative* response to a world we share. Not the shabby lie that this is the world itself.

The work is then judged not for what it represents, but for what it is itself.

For Sukenick the relationship between the artist and the world is complex in theory, but impressively effective in practice. " 'That's what Wordsworth is talking about,' " his character Sukenick argues in *Up*. " 'He tells how as a kid he had to grab hold of a wall to make sure the world was really there, but when he grew up the dead weight of reality almost crushed the sense of his own existence. It's when the world seems oppressive, dead, or to put it another way, unreal, that I get the feeling I'm walking around like a zombie.' " For such occasions art is not the discovery of reality, but " 'The Invention of reality. . . . Art seeks a vital connection with the world that, to stay alive, must be constantly reinvented to correspond with our truest feelings.' "

Tape

At the heart of this interchange between the ego and reality is the effect of the imagination in bringing the two into vital relation. I suspect that this is not merely a point of theory for Stevens but rather an intensely real experience upon which the theory was constructed. Faced with the depressing prospect of a reality that seems dull, plain, and irrelevant to the needs of the ego, the

*poet comes to feel that the world in which he lives is thin and insubstantial, so remote from his concerns that feeling he is part of it "is an exertion that declines" (*Opus Posthumous*, p. 96). When, through the imagination, the ego manages to reconcile reality with its own needs, the formerly insipid landscape is infused with the ego's emotion; and reality, since it now seems intensely relevant to the ego, suddenly seems more real.*

· · · ·

The mind orders reality not by imposing ideas on it but by discovering significant relationships within it, as the artist abstracts and composes the elements of reality in significant integrations that are works of art.

Tape ends

A CRITICAL DIGRESSION

Appreciated in this way, the novel is a spatial entity. When linear time, the single perspective, and even words themselves cannot express the full human vision of experience, spatial form can. "In a very real sense, the meanings of a novel constructed according to the architectonic procedure are not in the words. They are to be found, instead, in the relationships among the juxtaposed portions of the work, as in the image or concept that is derived from the collision of elements in Eisenstein's idea of montage composition. The meanings may be said to lie among the interstices of the structure." In this sense form may be the true servant of theme, for in an unreal world fiction can now deliver something that really counts, not a shabby lie about something hopelessly wrong in the first place. And the result is quite positive: "By abdicating his omniscient position, the author has acknowledged the inadequacy of one sole perspective to account for the totality of even his own personal view. The scope of reality has not been so much abandoned to chaos and irrationality as it has been expanded to include contradictory as well as complementary points of view." The new novel becomes closer to, rather than farther from, art, since not only can the writer "make sense of reality, he can extract its form and meaning, combine these with the attributes arising from his own perspective, and make from the two something new, a third being, a superior one: a metaphor, or, on a grander scale, a work of art, a microcosmic approximation of the originally controllable reality." The shock is not how far the new novel has gone, but how far we let the old novel desert the true ideals of artistic representation in favor of some wholly unreal documentation.

—Jerome Klinkowitz, from *Novel*, Spring 1973,
on Sharon Spencer's *Space, Time
and Structure in the Modern Novel*

III. WORKING IT OUT

Sukenick revises the form of the novel and the style in which to write it. His sentences defy simple grammar, even that as spoken in the streets. Instead he runs the end of one into the following, just long enough to plunge the reader on beyond the expected stop and keep him hurtling through the narrative at a speed faster than he'd customarily choose. In *Out*, the novel's larger design complements this speed: arranged like a countdown from chapters 10, 9, 8, through 3, 2, 1, 0, each section is designed with first 10 lines of type, then 9 lines to 1 of space, then 8 to 2, 7 to 3, until near the end the reader is racing through the pages at the rate of 9 lines of space to 1 of print, accelerating to section 0, when he is shot out like a cannonball. Once again, the book itself is the real thing. Even viscerally.

Tape

let's have a serious discussion says Empty Fox. What's your ambition.
  I want to write a book like a cloud that changes as it goes.
  I want to erase all books. My ambition is to unlearn everything I can't read or write that's a start. I want to

unlearn and unlearn till I get to the place where the ocean of the unknown beings where my fathers live. Then I want to go and bring back my people to live beside that ocean where they can be whole again as they were before the Wasichus came. That's why I like to travel this way.
                                    . . . .
the Wasichus make Disneyland of all this so they can sell it they get Indians to pretend they're Indians they make believe these beautiful mountains are beautiful they pretend that magic is magic they make believe the truth is the

truth otherwise they can't believe anything. There is a place with a billboard of a mountain in front of the mountain you Wasichus can't see without pretending to see so anyway you don't believe it. Anyway that's why you all have cameras you're not friends with your eyes only with

your minds you can't understand this.

Tape ends

The refusal to face our imaginations, the urge to suspend our disbeliefs, is to Sukenick the most debilitating feature of twentieth-century American life. As a novelist, he knows that the world as we know it is only a description; therefore, as he wrote in the *Village Voice* (1/25/73) about Don Juan and Carlos Castaneda, "The power of a sorcerer is a power of the feeling he can invest in his description so it is felt as a persuasive account of the world," which is precisely the job of the proper fictionist. Because of this orientation his sentences read differently and his chapters follow in almost bizarre fashion, but the object is to make us feel his account of the world as effectively as a sorcerer would have us. The death of the novel becomes the life of fiction, as the keys to its technique are revitalized for the living world.

IV. TWENTY DIGRESSIONS TOWARD A NON-DEFINITION OF ART

From Sukenick's essays in the Winter 1975 issue of *New Literary History* and the Winter 1976 issue of *Partisan Review*:

1. The hermeticism of the Moderns engendered, not without their implicit and, at times, explicit encouragement, a new and reductive academicism. . . . The hermeneutics of the New Criticism was, in part, a prophylaxis designed to protect life from the disruptive energy of art.

2. It was this essentially "Redskin" attitude toward experience in a new and explicit form that blew the lid off the closed and stuffy art of the Fifties, and released a flood of energy in a whole generation of creative artists. The improvisations of jazz, especially bebop, were the great examples, explicitly so in Kerouac's "Essentials of Spontaneous Prose." There was Olson's 1950 "Projective Verse" essay. . . . The first real explosion was abstract expressionism, which obliterated the demarcation between the painting and the experience of composing it. There was Frank O'Hara, whose poems are like casual notations of what happens as he goes along in a casual diction and flattened metric that reads quite differently from what one was used to thinking of poetry.

3. It seems to me that the real difference in question is simply that between an imposed order and one that develops as it goes along—"occurs as it occurs," as Stevens would say, "by digression" as Laurence Sterne would put it, or, in terms of jazz, by improvisation.

4. Henry Miller is for American novelists what Whitman is for American poets. The source of his vitality is the current that began flowing when he reconnected our art with our experience. Experience begins with the self and Miller put the self back into fiction. For a writer the whole point of literary technique is the fullest possible release of the energy of his personality into his work, and when one comes into contact with that force, the whole superstructure that one had assumed to be the point of literature begins to burn away.

5. The more we talk "about" a work, the less we participate in it, the less we are engaged by the experience of it. . . . When consciousness of its own form is incorporated in the dynamic structure of the text—its composition, as the painters say—theory can once again become part of the story rather than about it.

6. The impossible situation of the realistic novel was that the better an imitation it was of "reality" in the Aristotelian sense, the more it was an imitation of the other, Platonic sense: a shadow, a second-hand version, a counterfeit. The more intensely the novel was "about" life, the less it was part of it.

7. The collapse of illusionary time in realistic fiction parallels the collapse of illusionary space in perspective painting and serves a parallel function: the assertion of the validity of the work of art in its own right, rather than as an imitation of something else.

8. Just as one cannot say that a piece of music is "about" its melody, one should not say that a piece of fiction is "about" its subject matter—subject matter is just one element of the composition.

9. The words used meditatively in a literary work are not the same words used instrumentally in the world of action. Words in dreams do not mean the same thing as words in the newspaper. The word fog in Bleak House does not mean the same thing as the word fog in the dictionary, though its meaning in Bleak House, once developed, could be, probably has been, added to the general sense—one sees this process on any page of the OED. What language signifies in a literary work is different from what it signifies in its general sense, but then may be added to that sense.

10. Art as illusion is fundamentally a negative characterization which then must be circumvented by such awkward detours as the willing suspension of disbelief, which seems an adequate theory for children reading fairy tales but not for much else.

11. As artifice the work of art is a conscious tautology in which there is always an implicit (and sometimes explicit) reference to its own nature as artifact—self-reflexive, not self-reflective. It is not an imitation but a new thing in its own right, an invention.

12. Art is the regenerative part of experience as it generates new anti-entropic extensions of it that reestablish a vital connection with the data of reality in the energy field of the art work. That's why we can say that art makes life more real.

13. In a generative theory, formally, narrative would be the movement of the mind as it organizes the open field of the text. In a vitalistic sense, it would be the energy of personality reversing the entropy of experience—also known as the "subject matter," or "content," as it enters the field of the text. The result is a new experience, distinguished by the way it salvages energy from that constant dissipation characteristic of the flux.

14. The obligation of fiction is to rescue experience from history, from politics, from commerce, from theory, even from language itself—from any system, in fact, that threatens to distort, devitalize, or manipulate experience.

15. The fairy tale of the "realistic" novel whispers its assurance that the world is not mysterious, that it is predictable—if not to the characters then to the author, that it is available to manipulation by the individual, that it is not only under control but that one can profit from this control. The key idea is verisimilitude: one can make an image of the real thing which, though not real, is such a persuasive likeness that it can represent our control over reality.

16. Art delivers us from abstraction and solipsism with a newly vitalized sense of experience. It does not cage us in the crystal perfection of art.

17. The poem is not different from experience, it is more experience.

18. The contemporary novelist describes things with whose appearance we are already perfectly familiar . . . not to make us see those things but to test the language against them, to keep it alive to visual experience. . . . This kind of "truth" does not depend on accurate description of "reality" but rather itself generates what we call reality, reordering our perceptions and sustaining a vital connection with the world.

19. Art as a window implies that it is a means to reach some end other than itself. What? . . . This is the harvest of the doctrine of willing suspension of disbelief: if art is illusion, then documentary is better because it's the real thing.

20. The form of the traditional novel is a metaphor for a society that no longer exists.

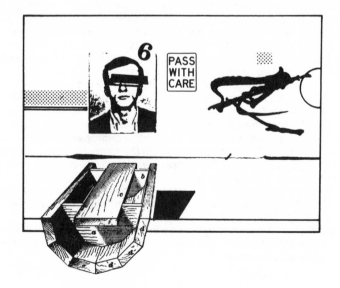

V. 98.6

Ronald Sukenick from Brooklyn, New York, sits in South Laguna, California, reading the paper he grew up on, the *Village Voice*. The news is not good: Bob Kuttner writes about lethal radiation experiments on indigent hospital patients, Dore Ashton describes the unimaginable in sado-masochistic theater, while Lucian Truscott IV gives a graphic report of death-cult sacrifices along the California beaches where Sukenick lives, and where he has come to write. New York may be sinking, but the State of California is in poor shape as well. Lousy subjects abound. What is there to write about?

As he writes his novel, Sukenick has dreams, dating them with the same objectivity as his footnoted newspaper sources. "7/14 he puts a dime in a slot and gets a newspaper. The series of murders that turned out to be part of another mass murder now turns out to be part of a series of mass murders." His dreams create a character who fits right into the news he's been reading—news that is frighteningly the same, whether it be the latest feature in the *Voice* or a commentary he's picked up on the Aztecs. Whether Mexico or America, 1541 or 1973, it's the same: "A civilization so deadened by its own proliferation that only death can renew its commitment to life." Imagining life among the Aztecs, Sukenick's character is caught in the formula of a nightmarish sacrifice, where "love ÷ power = sadism + masochism." With the knife about to fall "he wonders if there might be some way out through magic. Or through dream. Or acceptance. Or withdrawal. He decides the best thing would be to play his role through."

The state of America is Sukenick's apparent subject. A few years ago one of Kurt Vonnegut, Jr.'s characters coined the name *granfalloon* for any created agency "that was meaningless in terms of the way God gets things done . . . examples of *granfalloons* are the Communist party, the Daughters of the American Revolution, the General Electric Company, the International Order of Odd Fellows—and any nation, anytime, anywhere." Shortly after that the rock group Steppenwolf found political and aesthetic justification to call the U.S. a "Monster." In *98.6* Ronald Sukenick finds that his world of manners and of morals has become by straight dictionary definition a "Frankenstein": any agency or creation that slips from the control of and ultimately destroys its creator. But the behavior of this creature is despicable; even simple descriptive language is in such circumstances an abomination which reader and author can barely manage. Beyond what he reads in the *Voice* and finds so analogous in the Aztec book, there is nothing for Sukenick to write about. He can only write his way out.

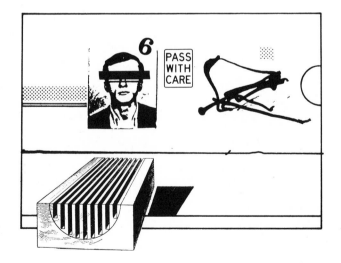

He begins with a collage of history and news, dreams and nightmares. His writer-character worries about being blinded "by the negative hallucination of our culture. A negative hallucination is when you don't see something that's really there." Hallucinations and their opposites form the first section of 98.6, "Frankenstein." Part Two, "The Children of Frankenstein," is a more conventional narrative account of a communal attempt to rebuild from this rejected past. The children have abandoned the nightmare, "the kind of trauma that can only happen when you wake up from a dream you think is the real thing." They get close to the rhythms of nature, but too soon their energy is misdirected and escapes. Their "normalcy" is false, as misleading as the steady temperature (98.6) of the woman miscarrying the commune's first child. Inevitably, the state of Frankenstein is created again.

In Section Three, "Palestine," Sukenick takes one more look at history and tries his ideal synthesis. It's hypothetical, of course, based on an explicit "if": "I wouldn't go on this way if that Arab wasn't such a lousy shot. They wouldn't tolerate this kind of writing under a Nixon administration. What Arab. The one where Rosy Grier broke his neck when he tried to assassinate Kennedy after the California primary two shots and all he could do was nick an ear lobe. Sir-what. That's why Robert favors high collars and wears his overcoat turned up. Yes Robert that's how he's known to his intimates. Bobby's only for the press. . . . So you think I'm crazy well let me tell you if those slugs had buried themselves in Robert's brain it all would have been very different."

Suddenly, in his writing, Sukenick has made everything perfect. "Palestine" becomes a trans-historical solution for Arab and Jew, just as his "State of Israel" is in fact a state of consciousness, a product of the imagination within the full control of its creator. "Here in Israel," he writes, "we have no need of cars. Automobiles have long been exiled from the cities and towns where transportation depends on various beasts of burden camels burros oxen. There are even a few llamas to be seen and modern experiments are underway with giraffes and zebras which in fact antedate the use of the horse in Africa and the Middle East." Ronald Sukenick, the Brooklyn kid transported to South Laguna, who has never been to Israel, continues: "We have an extensive intercity monorail system and colorful barges make their way among the canals." In the world of his own writing, Sukenick is improvising with reality as the best jazzman handles a change of chords. "Environmental planning is largely given over to the artists with the result that the native beauty of the Holy Land has been preserved and even heightened. The prestige of novelists along with other artists is such that no intermediaries are needed between ourselves and the public and we have the means to produce and distribute our own work which is in constant demand. Artists are recognized as the creators not only of esthetic works but of reality itself all scholars scientists and rabbis are acknowledged as artists each working in his appropriate sphere even politics is considered to be a certain kind of art."

"Palestine" is, of course, unreal. It is not even an ideal (remember the problems of "Frankenstein"), but instead an ideal of an ideal, where art holds beauty in free suspension. At the end Sukenick finds himself sitting in Laguna with the cat on his lap, listening to another improvisationalist, Jesse Lone Cat Fuller. The comparison is obvious: "yes ramble around settle in Calfornia pick up this and that adapt it to your style without sidemen the novelist is a one man band playing all the instruments." This has been the true subject of 98.6, far beyond the topicality of those Village Voice clippings.

"You can't judge a creative work by what it's 'about,' " Sukenick himself wrote in a letter to the Voice, 1/3/74. "A good poem or novel is always about something other than its subject material, and that's the difference between fiction and journalism." The point is the writing itself. Reviewing the work of novelist Paul Metcalf in Lillabulero #12 (Winter 1973). Sukenick noted that "Again we get a collage of fact and experience but what excites me here—what I feel most energy flowing from—is that the experience is direct experience, the author's presumably factual experience interacting with the fact of history, anthropology, and so on." Good writing fills the space between. In his continuing sections of "The Endless Short Story" (many of which have appeared in the Village Voice as oblique commentaries on "the news") Sukenick has argued for "poetry's perpetual plot against morality grammar and common sense in its latest transmogrification The Conspiracy to Destroy the English Language." Sukenick is the arch-conspirator, since once The Language has become "the coin of radio announcers school teachers and bureaucrats ratcaging us in the schizoid syntax of filing cabinets and crab louis," the fictionist must reinvent a true medium of discourse. The new writing comes across "as though someone in the middle of conversation suddenly started speaking in multi-colored bubbles instead of words. They are not surreal bubbles meant to contact The Absolute or The Unconscious they're just a way of chewing the fat."

As a result, he'd like someone to "tell the Eagle Scouts in the club house down here that it no longer matters if you can tie a line in more knots than Henry James or fly a sentiment higher than Matthew Arnold this is no longer serious stuff unless you're interested in the merit badge for belles lettres or editorial writing. And while the critics are out to lunch the writers gather in the back room where they are not thinking of Poetry or The Great Novel or Humanism or even of Experimental Writing or of anything more ponderous than stringing words together in ways that give pleasure and allow one to survive one's particular experience. And in so doing meet the only serious obligations of art in a world that constantly pushes in the direction of the impersonal and systematic and that is to be completely personal and unsystematic thereby saving experience from history from ideology and even from art."

In the Winter 1975 issue of *New Literary History* Sukenick has claimed that the more intensely the conventional novel has been "about" life, "the less it was a part of it." Fiction should instead be "an essentialized narrative—it embodies the progression of the mind as it confronts and affects experience." *98.6* is a combination of mind and matter in just such a narrative. Its final subject is invented, and is in fact its own language. Its final subject is Ronald Sukenick's own life of fiction.

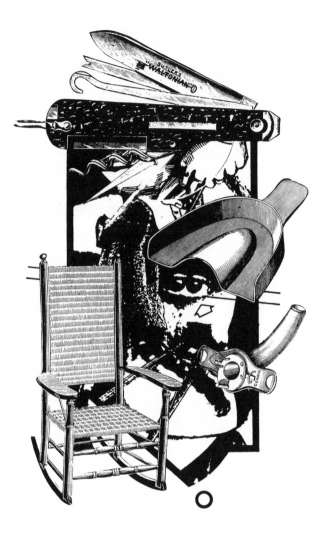

Chapter Three

Hunter S. Thompson is as much a gadfly to traditional journalism as is Ronald Sukenick to traditional publishing. Nor does he fit with the maverick New Journalists, who appropriate the methods of traditional fiction to flesh out their own reporting of documentary events, and who by so doing have set themselves up as polar opposites of the new fictionists. Thompson's own methods of composition are so similar to Sukenick's that he can wear with pride the label which the *Columbia Journalism Review* and *Time* have scornfully placed upon him: innovative fictionist.

The best works to compare are Thompson's *Fear and Loathing in Las Vegas* (New York: Random House, 1972) and Sukenick's *Out* (Chicago: Swallow Press, 1973). For what it's worth, both were written in the same year, 1971. Both deal with an identifiable historical field: the craziness of American life of the Sixties, climaxing at the turn of the Seventies. The structure of each is a journey into the heart of that life. The final subject of each book is the writer himself. But the method of composition is most important. Each writer makes the conditions of his own act of writing an integral part of the work itself. Sukenick uses every device possible to accelerate his narrative: dictating into a tape recorder, allowing himself just one hour to complete a section, syncopating his sentences with run-on punctuation so that the reader is impelled forward in concert with the writer's onrushing energy. Thompson thrives on the same methods of composition: fighting deadlines, sending in his material on tape and in unedited notebooks, doing his actual writing in the constantly self-described context of drugs, alcohol, and violence, until this very manner becomes part of his subject. There is no illusion whatsoever that there isn't a very real and stunningly idiosyncratic writer at the center of each work. That's the ultimate self-reflexiveness which makes Hunter S. Thompson a SuperFictionist. He has created his own mythology, his own life of fiction, against which subjects are to be tested and not just explained.

Thompson shares several techniques with one of his greatest admirers, Kurt Vonnegut, Jr. The quick cut, the strategic use of digression, the ability to propel himself through a narrative like a stunt driver, steering with the skids so that the most improbable intentions result in the smoothest maneuvers, the attitude of having one's personal craziness pale before the ludicrousness which passes for the normal in contemporary American life—on all these counts Thompson and Vonnegut share a basic affinity. This affinity extends to the way they both permeate the culture, even unread. Though their books reach millions of readers, millions more know Vonnegut from the films of his works and from the popularization of his attitudes. Thompson's own life of fiction was for several months running the subject of Garry Trudeau's *Doonesbury* comic strip series; the initial strips are collected in Trudeau's *"Speaking of Inalienable Rights, Amy"* (New York: Holt, Rinehart & Winston, 1976). Trudeau portrayed Thompson's lifestyle at his Woody Creek, Colorado, home; in a dramatization of his dream of receiving the governorship of American Samoa; and finally, in hyperbolic extension of Thompson's ambitions and behavior, as ambassador to the People's Republic of China. In 1975 Kurt Vonnegut, Jr., became the first American writer to be quoted by a starting pitcher in the World Series (Bill Lee of the Boston Red Sox) while at the same time having a song in the Top Forty ("Nice, Nice, Very Nice," adapted from *Cat's Cradle* by the recording group Ambrosia); the following year, Hunter S. Thompson became the first SuperFictionist to have his name placed in nomination for the vice-presidential candidacy of the Democratic party.

Beyond the trivia, which mounts every year, is the fact that writers of the New Fiction are becoming as established in our daily lives as were Hemingway and Fitzgerald in their own times. Like Vonnegut, Thompson has placed himself at the center of most important American events of the past ten years, and in the hands of a readership (most frequently that of *Rolling Stone*) inhabiting a world not shared by the celebrated Post-Modernist writers, whose works one can read without having any sense at all that they were written during the student revolution, the shift of recognition and eventually some sharing of power with ethnic minorities, the war in Vietnam, and countless other events from the major (the fall of President Nixon's administration) to the transitory (the Hell's Angels Motorcycle Club and the National Football League). Like Vonnegut, Sukenick, and the other SuperFictionists, Thompson has found a way to be in the world and at the same time be a fictive artist.

HUNTER S. THOMPSON

I. HUNTER S. THOMPSON IS NOT A JOURNALIST

One problem with Hunter Thompson is simply, as the Newsweek *slogan goes, that of separating fact from fiction.*

—Columbia Journalism Review

The President was not immediately available for comment on how he planned to spend his forty-five Big Ones, but Stans said he planned to safeguard the funds personally.

At that point, McGregor cracked Stans upside the head with a Gideon Bible and called him a "thieving little fart." McGregor then began shoving the rest of us out of the room, but when Stans tried to leave, McGregor grabbed him by the neck and jerked him back inside. Then he slammed the door and threw the bolt . . .

Jesus, why do I write things like that? I must be getting sick, or maybe just tired of writing about these greasy Rotarian bastards. I think it's time to move on to something else.

—Hunter S. Thompson,
Fear and Loathing: On the
Campaign Trail '72 *(San
Francisco: Straight Arrow
Books, 1973)*

In the context of journalism, here, we are dealing with a new kind of "lead"—the Symbiotic Trapezoid Quote. The Columbia Journalism Review *will never sanction it; at least not until the current editor dies of brain syphilis, and probably not even then.*

What?

Do we have a libel suit on our hands?
. . . .

THUMP! Against the door. Another goddam newspaper, another cruel accusation. THUMP! Day after day, it never ends. . . . Hiss at the alarm clock, suck up the headlines along with a beaker of warm Drano, then off to the morning class. . . . To teach Journalism: Circulation, Distribution, Headline Counting and the classical Pyramid Lead.

—Hunter S. Thompson,
"The Boys in the Bag,"
Rolling Stone #164
(7/4/74)

*

Some make the case that Hunter S. Thompson is a New Journalist, as Tom Wolfe uses the term. Thompson is so only to the extent that he employs some methods of traditional fiction to present his otherwise documentary material. In his critical anthology, *The New Journalism* (New York: Harper & Row, 1973), Wolfe argues that "Fiction writers, currently, are busy running backward, skipping and screaming, into a begonia patch that I call Neo-Fabulism." He adds that "the retrograde state of contemporary fiction" makes it easier to defend his own thesis: "that the most important literature being written in America today is non-fiction, in the form that has been tagged, however ungracefully, the New Journalism."

The New Journalists whom Wolfe admires are Rex Reed, Gay Talese, Michael Herr, Truman Capote, George Plimpton, Garry Wills, John Gregory Dunne, and Tom Wolfe. That's a fair selection from his anthology's table of contents. Many of these writers follow Wolfe's models, who include the chroniclers of European manners and morals during the eighteenth and nineteenth centuries. When he looks at contemporary fiction, Wolfe regrets the losses of character, scene-by-scene construction, realistic dialogue, third-person point of view, and symbolic detail that he was accustomed to finding in Trollope, Balzac, Fielding, and Thackeray. He prefers "the joys of detailed realism" which he finds woefully absent in the works of Borges and Coover, to name just two, but amply present in his own New Journalism and probably in his own fiction as well, since Wolfe's novel-in-progress is called *Vanity Fair*. The American Sixties, Wolfe insists, "was one of the most extraordinary decades in American history in terms of manners and morals." Therefore the techniques of the mannerists and moralists, which were discarded by the new fictionists, would have to be resurrected by the New Journalists in order to craft the definitive literary work of our time. And among the New Journalists Wolfe includes Hunter S. Thompson. But Thompson's methods, as we shall see, go beyond traditional fiction into those of more innovative art—techniques and styles tasting more of Sukenick and Katz than of Fielding and Thackeray. Plus he identifies with (and even becomes a part of) the action more than does Tom Wolfe or most of the other New Journalists. Thompson calls his new style "Gonzo Journalism," and its effect discredits Wolfe's thesis that the techniques of recent fiction are inappropriate for the serious literature of our age.

Thompson began this style with *Hell's Angels: A Strange and Terrible Saga* (New York: Random House, 1967). As he describes it, "By the middle of summer I had become so involved in the outlaw scene that I was no longer sure whether I was doing research on the Hell's Angels or being slowly absorbed by them." Yet Thompson maintains an interesting tension: despite his sympathy and identification with the Hell's Angels outrages, he constantly views them from a middle-class perspective. The values and sensibilities of Southern California's solid citizens are the backdrop for everything that Thompson has the outlaws do. If there is a literary style involved here, it's not that of Balzac or Trollope, but of Fitzgerald having Nick Carraway reserve judgment all the way until his final absorption into Gatsby. But as a SuperFictionist Thompson plays a tougher game than a Modernist character.

For one, there is the baiting. Covering the Kentucky Derby for *Scanlan's*, Thompson recounts his barroom conversation with a visiting Texan:

I shook my head and said nothing; just stared at him for a moment, trying to look grim. "There's going to be trouble," I said. "My assignment is to take pictures of the riot."
"What riot?"
I hesitated, twirling the ice in my drink. "At the track. On Derby Day. The Black Panthers." I stared at him again. "Don't you read the newspapers?"
The grin on his face had collapsed. "What the hell are you talkin about?"
"Well . . . maybe I shouldn't be telling you. . . ." I shrugged. "But hell, everybody else seems to know. The cops and the National Guard have been getting ready for six weeks. They have 20,000 troops on alert at Fort Knox. They've warned us—all the press and photographers— to wear helmets and special vests like flak jackets. We were told to expect shooting. . . ."

Another variation is Thompson's use of his British illustrator friend Ralph Steadman, to whom Thompson can play off his tales of rampage and paranoia against a chorus of "That's teddible, teddible." The Derby was Steadman's first visit to the U.S., allowing Thompson a conservative backdrop when the staid citizens themselves became more loony and depraved than the outlaw bikers of the Hell's Angels book. It all ends with Thompson driving his colleague to the airport:

Huge Pontiac Ballbuster blowing through traffic on the expressway. The journalist is driving, ignoring his passenger who is now nearly naked after taking off most of his clothing, which he holds out the window, trying to wind-wash the Mace out of it. His eyes are bright red and his face and chest are soaked with the beer he's been using to rinse the awful chemical off his flesh. The front of his woolen trousers is soaked with vomit; his body is racked with fits of coughing and wild choking sobs. The journalist rams the big car through traffic and into a spot in front of the terminal, then he reaches over to open the door on the passenger's side and shoves the Englishman out, snarling: "Bug off, you worthless faggot! You twisted pigfucker! [Crazed laughter.] If I weren't sick I'd kick your ass all the way to Bowling Green—you scumsucking foreign geek. Mace is too good for you. . . . We can do without your kind in Kentucky."

Finally, Thompson stretches another Fitzgerald technique, that of simultaneously leading the parade and heckling oneself from the curb, to capture the spirit of the age in himself. He turns himself into a laboratory for the study of what's going on in contemporary America. *Fear and Loathing in Las Vegas* (New York: Random House, 1972) captures the essence of this in Thompson's favorite drug for the occasion, ether. "This is the main advantage of ether: it makes you behave like the village drunkard in some early Irish novel . . . total loss of all basic motor skills: blurred vision, no balance, numb tongue—severance of all connection between body and the brain. Which is interesting," Thompson stresses, "because the brain continues to function more or less normally . . . you can actually *watch* yourself behaving in this terrible way, but you can't control it."

II. MAKING HIS OWN STORY

The only way to prepare for a trip like this, I felt, was to dress up like human peacocks and get crazy, then screech off across the desert and cover the story. Never lose sight of that primary responsibility.

But what was the story? Nobody had bothered to say. So we would have to drum it up on our own. Free Enterprise. The American Dream. Horatio Alger gone mad on drugs in Las Vegas. Do it now: pure Gonzo journalism.

. . . .

I needed this break, this moment of peace and refuge, before we did the Drug Conference. It was going to be quite a different thing from the Mint 400. That had been an observer gig, but this one would need participation—and a very special stance. . . . This time our very presence would be an outrage. We would be attending the conference under false pretenses and dealing, from the start, with a crowd that was convened for the stated purpose of putting people like us in jail. We were the Menace. . . .

—Fear and Loathing in Las Vegas

*

And unlike most of the others in the press box, we didn't give a hoot in hell what was happening on the track. We had come there to watch the real beasts perform.

—"The Kentucky Derby Is Decadent and Depraved"

What happened, in a nut, was that I got lost in a maze of hallways in the back reaches of the convention hall on Tuesday night about an hour or so before the roll-call vote on Nixon's chances of winning the GOP nomination again this year . . . and ended up in a big room jammed with Nixon Youth workers, getting themselves ready for a "spontaneous demonstration" at the moment of climax out there on the floor.

. . . .

They never came right out and said it, but I could see they were uncomfortable at the prospect of all three network TV cameras looking down on their spontaneous Nixon Youth demonstration and zeroing in—for their own perverse reasons—on a weird-looking, 35-year-old speed freak with half his hair burned off from overindulgence, wearing a big blue McGOVERN button on his chest, carrying a tall cup of "Old Milwaukee" and shaking his fist at John Chancellor up in the NBC booth—screaming: "You dirty bastard! You'll pay for this, by God! We'll rip your goddam teeth out! KILL! KILL! Your number just came up, you communist son of a bitch!"

. . . .

Now the others understood. A few laughed, but others muttered darkly, "You mean John Chancellor goes around putting LSD in people's drinks? He takes it himself? . . . He's a dope addict. . . ?"

"Golly," said the girl. "That explains a lot, doesn't it?"

. . . .

First I held up my "GARBAGE MEN DEMAND EQUAL TIME" sign at him. Then, when I was sure he'd noticed the sign, I tucked it under my arm and ripped off my hat, clutching it in the same fist I was shaking angrily at the NBC booth and screaming at the top of my lungs: "You evil scumsucker! You're through! You limp-wristed Nazi moron!"

—Fear and Loathing: On the Campaign Trail '72

III. SUPERFICTION (TAKE ONE)

Thompson does more than his colleagues who adapt the literary conventions of the eighteenth century to modern life in order to produce the New Journalism. Beyond this, he uses techniques of contemporary innovative fiction, and gets results similar to Sukenick's *Out*, Katz's *Saw*, or Barthelme's *Snow White*. For one thing, he details the action with the speed and effect of a drug rush, with no surrender to credibility once the circus is underway. "Terrible things were happening all around us," he claims in *Fear and Loathing in Las Vegas* as he tries to settle down for a drink in the hotel lounge. "Right next to me a huge reptile was gnawing on a woman's neck, the carpet was a blood-soaked sponge—impossible to walk on, no footing at all. 'Order some golf shoes,' I whispered. 'Otherwise, we'll never get out of this place alive. You notice these lizards don't have any trouble moving around in this muck—that's because they have *claws* on their feet.' " Still more: " 'We're right in the middle of a fucking reptile zoo! And somebody's giving *booze* to these goddam things! It won't be long before they tear us to shreds. Jesus, look at the floor! Have you ever *seen* so much blood? How many have they killed already?' I pointed across the room to a group that seemed to be staring at us. 'Holy shit, look at that bunch over there! They've spotted us!' 'That's the press table,' he said."

Another innovative technique is the collage method: in *Hell's Angels* Thompson incorporates verbatim, in their own form, quotes from *True Magazine*, the New York *Times*, personal comments from various observers, the Finch Report from the California attorney general's office, and so forth—all spatially organized as a graphic comment on the action. In his Superbowl coverage (*Rolling Stone* #155, 2/28/74) Thompson adds even more, with interpolations of tapes, letters, phone calls, news clippings, and fragments from the Old Testament prophets hurled in sermons from the twentieth-floor mezzanine of the Houston Hyatt Regency (" 'Beware,' I shouted, 'for the Devils also believe, and tremble!' "). And occasionally an epigraph from Milton or Dr. Samuel Johnson. "He who makes a beast of himself gets rid of the pain of being a man" is a favorite, cited many times.

But the key method which makes Hunter S. Thompson a SuperFictionist on the order of Sukenick and Katz is the self-reflexive manner of his work. He never disguises the fact that he is a half-cranked geek journalist caught in the center of the action. Right in the middle of a story he will often break down, but the breakdown itself carries much of the "information" about the country of the writer's own imagination which he is, like Sukenick, reporting. "Television can best give us the news, fiction gives us *our response* to the news," Sukenick has said in a statement which describes Thompson's work as well as his own.

The method is first used in *Fear and Loathing in Las Vegas* (which was published in *Rolling Stone* under the name of Thompson's alternate persona, Raoul Duke). Chapter Nine begins, "At this point in the chronology, Dr. Duke appears to have broken down completely; the original manuscript is so splintered that we were forced to seek out the original tape recording and transcribe it verbatim. We made no attempt to edit this section, and Dr. Duke refused even to read it." Thompson uses the technique several times in his campaign book (originally a year's worth of articles printed month by month in *Rolling Stone*), where under the pressure of deadlines he would resort to "tearing my Ohio primary notebook apart and sending about fifty pages of scribbled shorthand notes straight to the typesetter." At times the manner is old-fashioned *cinéma vérité* ("Damn! Fuck! I can't believe those fuckin' helicopters! I'll leave it on the tape just to remind me how bad it was"), and elsewhere it is just comic—in "Rude Notes from a Decompression Chamber in Miami" (*Rolling Stone* #140, 8/2/73) Thompson sends his reports out by a nurse "who copied Dr. Thompson's notes as he held them up, page by page, through the pressure-sealed window of his Chamber" where he was recovering from the bends.

The best example is from his Watergate coverage (*Rolling Stone* #144, 9/27/73). Any possible tedium in Thompson's twenty-one-page piece is relieved when the author himself comes apart. "Due to circumstances beyond our control," reads an editor's note midway through, "the following section was lashed together at the last moment from a six-pound bundle of documents, notebooks, memos, recordings and secretly taped phone conversations with Dr. Thompson during a month of erratic behavior in Washington, New York, Colorado and Miami." This is a second-power use of Thompson's own collage and breakdown methods. The one reinforces the other, and along the way his personality-at-the-center-of-the-action is given further embellishment: "His 'long-range plan,' he says, is to 'refine' these nerve-wracking methods, somehow, and eventually 'create an entirely new form of journalism.' In the meantime, we have suspended his monthly retainer and cancelled his credit card. During one four-day period in Washington he destroyed two cars, cracked a wall in the Washington Hilton, purchased two French Horns at $1100 each and ran through a plate-glass door in a Turkish restaurant."

IV. A HUNTER S. THOMPSON READER

Actually, their [the Hell's Angels] visits were marked by nothing more sinister than loud music, a few bikes on the sidewalk, and an occasional shot out the back window.

*

So I was not entirely at ease drifting around the casinos this Saturday night with a car full of marijuana and head full of acid. We had several narrow escapes: at one point I tried to drive the Great Red Shark into the laundry room of the Landmark Hotel—but the door was too narrow, and the people inside seemed dangerously excited.

*

Few people understand the psychology of dealing with a highway traffic cop. Your normal speeder will panic and immediately pull over to the side when he sees the big red light behind him . . . and then he will start apologizing, begging for mercy.

This is wrong. It arouses contempt in the cop-heart. The thing to do—when you're running along about a hundred or so and you suddenly find a red-flashing CHP-tracker on your trail—what you want to do then is accelerate. Never pull over with the first siren-howl. Mash it down and make the bastard chase you at speeds up to 120 all the way to the next exit. He will follow. But he won't know what to make of your blinker-signal that says you're about to turn right.

This is to let him know you're looking for a proper place to pull off and talk . . . keep signalling and hope for an off-ramp, one of those uphill side-loops with a sign saying "Max Speed 25" . . . and the trick, at this point, is to suddenly leave the freeway and take him into the chute at no less than a hundred miles an hour.

He will lock his brakes about the same time you lock yours, but it will take him a moment to realize that he's about to make a 180-degree turn at this speed . . . but you will be ready for it, braced for the G's and the fast heel-toe work, and with any luck at all you will have come to a complete stop off the road at the top of the turn and be standing beside your automobile by the time he catches up.

He will not be reasonable at first . . . but no matter. Let him calm down. He will want the first word. Let him have it. His brain will be in a turmoil: he may begin jabbering,

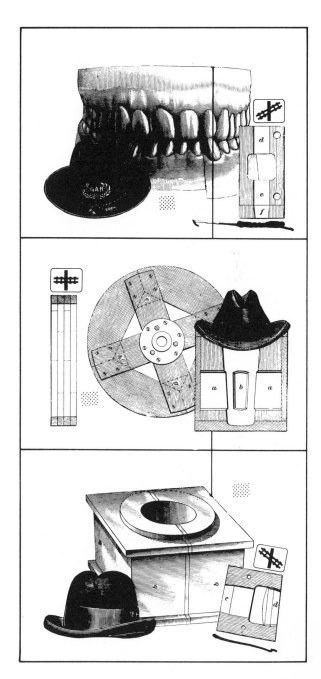

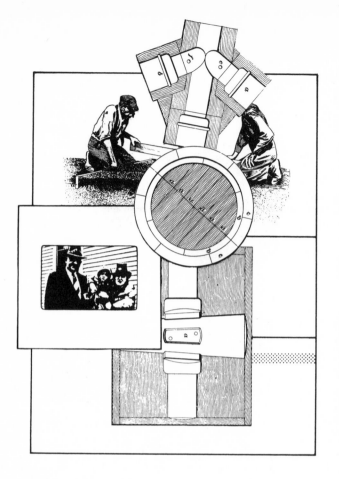

or even pull his gun. Let him unwind; keep smiling. The idea is to show him that you were always in total control of yourself and your vehicle—while he lost control of everything.

*

"Well, actually we were thinking about going out to Tex Colson's house and jerking him out of bed, tying him behind the car with a big rope and dragging him down Pennsylvania Avenue . . . then cutting him loose in front of the White House Guard Gate."

"You're kidding . . . You don't really mean that. You wouldn't do a thing like that, would you?"

"Of course not. That would be a conspiracy to commit either murder or aggravated assault, plus kidnapping . . . and you know me, Ralph; that's not my style."

. . . .

So I thought about it a little more, and it occurred to me what we should do was have these masks made up—you know those rubber masks that fit over the whole head . . . one of them would have to be the face of Haldeman, one the face of Erlichman, and one the face of Tony Ulasewicz . . . and after two or three days in the Emergency Ward, when he was finally able to talk, after coming out of shock, he would swear that the people who got him were Haldeman, Erlichman and Ulasewicz—and he would know they were mean enough to do it, because that's the way he thinks. . . . He'd testify, swear under oath . . . which would cause Nixon probably to go completely crazy.

V. SUPERFICTION (TAKE TWO)

Like all of the SuperFictionists, Hunter S. Thompson favors an expressive (as opposed to descriptive) view of life. As we've quoted from Ronald Sukenick, the descriptions of television give us the news, but fictional techniques give us our response to the news; and the truth of things, these writers agree, lies in our response. The value of their work depends, in turn, on how well that response is expressed in writing. "Thucydides is the first New Journalist I know anything about," Kurt Vonnegut, Jr., writes in the preface to his own book of journalism, *Wampeters, Foma, & Granfalloons: Opinions* (New York: Delacorte, 1974). "He was a celebrity who put himself at the center of the truths he was trying to tell, and he guessed when he had to, and he thought it worthwhile to be charming and entertaining. He was a good teacher," Vonnegut emphasizes, and the way for a writer to accomplish this is to put the truth he tells into strikingly human terms—so that his students will remember, and not go to sleep. "I am crazy about Hunter Thompson on that account," Vonnegut confesses. When he reviewed Thompson's campaign book for *Harper's*, Vonnegut described the lapses into paranoia, insult, and frenzy as almost beautiful, as "the literary equivalent of Cubism: All rules are broken; we are shown pictures such as no mature, well-trained artist ever painted before, and in the crazy new pictures we somehow see luminous new aspects of beloved old truths." Sukenick has talked about how banal and insipid and dull we find reality, how the allegedly real world is unreal to us in our inability to relate to it. Vonnegut observes that for Thompson, "reality is killing him, because it is so ugly and cheap." Therefore the Gonzo Journalist/SuperFictionist writes like a person under torture, thrashing about and saying things not expressed in other circumstances. Writers like Thompson, Vonnegut concludes, "are Populists screaming in pain."

"He makes exciting, moving collages of carefully selected junk. They must be experienced. They can't be paraphrased." That's Vonnegut's justification for calling Hunter Thompson the rare sort of American writer who must be read. The same has been said about Donald Barthelme. Vonnegut's analogy with Cubism and Barthelme's analogy with the collage art of Max Ernst tell us what both Gonzo Journalists and SuperFictionists are doing. Like the Cubists, they rearrange our visual censors so that we see all planes—all sides of the story—at once. Like the masters of collage, they take our neatly self-imposed human order and mix in the exotically strange and terrible elements which just may be a crucial part of our lives. Moreover, Thompson amplifies his own work and extends its dimensions—even multiplies its perspectives—so that it may more properly express the "strange and terrible sagas" about which he writes. This technique is more SuperFictional than Journalistic; indeed, it is the very opposite of both conventional journalism and conventional fiction, since it admits that the omniscient and omnipotent writer (whether he be the author of *Tom Jones* or Tom Wolfe himself) holds only a single perspective, which may be inadequate to account for even the complexity of his own vision. Here's how Thompson multiplies himself:

—*by making as much of the conditions under which he's writing as he does of the subject matter itself*. This is the technique of the self-reflexive novel as written by Gilbert Sorrentino, Ronald Sukenick, Steve Katz, Kurt Vonnegut, Jr., and the other SuperFictionists. There is even a contemporary scientific analogy: that of Heisenberg's Principle of Indeterminacy, whereby the experimenter must include himself as an influence on the experiment. The net result of this candor is a gain in the writing's completeness, beyond the traditional conventions of fiction or journalism.

—*by including references to his own mythology as a writer:* his extravagant behavior, his experiences with drugs (which in his *Playboy* interview of November 1974 he admits are sometimes fabricated), and his self-created image as the Mad Doctor of Gonzo Journalism. Like Vonnegut with his Kilgore Trout stories, Thompson makes constant reference to tales of madness outside the subject at hand; in his *Rolling Stone* piece endorsing presidential candidate Jimmy Carter (#214, 6/3/76), he gets off the subject for a while by speculating on what would have happened if Nixon had actually lost his mind during the Final Days and ordered a Third World War—"But it is still worth wondering how long it would have taken Haig and Kissinger to convince all those SAC generals out in Omaha to disregard a Doomsday phone call from the president of the United States because a handful of civilians in the White House said he was crazy. Ah . . . but we are wandering off into wild speculation again, so let's chop it off right here." But of course the reader's speculation runs on, because Thompson's incremental fantasy breeds a life of its own, becoming a *Dr. Strangelove* story about the Fall of Richard Nixon which the SuperFictionist can write by only *threatening* to write about it.

The ultimate master of this technique, beyond Thompson and even Vonnegut, may be Jorge Luis Borges, who in the prologue to his *Ficciones* (New York: Grove Press, 1962; originally published in Buenos Aires in 1956) writes that "The composition of vast books is a laborious and impoverishing extravagance. To go on for five hundred pages developing an idea whose perfect oral exposition is possible in a few minutes! A better course is to pretend that these books already exist, and then to offer a résumé, a commentary." Borges cites as examples Carlyle's *Sartor Resartus* and Butler's *The Fair Haven*, peculiar nineteenth-century works which Tom Wolfe avoids, but which in a strange way Hunter Thompson seems to reflect. "I have preferred to write notes upon imaginary books," says Borges. But for Borges and Vonnegut and Thompson, those books and stories and fantasies are born of the writer's own imagination. Hence the system of allusions is fully organic, completely self-contained, and expressive of the fullest dimensions of the writer's mind.

—*by dividing his own personality as a writer into mutually exclusive personae*. In *Fear and Loathing in Las Vegas* Thompson travels as himself, but arrives under the credit-card pseudonym of Raoul Duke; much of the extravagant behavior is then attributed to Duke (Thompson's own nickname), whom Thompson can properly deplore. Acting and observing at the same time, Thompson also extends his persona to a third level: bringing along his attorney, identified on the dustjacket as Oscar Zeta Acosta, who in the book is made to perform the more outrageous acts which Thompson can amplify and extend by his own expressions of horror and disgust. Still, Acosta *represents* Thompson, giving life to the metaphor of "power of attorney." For the *Las Vegas* book, Acosta is fictionalized, representing more of Thompson's imagination than his own self. Likewise, in Chapters Twelve, Fourteen, and Fifteen of Acosta's *The Autobiography of a Brown Buffalo* (San Francisco: Straight Arrow Books, 1972), Thompson is fictionalized as "Karl King." Acosta uses the same technique of detached astonishment to describe King's/Duke's/ Thompson's home in Woody Creek, Colorado, which he stumbles into after his own mad binge on the road:

I walked into the living room . . . it was the front of the ranch house. One wall was a window. You could see a green meadow with horses and cows at the base of a mountain of green, red, yellow and brown. There were large, thick leather couches around a cartwheel that served as a burnt-oak coffee table. That was normal. Nothing to get excited about.
    But did you ever see dried bats with silver needles in their white guts up against the wall? A brown moosehead with blood dripping from its sockets? And how about a stuffed owl with a black rat in its beak and blue policemen's badges for eyes?

The plain facts of Acosta's work as a Chicano lawyer are presented in one of the earliest pieces Thompson wrote for *Rolling Stone*, "Strange Rumblings in Aztlan" (#81, 4/29/71), but the expressive truth of the relationship between these two renegade writers must be found in their *Las Vegas* and *Brown Buffalo* books, which detail their respective lives of fiction.

—by constantly downgrading his own paranoid fantasies in proportion to the raving madness of the so-called straight world. He takes his favorite Vegas casino, the Circus-Circus, and remarks on how it "is what the whole hep world would be doing on Saturday night if the Nazis had won the war." Above the gambling tables are any number of bizarre circus acts, "so you're down on the main floor playing blackjack, and the stakes are getting high when suddenly you chance to look up, and there, right smack about your head is a half-naked fourteen-year-old girl being chased through the air by a snarling wolverine, which is suddenly locked in a death battle with two silver-painted Polacks who come swinging down from opposite balconies and meet in midair on the wolverine's neck. . . ." The madness goes on, twenty-four hours a day of gambling and circus, "but nobody seems to notice. . . . Meanwhile, on all the upstairs balconies, the customers are being hustled by every conceivable kind of bizarre shuck." There is a video projection screen upon which for only ninety-nine cents you can send your image, two hundred feet tall, above downtown Las Vegas. For an extra ninety-nine cents the promoter will throw in your voice message:

We will close the drapes tonight. A thing like that could send a drug person careening around the room like a ping-pong ball. Hallucinations are bad enough. But after a while you learn to cope with things like seeing your dead grandmother crawling up your leg with a knife in her teeth. Most acid fanciers can handle this sort of thing.
    But nobody *can handle that other trip—the possibility that any freak with $1.98 can walk into the Circus-Circus and suddenly appear in the sky over downtown Las Vegas twelve times the size of God, howling anything that comes into his head. No, this is not a good town for psychedelic drugs. Reality itself is too twisted.*

Thompson's career became successful as he developed from a journalist into a SuperFictionist. His days as a reporter for *Time* and then for the *National Observer* ended in a dispute over the Berkeley Free Speech Movement, to which he formed a personal allegiance (and which may have been what prompted him to ride with the Angels—to figure out why the bikers, with their socially radical lifestyle, could not join forces with the student radicals). A few years later it was the Chicago police riot at the 1968 Democratic National Convention which turned Thompson on to politics, but in a very personal way. His first *Rolling Stone* publication was "The Battle of Aspen" (#67, 10/1/70) which described his own campaign for sheriff in his adopted Colorado hometown, which he wanted to save from the big money developers. A major plank in his "Freak Power Party" platform was to rename Aspen "Fat City" as a way of deflating the real estate hype. His political tactic was "to spend his main energies on a series of terrifying, whiplash assaults on everything the voters hold dear. There are harsh echoes of the Magic Christian in this technique: The candidate first creates an impossible psychic maze, then he drags the voters into it and flails them constantly with gibberish and rude shocks." The technique is that of Thompson's writing, but in protesting the economic rape of Aspen he demonstrated its effectiveness as an approach to life as well as art. Thompson's party, which had candidates for mayor and coroner as well, lost by only six votes out of 1,200—by only one vote before five late-arriving absentee ballots were counted.

Living the life of fiction, writers like Thompson create fantasies which record the spirit—if not the misleading "actual" facts—of the life they've experienced. In *Playboy* (November 1974), Thompson tells interviewer Craig Vetter how he dealt with his own car in the context of riding heavy motorcycles with the Hell's Angels:

I was always getting pulled over. Jesus, they cancelled my car insurance because of that god-damn bike. They almost took my driver's license away. I never had any trouble with my car. I drove it at full bore all over San Francisco all the time, just wide open. It was a good car, too, a little English Ford. When it finally developed a crack in one of the four cylinders, I took it down to a cliff in Big Sur and soaked the whole interior with ten gallons of gasoline, then executed the fucker with six shots from a .44 magnum in the engine block at point-blank range. After that, we rolled it off the cliff—the radio going, lights on, everything going—and at the last minute, we threw a burning towel in. The explosion was ungodly; it almost blew us into the ocean. I had no idea what ten gallons of gas in an English Ford could do. The car was a mass of twisted, flaming metal. It bounced about six times on the way down—pure movie-stunt shit, you know. A sight like that was worth the car; it was beautiful.

Plus more fantasies on Nixon's Final Days, the book which Thompson was unable to write because Resignation stole the drama from Impeachment:

Thinking in football terms may be the best way to understand what finally happened with the whole Watergate thing: Coach Nixon's team is fourth and 32 on their own ten, and he finds out that his punter is a junkie. A sick junkie. He looks down the bench: "OK, big fella—we need you now!" And this guy is stark white and vomiting, can't even stand up, much less kick. When the game ends in disaster for the home team, then the fans rush onto the field and beat the players to death with rocks, beer bottles, pieces of wooden seats. The coach makes a desperate dash for the safety of the locker room, but three hit men hired by heavy gamblers nail him before he gets there.

Thompson was the only journalist to ride with both Richard Nixon and the Hell's Angels. These two poles of his experience influence each other, especially when they fuse in the person of the real subject of all these stories, Dr. Hunter S. Thompson.

VI. WHAT? DO WE HAVE A LIBEL SUIT ON OUR HANDS?

Hubert Humphrey is a treacherous, gutless old ward-heeler who should be put in a goddam bottle and sent out with the Japanese Current.

*

They don't hardly make 'em like Hubert anymore—but just to be on the safe side, he should be castrated anyway.

It was not until his campaign collapsed and his ex-staffers felt free to talk that I learned that working for Big Ed [Muskie] was something like being locked in a rolling boxcar with a vicious 200-pound water rat. Some of his top staff people considered him dangerously unstable. He had several identities, they said, and there was no way to be sure on any given day if they would have to deal with Abe Lincoln, Hamlet, Captain Queeg, or Bobo the Simpleminded. . . .

*

We had, after all, been together for the better part of two days, and the [Secret Service] agents were beginning to understand that there was no need to reach for their weapons every time I started talking about the blood on Dean Rusk's hands, or how easily I could reach over and cut off his ears with my steak knife.

*

She was gonna be an actress and I was gonna learn to fly. She took off to find the footlights and I took off to find the sky.

—The Divine Comedy, *trans.*
John Ciardi

*

Me? The first journalist in Christendom to go on record comparing Nixon to Adolf Hitler?

VII. FEAR AND LOATHING

For all of the charges against him, Hunter S. Thompson is an amazingly insightful writer. His "journalism" is not in the least irresponsible. On the contrary, in each of his books he's pointed out the lies and gross distortions of conventional journalism. As for "inventing" his material, his *Hell's Angels* documents just how the group was created by the conventional media and its "rape mania"—what Thompson calls "a publicity breakthrough, by means of rape, on the scale of the Beatles or Bob Dylan." Moreover, his books are richly intelligent. Against those who would fancy the Hell's Angels as heroic rebels and identify them with radical youth, Thompson argues that "there is more to their stance than a wistful yearning for acceptance in a world they never made. Their real motivation is an instinctive certainty as to what the score really is. They are out of the ballgame and they know it. Unlike the campus rebels, who with a minimum amount of effort will emerge from their struggle with a validated ticket to status, the outlaw motorcyclist views the future with the baleful eye of a man with no upward mobility at all. In a world increasingly geared to specialists, technicians and fantastically complicated machinery, the Hell's Angels are the obvious losers." Or in his Las Vegas book, where he charts the burning out of the Sixties: "What [Timothy] Leary took down with him was the central illusion of a whole life-style that he helped to create . . . a generation of permanent cripples, failed seekers, who never understood the essential old-mystic fallacy of the Acid Culture: the desperate assumption that somebody—or at least some *force*—is tending that Light at the end of the tunnel."

Thompson himself is capable of belief, and, like Vonnegut, hopes that there is a basic decency buried somewhere amid the junk-heap that contemporary life has become. Part of that very decency is Thompson's candid admission that he is a trash addict himself, that the conditions of our time have infected him even more than others. The reason is that he's placed himself at the center of the last decade's key events: the Berkeley Free Speech Movement and the subsequent nationwide college rebellions, the strange and terrible saga of the Hell's Angels motorcycle club, the 1968 Democratic National Convention in Chicago, the grassroots political reorganization of America, the violent reaction against the political organization of Chicanos and other minorities, the presidential campaign of 1972, the Watergate hearings, the House Judiciary Committee impeachment hearings, the fall of Saigon, and even America's very telling mania for brutal and oversized athletics—twenty years ago Thompson began his career as a sports reporter, and for the reporting of many of the events listed above he retained that designation on *Rolling Stone*'s masthead.

The June 3, 1976, issue of *Rolling Stone* featured Thompson's cover story; an endorsement, "with fear and loathing," of Jimmy Carter for the presidency. His attempt to explain Carter was made up mainly of explanations of himself, with the usual full run of self-reflexive and fabulative techniques. But Thompson uses this same style from his own life to spill over into his conversations with Carter, and the candidate's ability to pass Thompson's test establishes his credibility as needed material for the presidency. Thompson cites Adlai Stevenson to the effect that in a democracy people get exactly the kind of government they deserve; hence the ugly moods Thompson had been observing during the disruptions of the late Sixties and early Seventies yielded the inevitable results of Richard Nixon in 1968 and 1972. To Thompson, Carter reflects Thompson's own good intentions as voiced in Aspen, Aztlan, and the earlier stages of the McGovern campaign. To Thompson's relief, these intentions can be found in a viable candidate who hopes to reflect a true change in popular feelings.

Hunter Thompson has made his life and his writing style into a scourge for all that has gone bad in the world. That is the ultimate basis for his talent as a writer. In *Hell's Angels*, even with his constant middle-class perspective, Thompson was able to say of the bikers that "in this downhill half of our twentieth century they are not so different from the rest of us as they sometimes seem. They are only more obvious." Or at the end of his Kentucky Derby piece, after several days of drink and dope, looking for the ultimately depraved face from the crowd for Steadman to sketch:

My eyes had finally opened enough for me to focus on the mirror across the room and I was stunned at the shock of recognition. For a confused instant I thought that Ralph had somebody with him—a model for that one special face we'd been looking for. There he was, by God—a puffy, drink-ravaged, disease-ridden caricature . . . like an awful cartoon version of an old snapshot in some once-proud mother's family photo album. It was the face we'd been looking for—and it was, of course, my own.

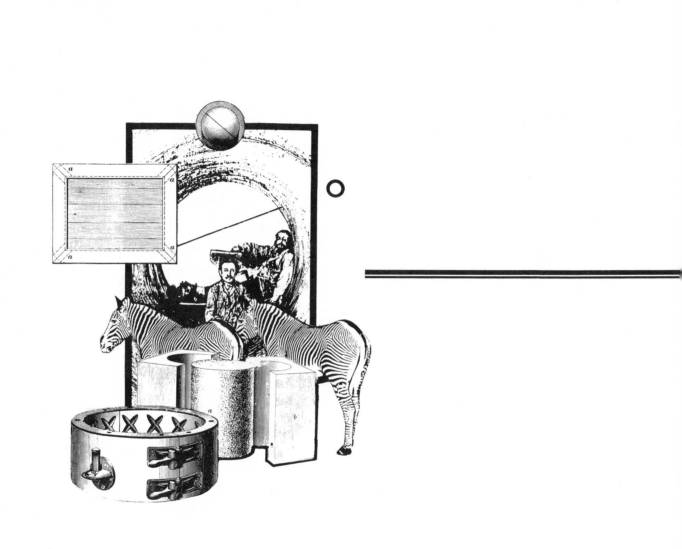

Chapter Four

Michael Stephen's first published novel was *Season at Coole* (New York: Dutton, 1972). It was a book so lively and riotous, by a young Irish-American so conscious of his lyrical Irish heritage, and with a tone so sympathetic to the cyclonic atmosphere of a poor Irish family on the Brooklyn borderline, that the *New York Times* could barely assess all the action and gasp for breath. "It is the night before Christmas," Martin Levin wrote in his review, "and all through their house every member of the Coole family is doing his own thing. Mother Rose is drinking vodka and muscatel in the laundry and conversing with the Virgin Mary; 300-pound Leland, an intermittently brilliant schiz, is going berserk in the basement. Upstairs, Oona and Sandra, age 16 or thereabouts, are tripping on hashish; in the attic, Terrence, age 14, is exercising his biceps, so he can one day assault his father in self-defense. Wolfe Tone, '11 or 12,' is daydreaming of the catcher's mit he will not get. Out in the great world, Michael (a writer) may be heading home for Christmas and Emmett (a hoodlum) may be doing likewise. And Leland Coole senior, the civil servant who heads this house in ferment, is stewing in his own choler. I've left out a few members of the immediate family, as well as the elder Leland's twin half-sisters, who root about in another house under the Williamsburg bridge—but they are originals too."

All of this family matter, which a conventional author might have turned into social reportage, becomes in Stephens's hands "a poem that soars." As with Flann O'Brien (the author of *At Swim-Two-Birds* and the Gaelic classic *An Béal Bocht*, and who has been named as an influence by nearly every contemporary innovator in fiction), Michael Stephens puts most of his action in his language. It is no mean feat to keep that equal to the action of the story, but such is Stephens's plan; as Fielding Dawson noted of the book, "The hysteria which at first is a trifle self-conscious becomes increasingly true without exaggeration." When story and language meet, it is like breaking the sound barrier. It seems as if the words will run off the page, but of course they don't, and that is Stephens's triumph.

In 1972 Jack O'Brien, Kathie Colonnese, and I were visiting Gilbert Sorrentino in New York. Justly acclaimed for his own poetry, fiction, and criticism, Sorrentino was lately being called "the Pound of our era." In the previous decade he had tutored Hubert Selby and, as an editor at Grove, fought for the publication of some of the Sixties' most exciting fiction. Now younger writers were coming to his attention: Kenneth Tindall, Clarence Major, and Michael Stephens—whose *Season at Coole* was sitting on his desk. Several years earlier he had accepted the twenty-year-old Stephens's first manuscript, an autobiographical novel titled *Gulfweed Voices*, but Grove Press was absorbed by Random House before the work could be published. Stephens then wrote *Season at Coole*, initially in the manner of *Gulfweed Voices* and then again in a more objective manner. Editor Hal Scharlatt acquired it for Dutton, and Stephens's career in the difficult waters of innovative fiction was launched.

By his own admission, Michael Stephens bears some resemblance to his writer-character Mickey Mack Coole. Finding Stephens in New York was almost as difficult as for Leland Coole to track down his errant son: the author of *Season at Coole* had shared at least six apartments in the previous five months, took his mail at addresses different from those where he received his phone calls, and kept disappearing to places like Amherst and Provincetown during business hours. When I did locate him, five very long flights up in sculptor Peter Reginato's Greene Street loft, the clatter of Reginato's workroom drove us to a nearby Soho bar, where we ate several cheeseburgers and knishes, drank a lot of dark beer, and spoke as in the transcript which follows. Stephens, it turned out, had resisted talking about his work before, confining his thoughts to notebook jottings. Our talk was like opening those notebooks, the existence of which probably explained Stephens's very coherent and considered view of his own work.

When Reginato had put down his tools for the day, we returned to the loft for even more intense conversation, and then some wine. This was on June 4, 1974: Michael had recently completed *Still Life* and was awaiting the imminent publication of his *Paragraphs* by Harry Lewis in Amherst. He was also trying to rewrite *Gulfweed Voices*, but the need for a clean and quiet workplace was apparent.

In early August I returned to New York and found Michael living Uptown in Mark Weiss's apartment near Columbia University. We added a few notes to the interview and looked at fresh copies of *Paragraphs*; ate a superb dinner at a Cuban restaurant on upper Broadway; and then walked over to the student-packed West End Bar, where a television set showed Richard Nixon resigning the presidency. We crossed the street, stayed a while at a quieter bar (until the first edition of the morning *Times* was out, reprinting Nixon's speech), and finally headed back to his sublet apartment. There we played a tape of Michael's reading at the West End earlier in spring. It was a chapter from *Season at Coole*, about Mother Rose drunk on vodka in her laundry room, ending: "Sleep soothes her for awhile, and dreams do not enter into this sleep. She is dreamless, alone, phantom-like in motherhood, a little Catholic school girl playing hooky from her holy family."

MICHAEL STEPHENS

March 17, 1974

Dear Jerry,

Thank you for your book, the essays, and especially the stamps, which I sorely need, I don't know how you knew this. As for digging, let us commence in terms of the literary archeological finds you are after. The first major point between writing about my writing and the other people you have pursued is that most of my best work has never been printed. There are a handful of people, like Gil [Sorrentino], who like my work enough so that I show them what I am doing. It is for this reason that I am reticent about giving clues to printed works' whereabouts simply because this work does not represent my output my vision my ideas etc. And I am also aware that it smacks a bit of Celtic Victorian preciosity and snobbery to write about a writer's writing which the reader cannot be availed either readily or through assiduous digging. I say this because I like very much the way you handled both Gil and Ron Sukenick, especially Gil who I feel is a greatly overlooked presence in the literary landscape today, as Cubby Selby told me when I met Cubby in LA some years back, "Gil is the Pound of our era." In the sense that he can respond to divergent talents outside his own realm of what is and is not literature. And he, like Selby, has been quite encouraging to me, in the sense that they consider me a writer. That's all a writer needs really, to hell with some other scribe picking away sentences, fixing grammar and spelling, and telling you to read Pound's ABC of Reading.

Does this sound like I am clearing my throat? Well, McNamara, it is St. Paddy's day, and even the tenor John McCormick, who I heard for the first time on the radio yesterday, had to clear his throat before he sang. And really this letter to you is like singing, in the criminal sense—an old Cagney movie say, OK, Mike, sing and we'll make it easy for you. Tell Officer Klinkowitz how you did it and why you did it, and we'll make it easy for you, he'll put in a good word for you. But you seem to have a humor about yourself out there in Iowa, and to think that you would like maybe to say something intelligent about my work, this is all quite flattering, I admit, and I suppose still if it gets you not everywhere, it gets you some place, only you must take it as a given what I suggested earlier, that my best work isn't printed, can't seem to get printed if my agent is any index of this truth, and I am reluctant to reveal the corpses of former works buried in those ugly old magazines that no one will ever find unless I talk.

You write with great sympathy and warmth for Gil and Ron. This is pleasing to see. Now I am like a stripper removing her clothes. I had stories in Evergreen, Feb. '71, which you say you read, a terrible story really; also May '71. An essay about Rudy Wurlitzer in April '71 Evergreen. The Voice printed an article on Dec. 26, 1968, Dec. 31, 1970, and Nov. 23, 1972. Also TriQuarterly 26—I find this story all right. I wish there were some way to get you Gulfweed Voices and the new book Still Life, but that would run into enormous money presently which I do not have—I am not a writer who makes money, never have been. Last year I made about $150 from writing, and the year before wasn't much better, and the year before that was much worse. Some of the paragraphs have appeared here and there, but there is no point in running that down because the book [Paragraphs] should be out by the end of April. In fact, if you are in no hurry, you can wait until then for the book, and an essay in the forthcoming Mulch magazine (you should write Harry Lewis/R.D. #1/Sugar Hill Rd./Williamsburg, Mass. 01096 for copies of mag and book, I already wrote him to send you same, but he might forget with book deadlines coming up, I am sure he is spaced beyond belief). Broadway Boogie/2680 Broadway/NYC, NY 10025 is coming out with a story called "Meat Lust," which I rather like. I'll also enclose in this letter a story everyone hates but which I find quite unusual for its natural flow and artless quality. It is called "Odalisque with Red Trousers"—after the Matisse painting of same name. That should keep you in reading for some time, also bring you up to where I am today—speechless. . . .

Our desires are simply stated. We are revolutionaries rampant in the Americas! Poets and statesmen, in the tradition of former Irish revolutionaries, men of letters, but also men of action. Our tactics are diverse, "total assault," as one Catholic anarchist, Ed Sanders, says. This is our intent, to motivate ourselves in the direction of a radical society, a cultural revolution.

Picture the disorientation on the part of the police, whether it be New York, Chicago, Los Angeles, or San Francisco. For all cops are Irish at heart. Their theory, get the commie gook mocky shine traitors, but the switch will be, the recalcitrants are micks. Erin Go Brau, alongside the NLF flag, they've been duped, what kind of shenanigans is this, officer?

The next step will be to invade the Irish-American societies throughout the country. Give them what

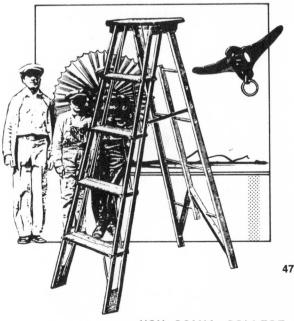

47

they should have, a Yeatsian second coming. Bring along blacks and browns and yellows, Mexican pachuco bandits, local Puerto Rican winos. All men are Irish at heart. Let the police arrest us on the demonstration lines, and when we appear before the red-faced, droopy-jowled judge, we will tell him, "We did it for Ireland."

I have spoken about such a program for years to many Irish men and women, in bars or at parties, over a glass of beer, and many of them agree with me, that this is the only relevant Irish tactic, the only patriotic gesture in remembrance of those men who liberated that great nation. Let us begin, then, when we raise up our glasses in salute, in every Blarney Stone or Blarney Rose bar, we will remember Che Guevara, a true Irishman, and raise our glasses high, we will toast, Venceremos! Venceremos!

—"The Black Irish Have Come to Roost"
(Village Voice, **12/26/68**)

The house was a museum, literally, of natural history, each inhabitant here made the center of his life a collection of things, the mother storing up children, the father collecting beer waste around his belly, the oldest son a collector of misanthropic dreams, the brother Emmett a collector of . . .
He reeled, thinking of them.

—Season at Coole

The particular time and place in this story of an Irish-American family is the occasion of son Michael's first visit home since he fled at age fifteen to be a poet. Earlier in the book each family member has had his or her chapter, except for the three youngest, who share one, and Michael—Mickey Mack, Mackool—who has none. In story terms, it's been the night before Christmas, climax of a time when, as a daughter describes it, " 'Daddy gets his period once a year and for two weeks before Christmas his blood drips everywhere.' " But this year things are worse for Leland Coole, Sr., and the rest of his family. For instance, "Leland Jr. sucked in his meat, tearing pieces from his plate, ravenously, for this Christmas he and the old man had decided to go off the edge of the planet like a brace of ducks in orange sauce together, a duet for father and son, where usually poppa does it now at Christmas, his son Leland will do it a few weeks or months later."

"Logic had failed these people years ago," we're told. Here is how some of them act, beginning with the customs inspector at the center of the chaos:

Leland Coole, Sr.:—**These sons, he thought, what a cross to bear, what a pain in the ass worse than the guineas on the docks and the wacky government he worked for, though he couldn't remember who was missing, since he couldn't remember any of their names at that moment, simply thinking to himself, "one of the chiefs must be in trouble." The phone kept ringing, ringing.**

He picked up the receiver.
"Hello, Coole residence."
In his most pleasant voice.
The voice at the other end of the phone could be heard screaming.

"I don't care whose residence it is, put your father on the phone."

This is what the Inspector heard:

"Your son Michael went crazy and would you please come to Manhattan or we'll have to take him to Bellevue."

But what he heard and what the police said, well, the police said:

"We have a relative of yours and would you please come to Manhattan or we'll have to take her to Bellevue."

But since all his daughters and wife were at home, it had to mean a son [. . .]

Leland Coole, Jr.:—They are scared shitless because of his size & the terror he inspires in them. Don't he know it, from mother to father on down the faces of the children, he could wipe them out, make page three of the Daily News.

FORMER MENTAL PATIENT GOES BERSERK
KILLS ENTIRE FAMILY WITH RAZOR

But Michael & Emmett would get out of that slaughter, because they don't come by anymore, he'd hunt them down like he did Michael once, when he knew Mackool was tapping his brain for ideas in those books he wrote, that nurd, he's the one Leland wants to get, cut off his typing fingers, bleed out his tongue, inject blue ink into his veins [. . .]

Emmett Coole:—"My trouble is, I'm alive at twenty-seven and I'm acting still like I'm fifteen about to die in one year."

The Inspector was downstairs with his badges, his Knights of Columbus card, an epaulet from his U.S. Government uniform: Leland was there with his underpants falling off, the children—how they were wonderful in these cases!—gathered around the police like a slew of Oliver Twists, poor and depraved looking like a Dickens dream of squalor, they were breaking hearts with their sobs and cries, Don't take our brother, we love him! He's only got six months to live!

Emmett was having his morning asthma attack on the porch, as the police marched in to arrest him. Leland was called from the other room.

"Remember the Post Office, Easter 1916, and who you were named after!"

Mother Rose turned to Leland.

"He was named after my brother Emmett."

Leland was annoyed.

"He was not!"

Inspector Coole was once again, blown-minded, stunned, looking to his wife and older son, the gathered children, the police surrounding Emmett.

"He was named after Robert Emmett," Leland said.

But Mother Rose insisted, he was named after her brother.

Terry stared at the police, who were trying to shoo the children from the room. Emmett's skinny body was draped over one cop's arms, like a cloth, and the piggish-beat-up cop with the bandage had to be restrained by two other officers.

Mother Rose was in the room now.

"He looks like John F. Kennedy this minute."

The police halted, amazed.

They couldn't believe what they heard and went ahead with their arrest, as though she had said nothing.

"Long live Leopold and Loeb!" Leland shouted, as his father attempted to get him to go into the cellar.

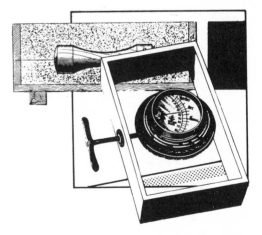

Patrick's chapter is really Mackool's, since Pat is the one who seeks out Michael for a talk. And when they meet, "they talked of their tribe, the usual way the conversation went was one Coole was trying to outdo in depravity the other Coole with a story about their, what they called, Family." In terms of the story, Patrick tells his brother about the latest mad confusion, how two bizarre Coole relatives (half-mad sisters, a story in themselves, which we get in time) are being detained by the cops (in lieu of Bellevue), and how the old man believes, and is acting out his beliefs, that it's Mickey Mack who's gone nuts.

Behind all these stories is the storyteller, Michael Coole. He is "the watershed child between the alcoholic nation of mother and father, Leland & Emmett," and the younger ones into drugs; he also defines the final triangle of the youngest, Deirdre, Terry, and Wolfe. The house of Coole has a dining room, a head room, and an attic, and only Michael inhabits them all: "just pick any room, cozy fertile bins where memory never ceased, where fantasy ruled, and he had come once again to wonderland." But this time Mickey Mack Coole is a person come to find that "the seeds of his imagination took their powers from these musty rooms, a seven room house fogged with a million crack ups, a clan of visionaries here," each with their own story but which only a supreme fictionist can fashion into art. We have the people, as real as can be; they tell us their stories, bizarre as they seem; but what simultaneously makes it fiction and makes it matter is the artistic intelligence in, about, above, and behind it. No matter what, says Beckett in the book's epigraph, "All is not then yet quite irrevocably lost."

Waiting for Steve Katz in a Spring Street bar, June 1974

Well, the perversity of my own nature is such that I can create a lot of humor out of my own personal pain. And so the tone of Season at Coole *comes out of that particular aspect of my own personality. When I was writing the book a lot of people felt I was brutal, and they were upset that my own family resembled too much the people in the book and that it was an offensive act on the writer's part to do that. In fact just the other day a doctor I know who comes in this bar occasionally had read the book, had read it twice, and was very upset about it.*

Q. Has your family read it?

Yeah, my family has read it, too. And that's what he wanted to know, and was very concerned by that. And what I was trying to explain to him is that first of all the members of my family—my real family—lived through a correspondent experience. It wasn't that actual experience, but there were enough things in it that were correspondent to it, so that it really was not offensive in the sense that it was a given day-to-day reality for them, to be poor like that and to find escape in that infighting, and the drunkenness and drugs and all those other things. So it may be shocking to someone who didn't grow up in experiences like that, but to someone who has lived that every day it's not terribly shocking, and it's also in another way triumphant, because it shows that you survived it. If you didn't survive it you wouldn't have been able to write about it.

My family background was very much Irish—Irish in the New York sense that they can really respond to someone writing a book, because language is a cultural heritage to them, even in an atrophied culture. And there is indigenous to an Irish literary life a certain kind of sadness and humor about it, a given in Irish literature from the beginning, and I was always very influenced by it. Even though my family never read that much, there was a built-in mechanism in my mother and father to respond to the fact that it was a lyrical achievement that could transcend any of the degraded quality of the subject matter.

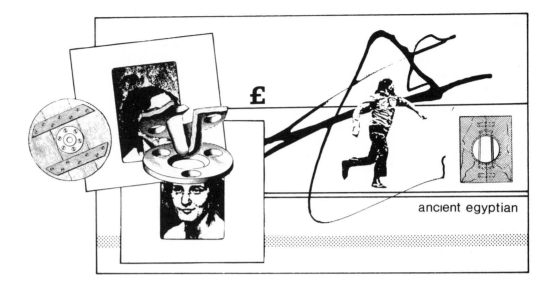

ancient egyptian

Later in Peter Reginato's Greene Street studio/loft, over burned coffee

You know, it's about everyone's family. We're all dissolving. It's an establishment. It does not work anymore. It's a bogus kind of system that destroys women and destroys men at the same time, destroys the children that come out of it. So that my writing about it was also being aware of other people's lives being wrecked by that social and cultural system, and that I was just being the voice of that collective experience. On a very profound level I don't really think that there are many evils left in the world. But on a really personal level I think the family thing is a destructive force in our lives, and it's one that I could really get going on. In some ways I'm not sure if I should because I know then I'm politicizing. You know, I'm not really talking about my art, although my art came out of it. I think about William Burroughs when he talks about family in that book of interviews called The Job *that Grove did. He starts talking about his family and he talks about revolution: you can't have a revolution because the family unit will always be there. Because it's the most reactionary and destructive force there is. And when I start thinking about it and get angry I realize that it's absolutely true. In some way when I was writing my book a lot of that was in my head—that I really wanted to go out and destroy that shit and make it look so ugly that no one would ever dare get themselves involved in it. And yet we all do and we all have our optimisms about it. And I don't really see any alternative to it, which is a profound problem of our time. But we all have a desire to procreate and to flatter ourselves by seeing children that in some way mimic us in a flattering way.*

The other profound evil that I've come to realize is poverty, having been in it all my life, and at a certain point it just begins to corrupt you in a very brutal and ugly way. Shaw and O'Neill were very sensitized to this, and lots of other writers, but Shaw and O'Neill in a way that I can see very visibly at the moment. Family and poverty are certainly themes in Season at Coole: *I was going after the evil of poverty and how it destroys any kind of talent, certainly like with the character Leland—a near literary genius who is done in by his . . . just the insanity of being poor, you know, and how it promulgates itself further. And then the other personal evil is the whole thing of family, and in my own case it was an exaggerated evil because it was so apparent. But I think that everyone I know, whether they cop to it or not, they have that strain running through their lives—a familial profundity that at times can approach despair, because they have a mother and father.*

Unhinged from the doors of my cell, Prince S's rabbit is in the room, I can't remember his name. The motherfucker speaks to me, & I'm loony, Michael Mad Dog, goddam, up & down the merry-go-round my head, it was on Second Avenue, he bummed a cigarette outside the Fillmore, he said, "tick with me tonight, I'll tell you all about her." I lit his cigarette & he opened a bottle of wine, we whispered into the stuff, got shitfaced together, she (I mean here the Prince S) was off rehearsing a piece of music by Schönberg, 12-tone Earl Scheib paint job, the bartender was speaking to me & the rabbit. The animal's tuxedo covered with New York soot, he voiced strong objections to, "the rats give the rodents a bad name, take myself. I'm clean, not aggressive, like to talk to people, make love, but that's not what I want to talk about, I'm always jumping off tracks," his ears drooped, lower. . . .

—"The Hare Apparent," Evergreen Review **(February 1971)**

High Tide

Scones for breakfast; shower, shave, watch a gull fly past the skylight. Sand covers the floor in the kitchen, because I forgot to empty my sneakers after walking along the beach at sun up. The pebbles on the linoleum grate along the soles of my bare feet. Besides, a postcard arrived from heaven. The angels are with me now; the angels approve of the way I make love to her. We were talking about a pheasant when the postcard came in the mail. A pheasant of such fine succulence that we would eat its feathers too. I doubt whether the angels understand this devotion to birds. Other mornings I spoke of writing a letter to an old girlfriend, but the thought of, she never answers, drove me to go swimming instead. A simple letter I could fold in thirds, double spaced, and with a direct statement. Dear S, miss you still, wish you were here. I guess it seems strange that I should write you after all these years, but my feelings never flagged, I wanted to tell you about my wife and child, but I suppose that isn't necessary. The boy has my eyes and your nose, his mother's temperament. The boss fired me three weeks ago for not taking an interest in my work, and I've been living on a wharf at the seashore ever since. My unemployment is transferable, we manage to cut expenses to a minimum and live a healthy, uncluttered life. Your breasts creep into my dreams, and your long body appears whenever I swim too far from shore. I imagine that you get better looking each day, my own face has assumed a distinct character since we last met. My curiosity would drive me to ask why you never say hello to me on the street, but then I realize it's none of my business, we all have our quirks. When I'm alone on the beach, I like to think that I've known nothing but good ladies. When I'm with friends, I tell them you are fine, that you are a complex woman who can't be explained in an evening. With most women, I assume their natural grace but realize you would have handled the situation with more poise. This keeps my head from wandering where it doesn't belong; I can understand how you might forget my first name after not seeing me for so long. My own memory relies on imagination most of the time. There is the sound of water breaking on the shore outside. I found out yesterday that the sound is called "plangency." To the best of my knowledge, there has never been a name for the sound of a man breaking past a woman's thighs, a name for the absence of this sound in my ears now. But the air is fresh, the wind is calm, I see the fishing boats coming in for the day. Today I had scones for breakfast; cheese, pears, burgundy for lunch; chicken wings, kale, raw clams, white wine, Portuguese bread, sweet unsalted butter for supper. Love,

—Paragraphs **(Amherst: Mulch Press, 1974)**

Writing paragraphs is a vocation that Stephens shares with Ronald Sukenick, Steve Katz, and Clarence Major. Sukenick's "Endless Short Story" is an attempt to define his work not by genre, but *as writing*—the art of "chewing the fat," as Sukenick would say. As Clarence Major describes his own efforts, "I've been struggling with this whole business of fixed forms, struggling to break out of that tight little restricted area that I feel when I'm working on something that has to be defined as a poem, for example, or defined as a novel, with a beginning, middle, and end. It's very satisfying to be working on something that has no name. That's what it's really all about, for me anyway, to try to do something like that—that surprises you, that's full of surprises for me." Or as Ronald Sukenick writes in the *Digressions*, "We work beyond form: form is the embodiment, the temporary manifestation of the imagination, an embodiment that is the consequence of the questioning of form by the imagination." Sukenick, Katz, Major, and Stephens "write beyond any definitions of form because we believe that fiction is always in process of defining itself," Sukenick concludes. Not "expression" in the Romantic sense of the term, since expression implies a sense of auto-biography or confession—neither of which are fiction-making activities. What we have from these writers instead is improvisation with both words and experience, factual or made up; an activity so free from the abstractions of pre-existing forms that the result can be fresh contact with the world. The paragraphs may be the ultimate SuperFiction.

Michael Stephens's *Paragraphs* is printed with illustrations by Fritz Bultman: a series of nudes seemingly sculpted with pencil. In his own short "Study with Nudes," Stephens writes that "Nudes don't excite me any more, yet there are people—I know a friend—who can create the nude in drawing as though they were the first to think of this idea, so original is their line of sensuosity, of pencil point turned lead to flesh." There is an inebriety with physical things which *Paragraphs* treats with the same sense of discovery. In order to write "I love you," Stephens literally fleshes out his imagination with colors, sounds, smells, tastes, and touches. A bowl of pears, a bowl of nectarines becomes "the center of my heart"; his writing makes associations so rampant that there is no abstract place for his feelings to hide, no preordained form to be imposed on his writing. For "Hemingway in Paris" Stephens takes a typical Montmartre cafe scene, right out of Carlos Baker or *A Moveable Feast*, and improvises with the stuff of Hemingway's life: "There was a brief second where the words Ketchum, Idaho shot through his brain like a bullet, and he wiped what felt like a burning tear of sweat from his forehead, he did not know where he was and looked from Mike Campbell to Lady Brett wondering who these startling creatures were." The three finish their white burgundy together, author and creations alike. *Paragraphs* is the language of dreams, the words of improvising thought, an attempt to deal with life's sensuosity in its full physical sense without the writing being confused with subject matter and turning into titillation. Stephens's hope, like Sukenick's, is for "composition" as we know it in the drawing. "A nude body in fiction is a prelude for a pornographic stunt," Stephens reflects, "yet in the drawing, life forever goes on within the limits of that frame, wild brushes of strokes, and ecstatic pulls and pushes of dramatic tensions made flesh by a pencil." Drawing is the process of a man's hand on paper, his muscles following "the dictates of his imagination." Imagination triumphs over boredom, life triumphs "over nothing." The writer of paragraphs faces his world with the elements of his own composition. "I am Michael, I am desperate, I am the love my words stand for. . . ."

Still later at Reginato's, with wine

Isaac Babel wrote novels that were about two pages long, literally. The Red Cavalry is just a series of brilliant novels, one after the other. They're very, very short, some of them are two pages, some five, but never much beyond that. How I did the paragraph was that it started out as an experiment because I was thinking about my own style and the units that I wrote in, and that I wasn't particularly interested in writing a poem, with a line break; and I wasn't particularly interested in writing a story, with a beginning middle and end. I was trying to find out how my thought process worked. I realized that it worked in paragraphs; I had one thing that was a paragraph and it would end there and then I would go into the next movement. So I just sort of started it as a way of refining the way I wrote and as I started doing it—I did about two or three hundred of them—I realized that a lot of them were separate entities and that they weren't just experiments or anything like that, or exercises, but that they were actually their own integral form. I liked that idea because it didn't have the burden of being called a poem which a poem does have today. And it didn't have the burden of having to tell a story, which is something that I've always felt to be a burden because I'm not interested in story. The thing with Season at Coole *is that there's practically no story at all. To this day why I still love Joyce is that he was probably one of the worst storytellers of all time. In* Ulysses . . . *I remember hearing Anthony Burgess speak one time and he was saying that the movie version of* Ulysses *was extrapolating the story and forgetting about the rest of it, making a movie of the story. He said the thing they didn't realize was that it was probably the worst story ever written, and that the beauty of his writing was something totally different. And I started thinking about that.*

Particularly Charles Olson, his essays, was the first influence in terms of how I wrote a sentence and a paragraph, making the paragraph a unit of writing, and using a comma instead of a period for breath pauses, and letting the ends of the paragraph be the real intaking of breath and the longest pause, almost a silence, and then going into the next one. I was talking with a friend of mine who's a very formal English instructor, and he said that to diagram a sentence in Season at Coole *is almost impossible because everything about the sentences in the book is grammatically incorrect. In Camus's notebooks he wrote that Balzac was not a genius in spite of his bad grammar but because of it. And since my own grammatical upbringing has been pretty negligible, you know, I went with that right away. Just thinking about American prose writers that I like, I liked Dreiser when I was really young, and maybe I liked it for that sort of sloppy American grammatical inaccuracy that he had. That is certainly valid to American speech, though. And Frank O'Hara has that in* The Lunch Poems, *you know, just that the constructions are slightly awry at times, and that's the thing that makes them so artful.*

From there [New York] Andrei Codrescu wandered to Detroit (because he read about that city in Céline's "Journey to the End of Night"), hooked up with John Sinclair's Artist Workshop, and learned, as on a tabula rasa, the American language via the street hippies, radical poets, rock records, and later from runaway girls he picked up on 8th Street, the countermen at Blimpie's on Sixth Avenue, and other unaccountable American Sources.

—**"These Poems Are Loaded,"** Village Voice
(12/31/70)

The truth is the consistency of the language, and its unnameable ability to create experience, not through language, but language as the experience itself.

—**"Reviews: Living at the Movies,"** Valley Advocate
(2/6/74)

My whole orientation to words is more lyrical than anything else. Anything I write has got to have a certain music to it or I don't bother with it. Very often in my work one of the problems is that the music often cuts off any story line. In Season at Coole *I happened to maintain that, it's true. But in other writing I've done since then the music got out of hand, but it is still a prerequisite that it has to have that music somewhere. The first person that ever really influenced me in terms of writing when I was young was Thelonius Monk. I often have this fantasy of someday doing a musical about his life, and putting words to all of his compositions, like "Round Midnight." I went through a whole period, when I was about fifteen or sixteen or seventeen, where I used to go see him everywhere; I used to go to the Five Spot every night and listen to him. That was the initial lyrical experience.*

I see two influences working in Flats. **The first is writers like Beckett and Robbe-Grillet; the second is cowboy pulp novels and Western movies. There is a feeling here like in John Ford's silent movie** Three Bad Men. **Just a couple of raunchy cowpokes shooting the shit at the fire in order to make it through the night, hoping that the sun shines once more so they can see the posse coming, the rattlesnake under a rock, or an Indian in the foothills.**

—**"A Voice at the Edge of Things,"** Evergreen Review
  (April 1971)

**What is a geography to say
what I say.
Let me be the figure of the inward.**

—Alcohol Poems **(Binghamton: Loose Change
  Press, 1973)**

**The seeds of his imagination took their powers from
these musty rooms. . . .**

—Season at Coole

It's one of the few things about the book that I had a really thoughtful kind of pre-writing reaction to. First of all I did about eleven drafts of the book to start with, and so a lot of the quality of my style that looks like a loose-ended spontaneity is a worked-out process that I go through to maintain the illusion that it just came out of me in one burst. With Mickey Mack the original version that Dutton accepted was done in the first person. So in other words I was the narrator; when I was discussing it with my editor and looking it over at one point, I felt that it was so obvious that it was my story that it would be better if it were in the third person. I never at any point try to give an objective reality of the story or of these people's lives or anything. So what I came to realize is that the voice of the narrator is so subjective that it wasn't necessary for a chapter about Mickey Mack Coole because it was his story all along, and that more than anything else the characters he created were projections out of his own fantasy.

Michael Stephens makes music of life, something out of nothing. He makes it a silent movie, a slapstick comedy, the "grotesque, situational poetry" which Kurt Vonnegut, Jr., says in *Slapstick* is "what life *feels* like to me." Vonnegut's models are Laurel and Hardy, who with their limited agility and intelligence "go on and on." The fundamental joke about them "was that they did their best with every test. They never failed to bargain in good faith with their destinies, and were screamingly adorable and funny on that account."

Stephens's model is Buster Keaton, renamed in the manuscript *Still Life* as Martin "Buster" Shigh. Well intentioned, he is forever beaten, fired, abused, and insulted, yet he can respond to life with an imaginative energy which makes it into a comic work of art—the life of fiction which for some may be a still-life portrait but which is "still life." His response to Vonnegut's cosmic joker is, like Vonnegut's characters, to take a pratfall. His hopeless seductions are performed with seltzer bottles and cream pies. But as long as he can make art of his life, life will go on; all is not then yet quite irrevocably lost.

Life is a farrago, I said.

I shimmied up the drainpipe, my keys locked in the building I shimmied up; the room whose window I shimmied toward was on the second floor where I slept.

Things were awry as I shimmied up the drainpipe toward the window, with its broken panes, within whose demesne my keys were located.

I shimmied up the drainpipe in this freezing cold pre-dawn, and I said, if life isn't a farrago then I'm drunk or crazy, of which I might be both. I tried shimmying up the drainpipe earlier, but quarter way I slipped, and downward I shimmied, which was not helpful or what I intended, I shimmied up to the window ledge with its broken pane, and I espied my key ring on the table, the keys locked within the magic circle of the ring. I reached out as though to embrace the keys, and I slipped—fully up the drainpipe I had shimmied now—and then I fell from the second story ledge, backward, onto the concrete, unhurt, because I was either drunk or crazy so the usual tensions that attend a person trying to break into a second story window did not attend my person.

I lay in the chunks of glass.

The brandy swelled in my head like a heat, the palms of my hands were bleeding.

I looked at my bleeding hands, I said, "I feel all right, I feel fine."

Chunks of glass stuck in my ass, which I picked, both the ass and the glass from the seat of my pants. I threw the pieces of glass into the bottle-broken street.

Then I felt a warm liquid oozing down my ass, down my trousers to the back of my knees.

I must be bleeding to death, I said, but then I realized that my pint of wine, in my back pocket, had broken. The only real damage was to my thigh, which bled like a holy red river down my leg, because the ballpoint pen in my right front pocket had punctured the cloth, punctured the flesh and muscle of my upper leg.

The pen had jabbed my leg as I fell, the pen's nib ensconced in my femoral. My sunglasses were cracked, and now that I thought about it, my ribs and my back were numbly aching, quavering from the fall. I concluded that this was not a graceful fall, nor was it a successful ascent, since the import of climbing was to gain access to the window, to enter the window into the room, and from the room to extract my key ring with the keys to the front door.

The day before I had seen an afghan leap from a fifth floor window around the corner. It was pure grace, as though its ears were desuetudinous wings that were about to come back to life. The afghan bounds to the next building; no, it splattered over the concrete below, yelping in utter pain, within minutes dying, it was dead. I neither yelped nor died from my fall. I learned one thing, and that was to be circumspect upon my next ascent up the side of the building to the room in which I slept. I shimmied up the drainpipe, I spoke to myself, I said:

Steady, Martin.

Or I said: Easy does it.

Or: You've got it now, Buster.

Watch your step, Mr. Shigh.

[That's pronounced "Shee," like the good people.]

I shimmied up the drainpipe toward the second floor window, I placed my cut hands on the window ledge, and with one burst of energy from my blood-wet and alcohol-dripped legs, I am inside the window, I am home safely.

But then my pants got stuck on the aluminum clasp on the drainpipe, and I hung, legs dangling, thrashing in the ozone, arms waving for help. Life is a farrago, I screamed. A man then walked past with his dog, whistling, I yelled for help but he kept walking, once looking up as though I were an apparition in the air, he muttered, "The things people do in this town." Then my pants ripped at the crotch, where all the weight was, and I burst from the sky.

—Still Life **(New York: Kroesen Books, 1977)**

Dear Jerry,

I think it was a good meeting last week and I look forward to seeing what you do with the material. Right now, shortly after my first verbal speak about a craft I've always maintained a silence about, I am reflecting on some of your questions and my answers to them. The most major addition I feel is necessary concerns the notion of using real people as the inspiration for one's characters. We all do this, but, I suppose, in my case, and probably in Gil's case too, the reader seems more concerned how much is real and what is imaginary. For me, they blend so easily, I cannot often find the demarcation line. But I do have several rules, which I didn't mention in the interview, and which I find essential before I sit down to type out a story or book. First, I say, never write to get even. It will always go against you. Second, be like Chekhov, love every character you write about. The second rule is essential—you can't get into a character, whether you criticize or praise, unless you love them first. Not like. LOVE. With an obsessive passion. The Cooles I love dearly, or I could never say what I say about them. Ditto in Still Life *with Buster Shigh and Lady Hand. Ditto in the stories. Well, amigo, I am sure more will follow at both ends of this correspondence. Be well.*

Michael

Chapter Five

Walter Abish began publishing fiction during 1970–71, first in the little magazine *Confrontation* (edited from Long Island University in New York), and then in the New Directions anthologies. Although his work has since appeared in *Paris Review, TriQuarterly, Fiction, Extensions, Fiction International,* and *Seems*, he is preeminently a New Directions writer. He's been represented in nearly every one of their anthologies since #23 (1971); New Directions is the publisher of his novel, *Alphabetical Africa* (1974), and his story collections, *Minds Meet* (1975) and *In the Future Perfect* (1977). Abish is also a contributor to the Fiction Collective's anthology, *Statements*.

Many of Abish's fictions are written in the manner which Donald Barthelme has made almost mainstream: stiff-upper-lip sentences, self-effacing characters, and just enough input from the outer world to make you think that everyone must be a lunatic out there. But to Abish the world is far less interesting than the language it uses—particularly language he can adapt into "self-exploring" fiction. This interest is most apparent in *Alphabetical Africa,* a novel constructed of chapters lettered "A" through "Z," then back from "Z" to "A" again. All the words in Chapter "A" begin with the letter *a;* in Chapter "B" words beginning with that letter are added, in "C" those words can be used, and so forth. The strategy is more than a device, since it forces a functional self-consciousness upon both author and reader (for instance, the first-person narrator cannot enter the story until Chapter "I"). Midway through, the book starts collapsing. First we lose the letter *z*, then *y*, then *x*, until by the end we are back to all *a* words. "The whole book is like taking a deep breath and letting it out," Lawrence Alloway has said. "I love the way the alphabetizing expands from one letter to the status of a full vocabulary. At first the world follows the words. Then, as one approaches Z, the word-gains divulge a full-scale narrative. After the situation is revealed, the lexical possibilities contract, but the word-loss is based on known characters and their deployment."

For all this linguistic emphasis, there is a good deal of action in *Alphabetical Africa*: the continent is attacked by an army of driver ants, chipped away by geographers (who seem to be reducing its size as it becomes "better known"), painted orange (as in map colors) by an aggressive neighbor, and finally used as the backdrop for a cloak-and-dagger intrigue about jewel thieves. Central to it all is Alva, the object of a great deal of sexual interest and anxiety. Both theme and technique serve Abish's purpose. "Feeling a distrust of the understanding that is intrinsic to any communication," he said of **Alphabetical Africa**, "I decided to write a book in which my distrust became a determining factor upon which the flow of the narrative was largely predicated."

Abish was born in Vienna and grew up in China. He lived in Israel for eight years, where he served in the tank corps of the Israeli army ("I'm afraid I was not much of a soldier," he admits). In 1960 he came to the United States as an urban planner; one of his projects included a survey of brownstones in New York City, where he learned that the exceptional sturdiness of their construction has abetted the lives of many older neighborhoods which would otherwise have disappeared years ago. Although he disclaims any immediate influence on his writing, it is remarkable that he should have learned the underlying structures of America before settling down to life in its particulars.

The literal perspective which Walter Abish has on New York City these days is nearly as remarkable. He works just a few blocks back from the old dueling grounds on the New Jersey bank, overlooking the Hudson River. It was here that Aaron Burr fatally wounded Alexander Hamilton; Hamilton's statue, on the approximate site of his death, figures in the cover design of Abish's poetry collection, **Duel Site** (New York: Tibor de Nagy Editions, 1971). To get to Abish's studio in New Jersey, one drives even higher through the narrow streets along the cliff, then follows on foot a steeply declining set of steps. The house itself is like a cottage from the Wisconsin or Minnesota lakes, although its patio and garden—on the nearly vertical hillside—are suggestively Mediterranean. On an unusually cool, rainy summer afternoon in 1974 we sat in the garden, sheltered by a canopy of trees and vines, talking without benefit of tape recorder or notes. Walter asked that we keep the tape from inhibiting our conversation; it would be better, we both agreed, to run through our questions and answers extemporaneously, then write them out afterward.

Occasionally the rain would drive us inside for coffee (espresso, of course), an exotically flavored ham on French bread, and later wine. When the weather broke we climbed the steps for a stroll around a nearby lake ("It is exactly two miles around from this point," Walter said), then returned for dinner with Cecile Abish, a sculptor exhibiting in New York at the time.

The environment was pleasantly unreal: our drive from midtown Manhattan had taken less than fifteen minutes, but it seemed we were hundreds of miles away. Sitting in the garden, waiting for the rain, there was no hint of New York City except for a slight break in the trees, which revealed a postcard view of the island, stretching from Riverside Park (just across from our location) down the West Side Highway, punctuated by the Empire State and other midtown buildings. Later, when the overcast lifted, the whole scene took on an H. G. Wells time machine effect, as the controllers at La Guardia sent jet after jet after jet up the river, almost at our altitude (it seemed), floating there before our eyes from this primeval garden. That evening, from my hotel on far West 42 Street, I tried to pick out the lights across the river. In the clatter and din of Manhattan, it hardly seemed the Abish studio and its garden could be there.

WALTER ABISH

IN THE GARDEN: I

By now I have given a number of different explanations of how I came to write Alphabetical Africa. *I believe that all, to a degree, are correct. To begin with I couldn't have attempted to write* Alphabetical Africa *without first having written "Minds Meet," in which each page or less than a page-long section was built around the key word in the alphabetically arranged subtitles. A message spelling out my concern with the formation of ideas in a literary context serves as a kind of theme. The message reads: Is there any other way to live? The alphabetically arranged subtitles are: Taken* aback *by the message, The* abandoned *message,* abased *by the message,* abashed *while receiving the message, once the knowledge of the message has* abated, *and so on.... The short pieces deal with the act of being taken aback, of abandonment, or being abashed, etc. The key words starting with the letter* a *in the title act as catalysts. The same characters appear in most of the sections. Instead of words authenticating the characters, I had hoped to accomplish the opposite. By questioning their authenticity, I wanted the idea, and the words as signifiers to stand out, delineating the entire process of the work.*

The abandoned message

Two million eight hundred and thirty-three thousand vehicles were abandoned in the countryside during the first quarter of this year. A sizable number of the abandoned cars contained people . . . some also contained pets. Of course, by the time a car is found it has already been stripped of its engine, its tires, and anything else that may be useful to another driver. In most cases the cars had run out of gas, and the driver, passengers, and pets, out of luck. Unwilling to abandon the car many people heroically sat with it. Technically, as long as they remain in the car, the car cannot be considered abandoned. At one time the film industry exploited the theme of abandonment. It went to great length to build up the myth of the abandoned husband. Although some of these films were made over thirty years ago they can still be seen on television. Generally the movie's climax, if it can be called that, is reached when the wife, returning from her millionaire lover, drives her Rolls over the body of her missing husband. Bewildered they stare at each other. She accompanies him to the hospital, abandoning her car. It is not too painful, he assures her, as millions of married men bite back their tears, and their wives, in panic at their husbands' distress, welcome the oblivion into which they have sunk. Still, the word "abandoned" is rarely used in the film. In actual life it is used all too frequently; i.e., we should abandon Harlem, or we abandoned our children. Abandoned children grow up to make love like other people. But there is a sadness, a lingering wet sadness on their sallow faces as they pick up a girl on the road, and then drive their cars in circles until they have run out of gas.

—**"Minds Meet,"** Triquarterly **#26 (Winter 1973), collected in** Minds Meet

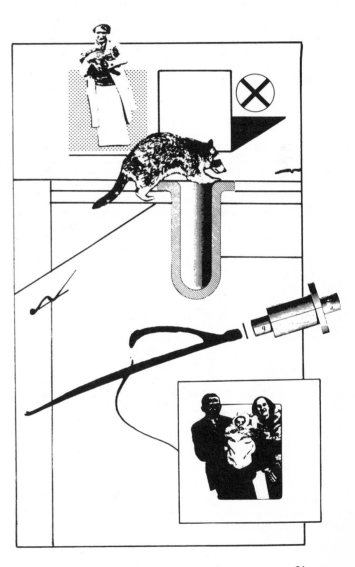

Despite his foreign background and experiences, Walter Abish is nonetheless thoroughly Americanized. Like Donald Barthelme, he plays with substitutions and inversions in the modern American landscape, taking our habitual mores and exposing the silliness they mask. Knowing he's from Vienna makes it all the more fun. In his story "More by George" from the New Directions #27 (1973) anthology, a couple together with hitchhiker and camper travel from Vienna, Maryland, to Vienna, Georgia (pop. 3,718). There the people are about to celebrate "the anniversary marking the defeat of the Turks, as well as, one hundred fifty years later, the publication of a slim volume of poetry entitled *Rambles of a Viennese Poet*, a book that was promptly outlawed when it first appeared in print." For the occasion a replica of the Stefan's Turm has been erected. "It was only one fifth the size of the original, but three times as large as the one in Vienna, Maryland, which had a population of 420."

Abish is also concerned with language. Often it is the subject of the story itself, as in the passage from "Minds Meet." Other times his characters treat the topic, as in "Crossing Friends," published for the first time in *Minds Meet*: "He presses his knife against Doug's throat because he found it difficult to rely solely upon language. Language contains all kinds of secret impediments. Language constricts."

Abashed while receiving the message

Harry is intensely sensitive to what others think of him. He is so afraid of asking the wrong question, or mispronouncing a word, that frequently he gets on a bus and rides all the way to the end of the line rather than ask the driver or one of the passengers where the bus is going. Many men, like Harry, are not certain what day of the week it is. Yet others have minds like clocks.

Harry steps into a bank in Queens and points a pistol at the bank teller. Let's have all your dough, he says. Dough, mocks the teller. What do you think this is, a bakery? Next thing you'll be asking for bread. Harry blushes furiously. He is being mocked. He feels abashed. It is a familiar quandary, so he shoots the bank teller, and then hops on the first passing bus outside the bank. Killing is a stabilizing factor in this society. But in no time Harry is again filled with a familiar panic, he doesn't know in which direction the bus is headed.

—"Minds Meet"

The characters in Abish's stories who are concerned with or confused about language are usually confused in their personal lives as well. The stories center on this confusion. "All those courses in psychology have not prepared me for a locked door," the narrator of "The Second Leg" (*Paris Review #55*, Fall 1972, collected in *Minds Meet*) confesses. "Logic 1. and 2. has not helped me achieve a measure of tranquility." Characters such as this narrator are constantly self-reflective, measuring every move they make; since their actions and (more often) musings constitute the core of the story, Abish's fiction itself becomes self-reflective. But never with the ponderous seriousness of Beckett. For some reason when American fictionists use this technique the result is more exuberantly funny. It never happens with the confessional poetry of Lowell, Plath, or Berryman; but put it in prose and the result is literary hysteria. "So far she has not made one single reference to sex. It must be my imagination . . . my restless, troubled mind that is plaguing me. . . . It must be my imagination . . . all the same I can hear her quite distinctly enunciate the ejaculatory words: fuck, balls, cunt. . . ."

Barthelme puts his characters through similar rigors; like Abish, he is drawn to the paranoiacally self-conscious narrator who undermines the seriousness of what he has to say by the way he goes about saying it. The art, of course, is in the way it is said; that much is held in common with Beckett and the French New Novelists. But as Barthelme has written of them in *Location* (Summer 1964), "The French new novelists, Butor, Sarraute, Robbe-Grillet, Claude Simon, Philippe Sollers, have . . . succeeded in making objects of their books without reaping any of the strategic benefits of the maneuver—a triumph of misplaced intelligence. Their work seems leaden, self-conscious in the wrong way." There is humor, even of an American variety, in Beckett—Buster Keaton, perhaps, especially as Michael Stephens uses him for *Still Life*. The appropriate model for Walter Abish's characters, however, would be the comedian Woody Allen, because as the story develops, a self-reflexive narrative figure has been created whose own self-doubting attributes are the story's point.

IN THE GARDEN: II

I am and have for some time been intrigued by the idea of fiction exploring itself . . . fiction turning inward and measuring by means of its mirror image of life forms, the encoded development of itself. Within that context the narrator often plays a double role, frequently an unreliable one, a role in which what he sees, and how he sees it can isolate and also mar the logical sequence of events that might have been expected to follow. When fiction explores itself it also explores how ideas are formed in fictional circumstances. I for one try not to forget that I am writing fiction while doing so, and that instability can be considered a form of breakdown in communication . . . or at least a threat of one. In my early work this is made manifest by the stability/instability of vision and language, affecting thereby the lineal order of an ordered set of objects I describe.

I think that in today's society we are more aware of instability and its permutations . . . certainly it pervades our day-to-day encounters, our actions, as well as our attempts to cope with the deluge of signals emitted by our brains, chiefly by blocking the never quite clear fluctuations of our emotional response to stress. But whereas instability has a curiously contemporary and psychological ring to it, its quasi-antithesis, stability, evokes a kind of nostalgic view of the past in which everyone aspired to an economical, political, psychologically gratifying stability that, at the time, seemed almost a feasible attainment. Goethe, I believe, condemned Kleist for being unstable. He also helped ruin Kleist's career. Sure enough, Kleist shortly thereafter committed suicide as if to prove Goethe correct. It's hardly surprising that Goethe became a culture hero for generations of Germans who above everything else dreaded disorder, and equated order with a moral rational development.

To this day our cultural divinations allow us to create a clear but utterly fallacious division between the stable and the unstable, as if they were self-contained units, uncontaminated by each other, and it is impossible to use either word without the loaded cultural references and values they encapsulate.

*

All evening I master forbearance. I decline to inquire into their true relationship. Why should it matter to me, a kind of stretched out weekend guest, what she and Victor do in the bathroom. It is so simple to jump to an erroneous conclusion. First Victor excuses himself, and leaves the table. Then she goes to the kitchen to fetch the dessert and coffee. Don't run off and desert me, I say jokingly. The next thing I hear is their boisterous shouts, their unabashed shrill laughter. They do nothing to restrain their mirth . . . or the sound of running water. It is seeping through from under the bathroom door when I get up to investigate. I keep myself in check and do not bring it to their attention. All things considered . . . not to overlook the soaked bedroom slippers, as well as the inexplicable presence of the two damp pillows on the toilet seat. I am at an utter loss for an explanation. Is this all being done for my exclusive benefit? I am resolved not to take too dark a view of all this horseplay.

—"The Second Leg"

Abish's protagonists are forever being excluded from the party. It's usually a matter of sex, as in "The Second Leg." In "The Istanbul Papers" (New Directions #23, 1971, collected in *Minds Meet*), Abish tells of a minor diplomatic functionary who attended Harvard with John Kennedy and Norman Mailer—and who is forever excluded from that company. "Don't you want to show them up," a colleague taunts, "and stride shoulder to shoulder with Norman and Jack down the corridors of power?" His ticket of admission is unlikely: an affair with Hitler's daughter. "Hitler Jugend be damned. If Jack can profess to be a Berliner, I don't see why I can't be the lover of Hitler's daughter." Again, the narrator becomes the excluded party, as the real issue becomes the interests of his colleague and the stamping of the girl's passport. "I often think of those hectic days, standing shoulder to shoulder with Norman and Jack in the quadrangle," he concludes. "Only their dreams have come true."

There is a possible reason why the self-reflexive character in fiction so often plays the buffoon. Among Communists the confessional strain is provided for by the structure of self-criticism, an adaptable tool for any political writing; Catholics (accounting for most of the confessional poets) have examination of conscience, and Confession itself. But without such a structure, the result is pure solipsism, drifting every so often into rampant paranoia. When it is either substanceless or hopelessly naive, it's funny. As are most of Walter Abish's stories.

The two musically gifted lovers do not wait for the auspicious moment as they set out to visit an aging aunt. They are all smiles as they ride to the station. The young man is the first to dismount. It is one of those incendiary moments when all of life is on the brink of a new discovery. The zip in his pants has burst open, and despite all desperate and feverish attempts refuses to close again. She felt a sudden relief as he, this pink cheeked lover of hers, rather than face her in this crisis, stepped in the path of the oncoming train.

—"Minds Meet"

The best of Abish's fiction offers a loony mix of the aesthetic with the ethic. His diplomat from "The Istanbul Papers" reflects, "Unfortunately, the Embassy library leaves a lot to be desired. But there are so many other rewards. I am carried away by the slow emollient pace of the city . . . by the magnificent mosques with their sun-basked courtyards . . . by the serene flow of the river, and by the shiny eager faces of the young boys who beg for a livelihood. Seldom has anything so succeeded in inspiring me. Tomorrow I'm to meet Hitler's daughter." Often disconcerting things will be converted to an aesthetic, not as a form of escape, but to make them manageable; then we as readers can come back to life (as we inevitably will) with a better appreciation. It's a question of long-term versus short-term gains. It is instructive to note the silliness of people who make something over nothing—confusing the ethical with the aesthetic. The converse is the silliness of making nothing over something. In this manner the aesthetic can help us locate what is real in life, and what is not:

This is an introduction to the ladders. They are still missing. The painters left in a truck four days ago. The driver drove along 14A as far as Grant's, then turned left. He could be anywhere by now. The ladders are stored in the local fire station. The firemen tried to conceal them from me. They tried to distract my attention from the ladders. But they are not very practiced at this sort of deception. I was able to count the ladders and, later, able to confirm their absence from the homes of the painters. What this means I cannot say.

—"Non-Site," Fiction, *1 (#4, 1973), collected in* Minds Meet

IN THE GARDEN: III

In my later work, Alphabetical Africa, *and "This is not a film, this is a precise act of disbelief," I try to achieve a neutral value in my writing, that is to say, I avoid the intentional and sometimes unintentional hierarchy of values that seems to creep in whenever lifelike incidents are depicted. Through the avoidance of a hierarchy that is related to values outside the actual work, language has a chance of becoming what Roland Barthes refers to as a field of action, and to quote him: "the definitions of, and the hope for a possibility." In other words, language ceases to be a "tool" that facilitates the realization of a lifelike atmosphere, and concomitant creation of "real" people . . . it also ceases to intensify the immediacy of action, thereby diminishing the somewhat misleading proximity between words and what they signify.*

Although the letters of the alphabet are independent of each other, people tend to ingest or read them, as the case may be, in small or large clusters that are called words. No matter what people say to each other, they are using words, not letters. When a word is not understood, the person using it is obliged to spell it aloud. This entails breaking the word into letters. However, if one is careful, one can speak for hours on end, even months, sometimes, without once being compelled to spell a word. . . . In the more rural sections of the U.S. people do not resort to spelling difficult words . . . instead they plunge a V-shaped knife into the other fella, who moans, "Ohhh." O also happens to be the fifteenth letter in the alphabet. For some reason it is often used by insecure people.

—"Minds Meet"

Walter Abish's first novel, *Alphabetical Africa*, includes his customary interest in the inability of people to communicate. An example from Chapter E shows both technique and theme at work:

Demure damsel eagerly clutches at Emperor's defenses, but Emperor, deeply embarrassed, draws back, coughing, a bit calculatedly, cough, cough, but by coughing Emperor accidently creates a complex code designed by bombing consultant. As Emperor considers balling Edna again, airplane erroneously bombs beleagured Ethiopian capital, eliminating everything below. Capital becomes antiquity dated A.D.

Abish's skepticism of understanding, which he feels is so often lacking in human communication, becomes in *Alphabetical Africa* "a determining factor upon which the flow of the narrative was largely predicated." His subject matter—Western uncertainty personified—is the white man's view of Africa.

Now when I was a little chap I had a passion for maps. I would look for hours at South America, or Africa, or Australia, and lose myself in all the glories of exploration. At that time there were many blank spaces on the earth, and when I saw one that looked particularly inviting on a map (but they all look that) I would put my finger on it and say, When I grow up I will go there.

—**Joseph Conrad,** Heart of Darkness

What made me take this trip to Africa? There is no quick explanation. Things got worse and worse and worse and pretty soon they were too complicated.

—**Saul Bellow,** Henderson the Rain King

The father and his worship is Asia; Europe is the precious self-centered forward-striving child; but the land of the mother is and was Africa.

—**W. E. B. Du Bois**

Africa—you know, that strange continent which serves as the subconscious of our planet. . . .

—**Ishmael Reed,** Yellow Back Radio Broke-Down

He is marching in front. Alva and Jacqueline are being carried in comfortable chairs far behind. Frequently both ends of the caravan are miles apart. Consequently, after a few months, certain linguistic difficulties arise as both ends, having developed different dialects, can no longer communicate.

*

It is difficult explaining a kidnapping in clicks.

—Alphabetical Africa

Abish has pushed both language and idea farther than one thought they could go. His Africa, colonized and exploited by two centuries of Europeans and Americans, is described as actually shrinking. The map itself changes colors, as one country after another wins its independence; hence when one new nation makes war against another, the prime weapons are paint and brushes, used to transform the landscape to the aggressor's hue.

IN THE GARDEN: IV

When my publisher, James Laughlin, read a short section of "Minds Meet" that had appeared in Extensions *magazine, he asked me if the rest of "Minds Meet" was still available. By that time, however, the remaining sections had already been accepted by* TriQuarterly. *Wishing to write something in line with "Minds Meet" for the New Directions anthology, I started* Alphabetical Africa . . . *utilizing some of the ideas in "Minds Meet." As in "Minds Meet," the system in* Alphabetical Africa *subverts the contents by the conspicuous limitations that are placed on the quasi-plot. In a sense it is a novel that feeds on its own meaning . . . and in which the gradual verbal accretion and then deconstruction is paralleled in the situations portrayed in the book, such as the shrinkage of the African continent.*

Finally, there is one more explanation which may show the reason for my choice of Africa. A few years ago Abercrombie and Fitch in one of their semi-annual sales advertised an African Diary that was reduced from approximately ninety dollars to five. When I called the store I was told that the diaries, some two hundred in all, would go on sale the next morning. When the store opened the next day there were fewer than twenty left, and these were snapped up before I reached the counter. I remember seeing a rather bulky brown package being handed to a man standing near me. My curiosity has never been satisfied. Why should an African Diary cost ninety dollars in the first place? And what on earth is an African Diary? I suspect that it was a diary for the use of the well-heeled traveler on a safari. The idea had occurred to me that I might use the diary as a system in a novel. When I was very young my parents and I had circumnavigated Africa in a passenger ship. Seeing the advertisement I felt I would like to enter Africa—so to speak—via the diary.

Abish's novel is "about" Africa only in the sense that certain notions about that continent provide a field in which Abish can generate the energy of his fiction. Ronald Sukenick has asked that fiction be appreciated in terms of its principles and elements of composition—like a painting, or like a piece of music. One can appreciate abstract art, or virtually any music, without recourse to the old debilitating question always asked of fiction: what is it about? Or, what does it mean? Only film is so monotonously subjected to the same question. Abish's special use of language—within the topographically familiar surfaces of the world we share—works to discredit the question. His stories reflect the methods of filmmaker Peter Kubelka, a fellow Viennese. Kubelka's films are based on the idea that their substance is not a panoramic view of the world thrown upon the screen, but the phenomenon of light passing through a celluloid stencil twenty-four times per second. Sequentially moving celluloid frames may very easily accommodate a realistic narrative, just as may the sequential arrangements of words upon a page. But that's just one of many things film and fiction may do; to restrict them to that sole function is to ignore the very makings of their art.

Therefore both Kubelka and Abish draw attention to their form of composition. A film catalogue description states that "Kubelka formulates the rhythm of his cuts, and counterpointing of imagery and soundtrack, the repetition and subtle variation of his imagery, playing a very similar role to the main theme or melody within a fugue." Kubelka gives us what has been called a "vertical montage" of sound against image. In a similar manner, Abish focuses his art on the words and phrases of our language. His sentences are often composed of radically different words and thoughts which collide at the caesura. By these collisions, the story moves forward: its subject is nothing other than itself. The subject of Kubelka's major work is also itself: it is titled *Our Trip to Africa*.

IN THE GARDEN: V

I most certainly detect an affinity to my view of my work. A parallel to Kubelka's stencil would be the word as a signifier.

I presume that Kubelka, like me, is interested in the way ideas are formed. Alphabetical Africa, *for instance, is a working idea, a novel that constructs and then deconstructs itself. The gradual accretion and enrichment of language that occurs in the first half of the book allows me to enlarge upon situations in the novel. In the novel, per se, as in life, one is confronted by an endless array of choices, a multitude of possibilities. The moment a writer selects one avenue over another, his choice curtails the subsequent events. I keep on being intrigued by the choices I find I can make. Character, plot, storyline are simply approaches that carry within themselves the limitations of the instantaneously recognizable compressions of a "truth" that for one reason or another is pertinent to us at this time. It comes as no surprise that great works can also be free of these literary conventions. John Ashbery's* Three Poems *is a book of incredible riches and will rank among the great books of prose. It is devoid of plot, of character, of story. It is and will remain meaningful because it illuminates the formation of thought.*
. . . .

In my writing I try to strip language of its power to create verisimilitude that in turn shields the reader from the printed words on the page that are deployed as signifiers. Writing as close as possible to a neutral content, everything—the terrain, the interiors, the furniture, the motions of the characters—is an aspect of a topography that defines the limits of the situation being explored. The first few lines in "This is not a film, this is a precise act of disbelief" are as follows: "This is a familiar world crowded with familiar faces and events. Thanks to language the brain can digest, piece by piece, what has occurred and what may yet occur." It is a casual statement. One might say that those first few lines serve as a marker or mold for everything that is to follow. What is conveyed is the dubiousness of the familiar. In another story, the characters ponder the meaning of a message that has been received from outer space. It reads: Is there any other way to live? In a sense, the question lies like a grid over the short self-contained sections in "Minds Meet." The question defamiliarizes everything. If the familiar world is not familiar, then nothing, not language, not the most accepted forms of conduct, can be taken for granted.

I avoid and also distrust a clearly defined and definable action, since it serves as an explanation and tends to dominate what would otherwise be a more neutral surface of information. The key word in each of the alphabetically

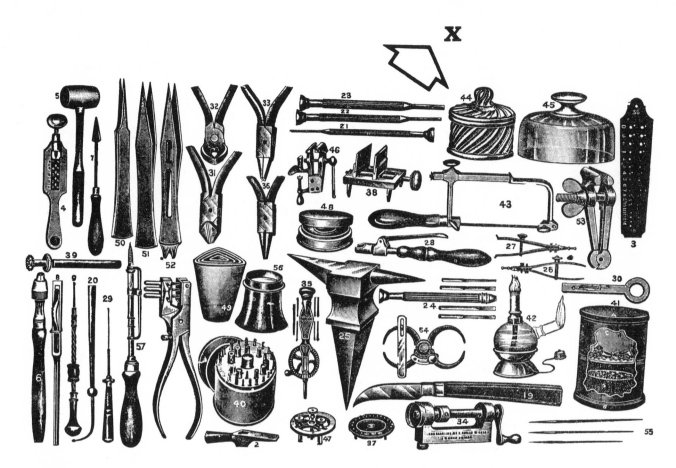

arranged subtitles of "Minds Meet" acts as a motivating force for the section that follows, defining and limiting each occurrence within the story. This idea was further developed in Alphabetical Africa, in which I used what John Ashbery described as a constrictive form. I was fascinated to discover the extent to which a system could impose upon the contents of a work a meaning that was fashioned by the form, and then to see the degree to which the form, because of the conspicuous obstacles, undermined that very meaning. For example, I could not introduce the first person singular until I had reached the ninth section. Frequently I intended to follow one direction and was compelled to follow another. However, forms, systems, structures, constrictive and otherwise, are not alien to life or literature. We simply have not developed an orientation in literature that would acknowledge them. I am reminded of a description of a Bororo Village by Lévi-Strauss in Triste Tropique. The huts were built in a large circle. The circle was divided in half, and all kinds of elaborate rules and etiquette restricted the conduct of each half-circle to the other half. For instance, marriage could only take place between a man and woman from opposing halves of the circle. So vital to the Bororos was this structure that missionaries wishing to convert them finally induced the Bororos to abandon their circular village and move into one in which the huts were laid out in parallel rows. I was extremely excited when I first realized that content and meaning are never free of systems . . . and in fact, frequently come into being on account of them.

"This is not a film, this is a precise act of disbelief" is Abish's novella, first published in *Seems* (#5, 1975) and subsequently collected in the volume *Minds Meet*. Its field of action is a small American town, run by a small-town oligarchy—mayor, businessman, architect, developer—who control the surfaces which reflect their needs. Within these needs are the absolute truths of their lives; but the surfaces are only introductions, familiar at first but slightly unstable, until the skeletons in the closets rattle too loudly.

In story after story Abish uses a few key elements: the familiar surfaces, the lurking needs, and ultimately the sexual provocation which shows the vertical montage when one is counterpointed with the other. Abish disrupts the smooth system of language, so that superficial conventions are revealed as just that. As Sukenick says, good art deconditions us from our accepted view of reality. When we live only on the surface, we find our needs too easily satisfied by the perfect home, the perfect job, the perfect place for a new table, chair, or plant. In "The English Garden" (*Fiction International* #4/5, 1975) Abish takes his epigraph from John Ashbery's *Three Poems*: "Remnants of the old atrocity subsist, but they are converted into ingenious shifts in scenery, a sort of 'English Garden' effect, to give the air of naturalness, pathos and hope." Abish's own story is about a modern German town, with bright new buildings full of neatly planned apartments in turn filled with nicely arranged furniture—all built on the site of a former concentration camp, the topography of which has been effaced by a newer surface. The narrator compares it to the stenciled coloring book he buys as a souvenir; all is jolly and smiling, all is facade, and nothing is intrinsic "until it receives its color." In "This is not a film . . ." Bontemps shoots his films in color so that people will remember his images; the opposite are the unpenetrating citizens who simply polish the surfaces of their lives, understanding little beyond the brand names and commercial lifestyles around them, and hence not communicating at all. "Rudolf Arnheim speaks of order as anything the human mind is to understand," Abish has said; "I think by undermining order, as we in our culture understand it, writers bring about a new understanding."

IN THE GARDEN: VI

I must admit that I lack the proper enthusiasm or care for the characters that appear in my work. I would be incapable of ever saying: Madame Bovary, c'est moi. *Characters are, if anything, points of departure. With a few words they rapidly take on an existence, and I try to interfere with it as little as possible. I am convinced that the characters' actions are open to psychological interpretation, but my writing, and the kind of information that is made available to the reader, does not invite it. As I stated before, the narrator, when he does exist, is not necessarily a reliable observer. His self-interest might be at stake, and what he describes cannot be taken at face value.*
. . . .

To the degree that the central character or characters play a lesser role in my current work, I suppose I have moved away from the humanism to which you refer. Humanism, I feel, is a word that has steadily been depleted of any meaning it once may have had. I suppose certain writers who concentrate on human conduct within the framework of "real" life can be said to center the contents of their work in humanism. Humanism becomes less evident when the content, the narrative, the story line is influenced, even predicated on a system or form. . . . While no one could accuse Beckett, Burroughs, Handke, Barthelme, Borges, Harry Mathews, to name a few, of not dealing with the human condition, one could hardly state that that was their primary concern.

Heidegger refers to being as something that does not take place within the skin. Existence, itself, means to stand outside oneself. Being is spread over a field, analogous to a field of matter, which represents its concerns. I think that everything, even the most contradictory could be on the surface of the same field. . . . Humanism with its specific values imposes a kind of center from which everything radiates . . . in the novel it affects the most diverse things . . . a scuffed carpet, a crack in the wall becomes intentionally or unintentionally incorporated in that humanistic field, presenting to the reader a kind of pattern he can instantly recognize and evaluate. This in itself is enough to destroy the possibilities I see in the novel. I think the novel should do more than reflect the current attitudes and anguished "human" values of the Thirties, the Forties, the Fifties, the Sixties, the Seventies, and so on. . . .

Humanism in a literary context is a surface phenomenon, then, when it imposes itself as the necessary grand subject matter for fiction. No matter how worthy its aims, it is only one more system; and systems, as Sukenick and Abish and Stephens have told us, make it impossible for us to communicate the needs which lie beyond them. As Sukenick has said in his *Digressions*, language is a self-contained system, "But the art of fiction and poetry lies precisely in opening that system up to experience beyond language" as it has become systematized. "The obligation of fiction," one must recall, "is to rescue experience [for Abish, read "our needs"] from history, from politics, from commerce, from theory, even from language itself—from any system, in fact, that threatens to distort, devitalize, or manipulate experience. The health of language depends on its contact with experience, which it both embodies and helps to create."

*

[On Hellmut Wilhelm lecturing on the I Ching **to the German community in Nanking, at a time when the youngster Walter Abish was in China]: I can see the heavy German faces and brains that are stocked with recollections of Meissen chinaware, Dürer-like landscapes and damask drapes, ponderously turning to the ancient Chinese text, a text that was able to magnify the elements of chance so alien to the interior of their European apartments in which even the arrangement of the furniture acknowledges an awareness of causality.**

—"Self Portrait," Individuals:
Post Movement Art in America
(New York: Dutton, 1976)

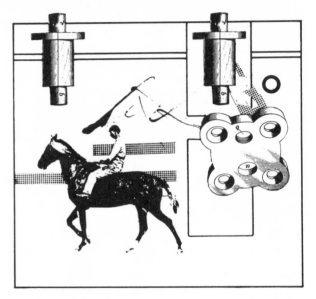

IN THE GARDEN: VII

I spent my childhood in China during the Second World War. I can recall on my way to school passing dead or dying Chinese infants wrapped in newspaper, abandoned because their parents were destitute and could not feed them. Quite vividly I can recall seeing two Chinese policemen playing football with a baby that seemed to be still alive. I mention this because my friends and I had become pretty well anesthetized to this kind of brutality. Perhaps I should add that the brutality was largely invisible, since we had all learned not to see it. Unlike most of my friends at school, I was immensely intrigued by Shanghai, and frequently on my own explored the city. . . . I recall that the red-light district which covered a large section of the city became a source of great fascination to me. The somewhat mystifying sexual transactions I observed as a child seemed doubly mystifying in their stagelike Oriental setting. . . . I suppose that my reluctance to employ straightforward explanatory action in my work stems in part from growing up in a world that was bewildering in its profusion of stylized drama, a drama that remained forever highly elusive. Whenever I see any of Cartier-Bresson's magnificent photographs of China I think I understand why a purely linear thread of development is so foreign to my work. All the same, China did not really encroach on the more or less conventional middle-class European lives my parents led. I did not know any Chinese people, or their customs, or their literature. In the English-speaking schools I attended, I don't believe that China was ever referred to . . . as if its incredibly rich history and culture did not exist. What I would like to emphasize is that the European communities, and there were quite a number, maintained in their apartness an extraordinary attachment to order and stability. They had their rituals, coffee houses, bridge clubs, tennis and soccer which were played with a great fervor. There was a social hierarchy in which the doctor, lawyer, professor, engineer, and businessman, like my father, took their roles quite seriously, oblivious of China.

*

The Pueblo Indians used to build roads that dissolved in the vastness of what lay outside their experience.

—"How the Comb Gives a Fresh Meaning to the Hair,"
New Directions #29 **(1974)**

Chapter Six

In 1962 Donald Barthelme, newly arrived in New York City from Houston, became the managing editor of Harold Rosenberg's and Thomas B. Hess's journal of art and literature, *Location*. Only two numbers of the journal ever appeared: Spring 1963 and Summer 1964. But both were influential. In the premier number Rosenberg talked about the need for literature to show the same liveliness so evident in postwar American painting and sculpture. "The formal vivacity" of these arts, Rosenberg argued, "was an outcome of their revolt against 'the forms.' Every idea of what was fundamental to a painting was misused or eliminated—gainfully." To what end? The foremost critical advocate of abstract expressionism answered in terms which a decade later would adequately describe his own managing editor's fiction: "In order to liberate the creative processes by elevating them above all preconceived aesthetic objectives, American painting and sculpture have constituted themselves a laboratory for accumulating data on bringing novelties into being."

In the American literature of the time, however, Rosenberg found a moribund devotion to established forms—"which actually exalts subject matter, since subject matter alone determines the difference between one conventional work and another." As Ronald Sukenick would later argue in the pages of *Partisan Review* and *New Literary History*, and as writers such as Gilbert Sorrentino, Michael Stephens, and Walter Abish would show in their own fiction, composition—and not subject matter—would have to become the prime criterion if literature were to share the renaissance of the American graphic arts. "Nothing comparable has taken place in literature," we heard from Rosenberg in 1963. "On the contrary, explorations begun long ago have been abandoned." Sukenick's own thesis was anticipated by Rosenberg's indictment: "For twenty years poetry and fiction have had their goals set by a traditionalist imagination in harmony with the formal conservativism of mass media. The result has been an incredible naivete in regard to the processes of composition. A poet who has devoted a lifetime to scratching at problems of structure is today likely to have less grounding in the production of a work of art and the distinction between the spontaneous, the automatic and the immediate than a 10th Street painter with two or three years of looking and listening."

Since his arrival in New York, Barthelme has lived among the painters—in his case, on the Village's West 11th

Street—and has been closely associated with the gallery life which had propelled him from Houston's Contemporary Arts Museum and the *University of Houston Forum* to New York, *Location*, and the *New Yorker*, where his stories began appearing with regularity in 1963. He too agreed with Rosenberg that "The conditions of psychic self-enslavement and joylessness under which most current literary works are produced makes reading difficult for anyone but a sadist." In the second (and final) issue of *Location*, Barthelme pondered what in literature might come "After Joyce." His conclusion was that new writers would indeed make objects of their books, refusing to let them stand as reflections or expressions of something else; but from his vantage point in 1964 the only writers doing even that much were the French practitioners of the **New Novel**, who did so "without reaping any of the strategic benefits of the maneuver—a triumph of misplaced intelligence." Barthelme complained that their works were leaden with tedious self-consciousness, slow-paced, "with no leaps of the imagination." In short, with none of the playful exuberance which his own fictions were to exhibit in the years to come.

Donald Barthelme stands beyond the Post-Modernists because his fictions, drawing their cue from the title of his *Location* essay, stand "After Joyce"—and after Beckett, Robbe-Grillet, Robert Musil, and Raymond Roussel as well. He sees no need for his fictions to demonstrate the chaos of existence, the loss of the self, the nightmare of daily life. Nor are his books protracted examinations of the ability (or inability) to write. Instead, they are playful musings with the world as is, taking materials of that world as compositional elements and making new and pleasing artifacts of them, which when added to the world make it a more enjoyable place to live. For Rust Hills's anthology *Writer's Choice* (New York: David McKay, 1974), Barthelme discussed the method of his favorite story, "Paraguay," from the collection *City Life* (New York: Farrar, Straus & Giroux, 1970). "Mixing bits of this and that from various areas of life to make something that did not exist before is an oddly hopeful endeavor," Barthelme confessed. "The sentence 'Electrolytic jelly exhibiting a capture ratio far in excess of standard is used to fix the animals in place' made me very happy—perhaps in excess of its merit. But there is in the world such a thing as electrolytic jelly; the 'capture ratio' comes from the jargon of sound technology; and the animals themselves are a salad of the real and the invented."

Barthelme takes the flat objects of life and makes them round; he takes what we assume to be a banal, insipid, and dull existence and shows how it can be made shockingly funny. For a world we might otherwise reject, with no alternative, Barthelme shows us how it can be fun to live there. He's the best argument against alienation since Jack Benny, Fred Allen, and the Marx Brothers—who in another period of Depression showed how another day's life was not the unimaginable horror that some feared it would be.

DONALD BARTHELME

"Fragments are the only form I trust." This from a writer of arguable genius, whose works reflect the anxiety he himself must feel, in book after book, that his brain is all fragments . . . just like everything else. Passive, drifting, witty, melancholy-hilarious, surrealist (though nearly seven decades have passed since Alfred Jarry wrote "Ubu Roi") . . . even the construction of his sentence is symptomatic of his role: It begins with "fragments," the stern healthy noun, and concludes with the weak "I." But. There is a point in history at which Wilde's remark comes horribly true, that life will imitate art. And then who is in charge, who believed himself cleverly impotent, who supposed he had abdicated all conscious design . . .?

—Joyce Carol Oates, "Guest Word,"
New York Times Book Review,
6/4/72

FRAGMENT A.

". . . something's always left, a bit of business left undone, lawyer's texts, children, pewter, friends, joint tax returns from some as yet unaudited year . . ."

—"The Bed" (Viva, 3/74)

FRAGMENT B.

"Yesterday you asked me for the Princeton University Press. 'The Princeton University Press is not a toy,' I said."

—"You Are as Brave as Vincent Van Gogh"
(New Yorker, 3/18/74)

FRAGMENT C.

The attached photographs of the human soul (Figs. 1 and 2), taken by Pioneer 10, the first spacecraft to navigate the outer solar system, were made on December 14, 1973, as the craft was leaving the magnetic field of Jupiter. The "photographs" (actually coded radio signals from the device's nine-foot dish antenna beamed back to earth) were, of course, incidental to the photographing of Jupiter itself, one of the mission's chief aims. They were made by Dr. Reginald Hobson, F.R.S., of Britain's Cavendish Laboratory, using Kodak spectroscopic plates type IIIa-J baked for five hours at 65° C. under dry N_2 before exposure.

—"The Photographs" (New Yorker, 1/28/74)

To the Editor:

The fall 1973 number of the Carolina Quarterly contains a story called "Divorce" and signed with my name. As it happens, I did not write it. It is quite a worthy effort, as pastiches go, and particularly successful in reproducing my weaknesses. A second story, titled "Cannon," also signed with my name, appears in the current issue of Voyages. As a candidate-member of the Scandinavian Institute of Comparative Vandalism, I would rate the second item somewhat inferior to the first, but again, I am not responsible. May I say, as a sort of notice to mariners, that only manuscripts offered to editors by my agent, Lynn Nesbit, are authentic—not good or bad, but at least authentic.

—Donald Barthelme
New York City
(New York Times, 12/23/73)

I tipped off the editors I knew but catching this guy was like swatting cockroaches: turn on the lights and he's scurrying off to the next magazine. Pretty soon he was hitting the big-time slicks like Ladies' Home Journal and Esky—books I normally don't sell so I don't know the editors well. As far as they were concerned, they couldn't care less who was the real Al Laveen, so long as the copy they were getting was hot—they didn't even care that he wasn't agented. The last straw was when he did a profile of some highbrow South American writer named Castanet, or something like that, for the Paris Review. Not only had this guy stolen my name, he was better than I was.

> —Richard Lingeman,
> "Steal My Name and You Got Trash"
> (New York Times Book Review, **2/3/74**)

Sirs:

This is to approximate a reply to the reply of Doug LeDuff to our publicity of 29 December which appeared in your journal. . . . We need only point to the 1958 exposition at the Galerie Berger, Paris, in which the "asterisk" series of Bruno was first inserted, to see what is afoot. The American makes the claim that he has been painting asterisks since 1955—we say, if so, where are these asterisks? In what collections? In what expositions? With what documentation?

> —*"Letters to the Editore"*
> (New Yorker, 2/25/74)

FRAGMENT D.

"And now the tender tears of dusk settle over the caduceus tree, thought Franz Kafka."

> —**"Divorce"** (Carolina Quarterly, **Fall 1973**)

FRAGMENT E.

"And now the silver wings of dusk settle over the Laredo Bowling Alley. Sitting on the porch of the Hotel Laredo, the detective thinks back to that morning."

> —**"Cannon!"** (Voyages, **#14/15, 1973**)

FRAGMENT F.

" 'And now the purple dusk of twilight time/steals across the meadows of my heart,' the Dean said."

> —**"Porcupines at the University"** (New Yorker, **4/25/70**)

In Fall 1973 critic and SuperFictionist Raymond Federman presented a paper at a conference, "Imagine Dead Imagine: The Self-Reflective Artwork in Contemporary Art & Literature." Federman's title was "Imagination as Plagiarism," and in it he argued that artistic genius consisted in the playful reorderings of already established principles.

In Spring 1974 Donald Barthelme discovered that his namesake plagiarist had cashed a $100 check made out in "their" name. Finding the party, Barthelme asked him to stop. But since July 1973 Barthelme had contributed pieces to the *New Yorker* and even the New York *Times* Op-Ed page under the pseudonym "Lily McNeil." Ms. McNeil was described as "a contributor to the *New Yorker*."

FRAGMENT G.

"Just a moment, Major Kinsolving. A dispatch rider is due, carrying word of the ftate of the heating plant in my houfe in Virginia. It's been acting awfully cranky. And another dispatch rider is due, bringing news of the well that is being dug at my estate at Fig Island, off the Carolinas. . . . And I await ftill another messenger, carrying intelligence of my summer home in Georgia. We've been having a few problems with the fenestration. Rude boys have been breaking windows by throwing giant crayfish at them. It's moft annoying". . . .

"You certainly have a lot of houfes, General. Although I'm not being critical. I understand. Everybody understands. The four million pounds that these houfes have coft the infant Republic doesn't bother us a bit."

> —*General Washington to an aide,*
> *"A Dream" (*New Yorker*, 9/3/73,*
> *signed "Lily McNeil")*

CRITICAL FRAGMENT A (from the introduction to Klinkowitz and Somer, *Innovative Fiction* [New York: Dell, 1972])

After the violent, wrenching alienation following the World Wars, the new writers found that life had settled down into something banal, insipid, and dull. Donald Barthelme is the most vehement: [in *Snow White* his character reports that] "The per-capita production of trash in this country is up from 2.75 pounds per day in 1920 to 4.5 pounds per day in 1965 . . . and . . . may very well soon reach a point where it's 100 percent." Barthelme's solution is to place himself on "the leading edge . . . of the trash phenomenon," paying particular attention to language when it might be "fill," "blanketing," or "*dreck*," and then somehow recycling or reviving it for human use. Ronald Sukenick states the problem [in *Wallace Stevens: Musing the Obscure*]: "Adequate adjustment to the present can only be achieved through ever fresh perception of it, and this is the effort of [Stevens's] poetry." Fresh perception is the stuff of Sukenick's and especially Barthelme's stories. The latter revitalizes tired forms by toying with imaginative content: the insipid talk of engineers is recharged when Barthelme shows them boasting, "We have rots, blights, and rusts capable of attacking [the enemy's] alphabet," and further developing "real-time online computer-controlled wish evaporation" in order to meet "the rising expectations of the world's peoples, which are as you know rising entirely too fast." He seizes the phraseological structures of such technocrats and deftly inserts his own absurdity, and suddenly the form itself is more interesting. Watching the Ed Sullivan Show, his narrator becomes bored with an Ed Ames song which is "sub-memorable." He quickly substitutes, as the medium itself might, "Something memorable: early on Sunday morning a pornographic exhibition appeared mysteriously for eight minutes on television station KPLM, Palm Springs, California. A naked man and woman did vile and imaginative things to each other for that length of time, then disappeared into the history of electricity. Unfortunately, the exhibition wasn't on a network. What we really want in this world we can't have."

CRITICAL FRAGMENT B (from a review of Donald Barthelme's *Sadness* by Jerome Klinkowitz [*Chicago Review*, Summer 1973])

Barthelme's *Sadness*, although arranged as a collection of stories, has the consistency and effect of a novel, drawing its substance from the title of its first piece, "Critique de la Vie Quotidienne." From the start of his career Barthelme has shown the ability to seize our mundane moments and make them lucid, usually by an apt metaphor or deft refocusing of language and idea. Nobody ever faulted Barthelme for his perceptions, but by themselves they could be called subjective, lyrical, poetic, or any of the other terms used to disqualify them as fiction. *Sadness*, however, gives his visions a clarifying run through our very familiar and objective lives. . . .

CRITICAL FRAGMENT C (from a review of Donald Barthelme's *Guilty Pleasures* by Jerome Klinkowitz [*New Republic*, 12/14/74])

Turning such perceptiveness into fiction is a short step. Given the state of our culture, how else is there to write? "The new opium of the people," Barthelme says in Joe David Bellamy's *The New Fiction* (University of Illinois Press), "is opium, or at least morphine. In a situation in which morphine contends with morpheme, the latter loses every time." With a field as varied as *New Yorker* fillers, Barthelme can be nearly as prolific and twice as fun. There is something of the bizarre in nearly everything these days; in *Guilty Pleasures* Barthelme transforms it into fiction. . . . Included in the volume are some of Barthelme's collage pieces, such as "A Nation of Wheels," where he superimposes a tire from a magazine advertisement on paintings and engravings to revive this dead metaphor. Other times his target is broader, but always the point is to throw imaginative cold water on some narcotic of our lives. . . . Against the boredom and silliness of life, Barthelme offers us these solitary vices. Guilty pleasures are the best.

CRITICAL FRAGMENT D (from a review of Donald Barthelme's *The Dead Father* by Jerome Klinkowitz [*New Republic*, 11/29/75])

In order to tell a story, Barthelme must reinvent a language which will bear it, and then perform a resuscitation act upon his readers so that the new words carry through. It's easy for attention to wander when bombarded by a list of things computers can do; Barthelme throws in the craziness of "wish evaporation" to shake us back to our senses. His so-called fragmentary forms do the same job. There's an energy which comes from rapid changes of context, the mixing of comic scenes, and the fracturing of linguistic modes. It's the basic method which has made cinema the prime attention-getting medium of our times: montage, quick-cut, a whole repertoire of techniques which work as well for tragedy as for comedy—which have, indeed, become the tempo of our modern lives.

With the publication of *Guilty Pleasures* in 1974, Barthelme for the first time identified a more immediate form of cultural commentary he had been writing: "Comment" pieces for the *New Yorker*'s "Talk of the Town" section. He had built his career as a fictionist through this magazine, and many of his artistic devices were extensions of *New Yorker* characteristics. Barthelme's trick of imaginative substitution reflected the magazine's delight with column fillers of *faux pas* from other print media; his stories themselves, in their deft understatement of life's idiocies, seemed like cartoon characters come alive. The "Talk of the Town" column allowed Barthelme to comment more directly, letting the world itself provide the mirth.

FRAGMENT H.

It is April, and Heliotrope, the Open University of San Francisco, is once again turning toward the sun of felt needs and marigold-yellow fulfillments. . . . We can begin Alpha & Theta Brain Wave Training (D-8), Belly Dance (D-30), Bicycle Repair and Maintenance (D-31), Common Medical Problems (D-38), or Divorce Before & After (D-47). . . . Ah, happy Heliotrope, with its Kung Fu, Tai Chi Chuan, Tap Dancing, Group Bio-energetic Reëducation, and Gestalt for Women Over 35! Come. You, dear friend, can teach a course in Paying the Telephone Bill, and we will teach one in Sleeping, and we will all, at long last, be avenged upon that fancy-Dan Lionel Trilling.

—New Yorker, 4/1/74

FRAGMENT I.

The palace was partly designed by Breuer, but then Mies came over one day while the thing was still a-building and said something about how wouldn't it be nice if the travertine that covers the west wall ran this way instead of that way (waving his hands in the air, which is how architects do their thinking), and Breuer, who is the most modest of men, said, "Mies, just for fun, why don't you do part of it, and we'll see what happens." Well, Mies liked to play, too, so he agreed, and then when Corbu visited the site he wanted to get in on it, and, in fact, the entire east wing is Corbu's. And then Nervi and Aalto and Neutra and Saarinen and Louis Kahn and all sorts of other people, all geniuses, got interested, contributed bits, ideas, little pieces, because none of them had ever done a palace before—I mean a real, honest-to-God palace, as opposed to a corporate headquarters. The king came down to the site every day wearing a blue hardhat and was just beside himself. I have never seen a king, even a limited constitutional monarch, take so much pleasure in anything. . . . Everyone wondered what Wright would have done if he had been around to participate, and Venturi jumped up and down and clapped his hands in glee and sent a telegram to Paolo Soleri, out there in the desert, and ordered forty dozen wind bells and wondered telegraphically if Soleri would be interested in doing the grand ballroom. Soleri was enchanted with the idea of doing a grand ballroom, and the next day the model arrived by air express, together with a blueprint forty feet long and so splendid in conception that everybody agreed it gave new meaning to the words "grand" and "ballroom." And the throne room, done by Simon Rodia, who did the Watts Towers, is as gaudy as Gaudí, and the royal kitchens, by Edward Durell Stone, make you want to get in there and cook your heart out.

—New Yorker, 12/24/73

FRAGMENT J.

Last week, a wan and scruffy dragon came to the city looking for a disease. He had in mind ending his life, which he felt to be tedious, unsatisfactory, tax-troubled, lacking in purpose. . . . At that moment, a Colonel of Sanitation came striding by, in his green uniform. . . . "But you—you have a strange aspect. What kind of a thing are you? Are you disposable? Biodegradable? Ordinary citizen out for a stroll? Looking for work? Member of a conspiracy? Vegetable? Mineral? Two-valued? Hostile to the national interest of the Department of Sanitation? Thrill-crazed kid? Objet d'art? Circus in town?"

"You suffer, however, from a sort of general meaninglessness."
"Since the thirteenth century."

—New Yorker, **2/26/72**

Although Barthelme's targets seem as broad as the cultural milieu itself, perhaps limited only by a *New Yorker* brand of urban wit, his fictions and satires often include elements close to his own life.

He is actually Donald Barthelme, Jr. His father is a famous architect with a teaching position at Rice University and a list of credits in the newly made city of Houston. Although born in Philadelphia, where his parents were in graduate school, Barthelme grew up in Texas—references to cowboys, cactus, and chili dogs appear with increasing regularity in his fiction through *Sadness*. His background is also Catholic: dogma and litanies are more prominent in his early work, which includes this confession from "A Picture History of the War" *(Unspeakable Practices, Unnatural Acts)*— "Bless me, Father, for I have sinned. I committed endoarchy two times, melanicity four times, encropatomy seven times, and preprocity with igneous intent, pretolemicity, and overt cranialism once each."

*

FRAGMENT K.

The Teachings of Don B./A Yankee Way of Knowledge

While doing some anthropological field work in Manhattan some years ago I met, on West 11th Street, a male Yankee of indeterminate age whose name, I was told, was Don B. I found him leaning against a building in a profound torpor—perhaps the profoundest torpor I have ever seen. He was a tallish man with an unconvincing beard and was dressed, in the fashion of the Village, in jeans and a blue work shirt. After we had been introduced, by a mutual acquaintance, I explained to him that I had been told he knew the secrets of certain hallucinogenic substances peculiar to Yankee culture and in which I was professionally interested. . . .

He then led me into the building against which he had been leaning. He showed me into a small but poorly furnished apartment containing hundreds of books stacked randomly about. In the center of the room a small fire was blazing brightly. Throwing a few more books on the fire, Don B. invited me to be seated, and we had the first of what proved to be a long series of conversations. The following material, reproduced from my field notes, has been edited somewhat to eliminate the dull parts, but in the main reflects accurately what took place during the period when I was Don B.'s apprentice.

. . . .

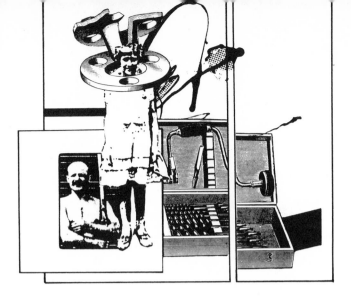

I did as Don B. bade me, and drained the glass in one gulp. Immediately a horrible trembling convulsed my limbs, while an overwhelming nausea retracted my brain. I flopped about on the floor a lot. I became aware of (left to right) a profound sadness, a yellow warmth, an indescribable anguish and a pink luminosity. . . . and, suddenly, standing with one foot on the profound sadness/yellow warmth and the other on the indescribable anguish/pink luminosity, a gigantic figure half-human, half-animal, and a hundred feet tall (roughly). A truly monstrous thing! Never in the wildest fantasies of fiction had I encountered anything like it. I looked at it in complete, utter bewilderment. It was strange and eerie, yet familiar. Then I realized with a shock of horror, terror and eeriness that it was a colossal Publisher, and that it was moving toward me, wanted something from me. I fainted. When I revived, it took me to lunch at Lutece and we settled on an advance in the low 50's, which I accepted even though I knew I was not yet, in the truest sense, a man of knowledge. But there would be other books, I reflected, to become a man of knowledge in, and if I got stuck I could always go back and see good old Don B.

—New York Times Magazine, 2/11/73

Other occupations of Donald Barthelme:
   a. **Newspaper reporter (Houston** Post)
   b. **Intellectual quarterly editor (University of Houston** Forum)
   c. **Art museum director**
   d. **Managing editor** (Location)
   e. **University professor (SUNY-Buffalo, Boston University, CUNY)**
   f. **Layout and design man** (Fiction)
   g. **Collectivist (the Fiction Collective)**

*

Evidence suggests that Barthelme is happier in category "f" than in "e." "I enjoy doing lay-out—problems of design," he said in 1972. "I could very cheerfully be a typographer."

Barthelme's first teaching position was as John Barth's replacement, for Fall 1972, at Buffalo. Allowing for the distance between typewriter and printed page, he did hardly any stories for the *New Yorker*. Of the following fragments, the first can be dated from his tenure at Buffalo, the second from his return to West 11th Street.

FRAGMENT L.

Lose yourself in the song of the instructions, in the precise, detailed balm of having had solved for you that most difficult of problems, what to do next.

. . . .

Many famous teachers teach courses in themselves; why should you be different, just because you are a wimp and a lame, objectively speaking? Courage. The anthology of yourself which will be used as a text is even now being assembled by underpaid researchers in our textbook division, drawing upon the remembrances of those who hated you and those (a much smaller number) who loved you. You will be adequate in your new role. See? Your life is saved. The instructions do not make distinctions between those lives which are worth saving and those which are not. Your life is saved. Congratulations. I'm sorry.

—*"What to Do Next" (New Yorker, 3/24/73)*

FRAGMENT M.

The tiny matchbook-cover press is readied, the packing applied, the "Le Foie de Veau" form locked into place. We all stand around a small table watching the matchbook press at work. It is exactly like a toy steam engine. Everyone is very fond of it, although we also have a press big as a destroyer escort—that one has a crew of thirty-five, its own galley, its own sick bay, its own band. We print the currency of Colombia, and the Acts of the Apostles, and the laws of the land, and the fingerprints.

. . . .

We do the Oxford Book of American Sin.

. . . .

I was watching over the imposition of the Detroit telephone book. Someone had just dropped all the H's—a thing like that happens sometimes.

"Don't anybody move! Now, everybody bend over and pick up the five slugs nearest him. Now, the next five. Easy does it. Somebody call Damage Control and have them send up extra vodka, lean meat, and bandages. Now, the next five. Anybody that steps on a slug gets the hammer in the mouth. Now, the next."

—*"Our Work and Why We Do It" (New Yorker, 5/5/73)*

*

In your story "See the Moon" one of the characters has the line, "Fragments are the only forms I trust." This has been quoted as a statement of your aesthetic. Is it?

No. It's a statement by the character about what he is feeling at that particular moment. I hope that whatever I think about aesthetics would be a shade more complicated than that. Because that particular line has been richly misunderstood so often (most recently by my colleague J.C. Oates in the Times) *I have thought of making a public recantation. I can see the story in, say,* Women's Wear Daily:

WRITER CONFESSES THAT HE NO LONGER TRUSTS FRAGMENTS

Trust 'Misplaced,' Author Declares

DISCUSSED DECISION WITH DAUGHTER, SIX

Will Seek 'Wholes' In Future, He Says

CLOSING TIME IN GARDENS OF WEST WILL BE EXTENDED, SCRIVENER STATES

New York, June 24 (A&P)—Donald Barthelme, 41-year-old writer and well-known fragmentist, said today that he no longer trusted fragments. He added that although he had once been "very fond" of fragments, he had found them to be "finally untrustworthy."

The author, looking tense and drawn after what was described as "considerable thought," made his dramatic late-night announcement at a Sixth Avenue laundromat press conference, from which the press was excluded.

Sources close to the soap machine said, however, that the agonizing reappraisal, which took place before their eyes, required only four minutes.

"Fragments fall apart a lot," Barthelme said. Use of antelope blood as a bonding agent had not proved . . .

Chapter Seven

"This is the closest I will ever come to writing an autobiography," Kurt Vonnegut, Jr., says in his eighth novel, *Slapstick; Or, Lonesome No More* (New York: Seymour Lawrence/Delacorte Press, 1976). An autobiographical impulse runs through all of Vonnegut's novels, becoming more pronounced as he develops the facility to deal first with a very personal subject—his experience during the World War II firebombing of Dresden—and finally with his own technical role as fictionist.

Like the other SuperFictionists, Vonnegut is not a writer of sweeping narratives. His own method is to compose page by page, relying on the energy of his self-described "jokes" to move the action forward. Vonnegut claims that finishing a page is like setting a mousetrap; the reader's act is simply to spring the trap. The larger method of Vonnegut's fiction is random but necessary, similar to the release of energy that one would witness after tossing a ping-pong ball onto a floor covered with mousetraps.

The mousetrap analogy is Vonnegut's own, and speaks for the same lack of pretentiousness which characterizes his sources as well. "I would like to say something about American comedians," he writes in the preface to *Between Time and Timbuktu* (New York: Seymour Lawrence/Delacorte Press, 1972); "they are often as brilliant and magical as our best jazz musicians, and they have probably done more to shape my thinking than any writer." Vonnegut admits that he often expresses "pious gratitude" for the examples of Twain, Orwell, and even Joyce, "But the truth is that I am a barbarian, whose deepest cultural debts are to Laurel and Hardy, Stoopnagel and Bud, Buster Keaton, Fred Allen, Jack Benny, Charlie Chaplin, Easy Aces, Henry Morgan, and so on." Two of his contemporary heroes are the radio comedians Bob and Ray; in his preface to their book, *Write if You Get Work: The Best of Bob and Ray* (New York: Random House, 1975), Vonnegut talks about the "refreshing and beautiful innocence" of their work. Instead of basing their comedy on celebrities and news of the day, Bob and Ray use more commonly indigenous material: "They feature Americans who are almost always fourth-rate or below, engaged in enterprises which, if not contemptible, are at least insane." They do not show persons hopelessly tormented by an evil universe; instead, "Bob and Ray's characters threaten to wreck themselves and their surroundings with their own stupidity. . . . Man is not evil, they seem to say. He is simply too hilariously stupid to survive." In *Slapstick*, Vonnegut's models are Laurel and Hardy, who in their films "were not very good at living" but who "did their best with every test," never failing "to bargain in good faith with their destinies, and were screamingly adorable and funny on that account."

In his own fiction Kurt Vonnegut, Jr., improvises with the materials of life, creating lyrical tricks which—in Donald Barthelme's manner—make that life a little easier to live. "Comedians and jazz musicians have been more comforting and enlightening to me than preachers or politicians or philosophers or poets or painters or novelists of my time," he claims. "Historians of the future, in my opinion, will congratulate us on very little other than our clowning and our jazz." From an otherwise impossible situation Vonnegut makes a work of art, turning possible disaster into a ballet of pratfalls.

As a strictly literary influence, he admires Louis-Ferdinand Céline, especially the Céline he quotes in *Slaughterhouse-Five* (New York: Seymour Lawrence/Delacorte, 1969): "The truth is death. . . . I've fought nicely against it as long as I could . . . danced with it, festooned it, waltzed it around . . . decorated it with streamers, titillated it. . . ." In his first six novels, leading to the Dresden experience of *Slaughterhouse-Five*, Vonnegut becomes successively more aggressive and more adept at his duty-dance with death, using his artistic imagination to reorganize the arbitrary factors of life so that the one inexorable fact—death—may be faced. *Breakfast of Champions* (New York: Seymour Lawrence/Delacorte Press, 1973) takes the artistic self-consciousness emerging in the earlier novels and makes it part of the novel's subject, in the manner of Sukenick, Thompson, and Katz. In *Slapstick* Vonnegut can face the world squarely, taking the strength of his own experiences in the world and combining it with his author's sense of self, so that his final product matches the exuberantly playful art of his favorites, Laurel and Hardy.

Vonnegut's talent is finding an attitude which allows such productive combination of subject and technique. In his introduction to Céline's *Rigadoon* (New York: Penguin Books, 1975), Vonnegut tells how a reading of *Journey to the End of the Night* led him to fashion his own phrase, "So it goes," for *Slaughterhouse-Five*, where it is repeated every time someone or something dies. "It was a clumsy way of saying what Céline managed to imply so much more naturally in everything he wrote," Vonnegut says. "In effect, 'Death and suffering can't matter nearly as much as I think they do. Since they are so common, my taking them so seriously must mean that I am insane. I must try to be saner.'"

KURT VONNEGUT, JR.

I. A LIST OF DESTRUCTIONS

In his first six novels, Kurt Vonnegut, Jr., destroys persons, places, or things:

Player Piano (1952)—Ilium, New York
The Sirens of Titan (1959)—a Martian army
Mother Night (1961)—Howard W. Campbell, Jr.
Cat's Cradle (1963)—the Earth
God Bless, You, Mr. Rosewater (1965)—Indianapolis, Indiana
Slaughterhouse-Five (1969)—Dresden, Germany

But in each novel, Vonnegut also rebuilds—in each case, by reinventing his world according to the particular needs manifested by the story:

Player Piano and *God Bless You, Mr. Rosewater*: the social ethic;
The Sirens of Titan, Mother Night, and *Cat's Cradle*: the moral theology;
Slaughterhouse-Five: space and time.

There is a hierarchy to these reinventions: as Vonnegut came closer to the central subject matter of his career—the firebombing of Dresden—he became more massive in his reorderings, until the trauma of Dresden forced the reinvention of the two basic elements of existence. From both a technical and a thematic standpoint, then, it would seem that the writing of *Slaughterhouse-Five* has exhausted his art and completed his fictional canon.

II. A LIST OF DEPARTURES

1. He's offended by the amount of money he now makes. "It's silly, not gratifying." So he threw away his latest novel, Breakfast of Champions, *because he didn't think it was very good and he knew it would make him more money. "I don't know what the hell I'm going to do next."*

—Chicago Tribune, 11/15/70

2. "I am in the dangerous position now where I can sell anything I write. I am like an animal in a wicker cage, if you want to know what my life is like now. I'm scrambling. For so long money motivated me and now there is nothing to move me off center. I don't know what to do."
. . . .

Vonnegut says repeatedly that he is through writing novels. I took it at first as a protective remark, but then began to believe it. . . . After Slaughterhouse-Five, *Vonnegut began work on a novel called* Breakfast of Champions, *about a world in which everyone but a single man, the narrator, is a robot. He gave it up, however, and it remains unfinished.*

—New York Times, 1/24/71

3. "I'm not going to write any more novels," he says firmly. "I've been writing the novel-short-story thing for twenty years. I'm written out as far as that sort of deal goes. Now, I'm going to concentrate on plays. Novel writing is a lonely business, and while I was rewriting Wanda June *for the stage I found I enjoyed the community aspect of the theatre. It refreshed me—if you'll pardon the poetic phrase."*

—Harold Heffernan, syndicated 6/8/71

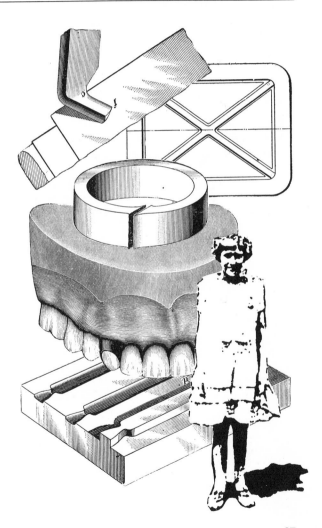

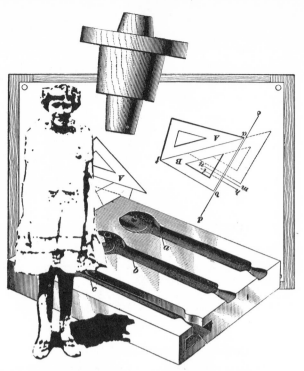

4. *This play is what I did when I was forty-seven years old—when my six children were children no more. It was a time of change, of good-bye and good-bye and good-bye. My big house was becoming a museum of vanished childhoods—of my vanished young manhood as well.*

. . . .

I was supposedly a right-handed person, but I found myself using my left hand more and more. It became the hand that did most of the giving and taking for me. I asked my older brother what he knew about this. He said that I had been an ambidextrous infant. I had been taught to favor my right hand.

"I'm left handed now, and I'm through with novels," I told him. "I'm writing a play. It's plays from now on."

—*Preface,* Happy Birthday, Wanda June *(1971)*

III. DISCLAIMING THE DISCLAIMER

I have become an enthusiast for the printed word again. I have to be that, I now understand, because I want to be a character in all of my works. I can do that in print. In a movie, somehow, the author always vanishes. Everything of mine which has been filmed so far has been one character short, and the character is me.

—**Preface,** Between Time and Timbuktu **(1972)**

IV. BREAKFAST OF CHAMPIONS

This book is my fiftieth birthday present to myself. I feel as though I am crossing the spine of a roof—having ascended one slope.

. . . .

I think I am trying to clear my head of all the junk in there. . . . I'm throwing out characters from my other books, too. I'm not going to put on any more puppet shows.

. . . .

"I am approaching my fiftieth birthday, Mr. Trout," I said. "I am cleansing and renewing myself for the very different sorts of years to come. Under similar spiritual conditions, Count Tolstoi freed his serfs. Thomas Jefferson freed his slaves. I am going to set at liberty all the literary characters who have served me so loyally during my writing career."

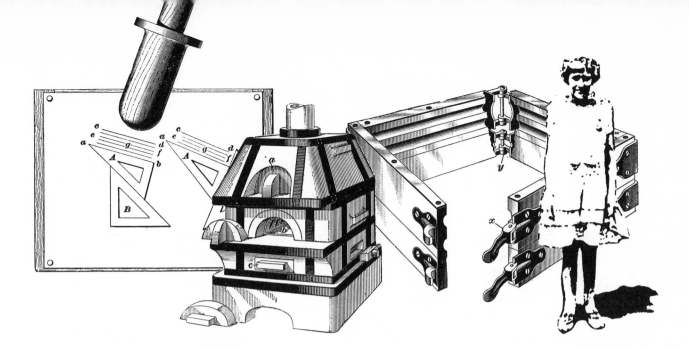

V. THE CONSUMMATE INVENTION

For the first twenty years of his career, Kurt Vonnegut, Jr., was the autodictatic novelist. He formed associations with neither universities nor "serious" novelists; instead, he made his living through the decidedly lower-level medium of slick magazine fiction and pulp paperbacks. By 1965, even with five highly idiosyncratic novels to his credit, he was not associated with the higher practitioners of the art: Bellow, Updike, Malamud, or Roth, and certainly not with the innovationists Barth, Kesey, Heller, and Pynchon. There was little evidence in the novels that Vonnegut was aware of them, either. Only for the writing of *Slaughterhouse-Five* did Vonnegut find himself in an environment (Iowa City) with knowledgeable friends (Robert Scholes, Vance Bourjaily) and innovative reading material (Céline). Under these circumstances, he produced his most technically complex novel—and apparently exhausted his themes and techniques.

Taken aback by his sudden fame, Vonnegut proposed to write no more novels. One might have wondered where his fiction could go from here, anyway. *Slaughterhouse-Five* carried his mode of reinvention to the ultimate limits of time and space. Therefore, when he did turn back to *Breakfast of Champions* (for a major rewriting), the subject had to be invention itself. In the interim Vonnegut had caught up with the decade's fiction: in New York, he formed a friendship with Donald Barthelme, became a vice-president of the P.E.N./American Center under Jerzy Kosinski, and was active in publishing circles. Vague hints of the more innovative fiction of Ronald Sukenick and Steve Katz appeared in *Breakfast of Champions*. All in all, it was a much more self-conscious novel. The circumstances of Vonnegut's career had brought him in line, for once, with the development of serious fiction.

Part of the action of *Breakfast of Champions* concerns the literary invention accomplished by the science fictionist Kilgore Trout when Dwayne Hoover reads his novel, *Now It Can Be Told*. The form of this novel is a letter from the Creator of the Universe, addressed to the reader: "Dear Sir, poor sir, brave sir: You are an experiment by the Creator of the Universe. You are the only creature in the entire Universe who has free will. You are the only one who has to figure out what to do next—and *why*. Everybody else is a robot, a machine." These machines exist for the testing of a free-will prototype, whom Dwayne reads literally to be himself (he's on the verge of going crazy anyway). "Of course it is exhausting," the letter continues, "having to be reasonable all the time in a universe which wasn't meant to be reasonable."

VI. THE ARBITRARY CONVENTIONS OF FICTION

I thought Beatrice Keedsler [the Gothic novelist in *Breakfast of Champions*] had joined hands with other old-fashioned storytellers to make people believe that life had leading characters, minor characters, significant details, that it had lessons to be learned, tests to be passed, and a beginning, a middle, and an end.

As I approached my fiftieth birthday, I had become more and more enraged and mystified by the idiot decisions made by my countrymen. And then I had come suddenly to pity them, for I understood how innocent and natural it was for them to behave so abominably, and with such abominable results: They were doing their best to live like people invented in story books. This was the reason Americans shot each other so often: It was a convenient literary device for ending short stories and books.

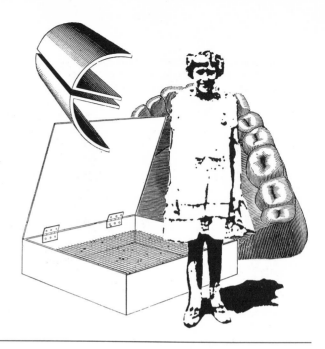

VII. THE ARBITRARY CONVENTIONS OF LIFE

Vonnegut begins *Breakfast of Champions* with descriptions of some of the most obvious and familiar elements in our lives. For instance, the national anthem: Vonnegut copies it out, and then observes that our country "was the only one with a national anthem which was gibberish sprinkled with question marks." Likewise for the symbols on our currency. "A lot of the nonsense was the innocent result of playfulness on the part of the founding fathers of the nation of Dwayne Hoover and Kilgore Trout. The founders were aristocrats, and they wished to show off their useless education, which consisted of the study of hocus-pocus from ancient times. They were bum poets as well."

There is a serious side to this arbitrariness-taken-for-the-absolute. Kilgore Trout speaks for it when he receives the Nobel Prize for Medicine in 1979:

"There were two monsters sharing this planet with us when I was a boy, however, and I celebrate their extinction today. They were determined to kill us, or at least to make our lives meaningless. They came close to success. They were cruel adversaries. . . . Lions? No. Tigers? No. Lions and tigers snoozed most of the time. The monsters I will name never snoozed. They inhabited our heads. They were the arbitrary lusts for gold, and God help us, for a glimpse of a little girl's underpants.

"I thank those lusts for being so ridiculous, for they taught us that it was possible for a human being to believe anything, and to behave passionately in keeping with that belief—any belief.

"So now we can build an unselfish society by devoting to unselfishness the frenzy we once devoted to gold and to underpants."

Vonnegut has said similar things before. In *God Bless You, Mr. Rosewater*, he took his millionaire protagonist to a science fiction writers' convention, and there had him pass out checks worth hundreds of dollars. "Think about the silly ways money gets passed around now," Rosewater advised them, "and then think up better ways." Such an ability to imaginatively transcend reality is at the heart of Vonnegut's reorderings, making invention possible even for those without the pragmatically necessary means.

But along with an absolute faith in the rigidity of conventions, people lost the power of ideas. "Ideas on Earth were badges of friendship or enmity," Trout continues. "Their content did not matter. Friends agreed with friends, in order to express their friendliness. Enemies disagreed with enemies, in order to express enmity."

VIII. CONVENTIONS: IN AND OUT OF THE KNOW

It was New Year's Eve, and Billy was disgracefully drunk. . . . Billy found himself out in his automobile, trying to find the steering wheel.

The main thing now was to find the steering wheel. First, Billy windmilled his arms, hoping to find it by luck. When that didn't work, he became methodical, working in such a way that the wheel could not possibly escape him. He placed himself hard against the left-hand door, searched every square inch of the area before him. When he failed to find the wheel, he moved over six inches and searched again. Amazingly, he was eventually hard against the right-hand door, without having found the wheel. He concluded that somebody had stolen it. This angered him as he passed out.

He was in the back seat of his car, which was why he couldn't find the steering wheel.

—Slaughterhouse-Five

Some examples of arbitrariness from *Breakfast of Champions*: seeing trucks along the highway lettered "PYRAMID," "AJAX," and so forth, "Trout wondered what a child who was just learning to read would make of a message like that. The child would suppose that the message was terrifically important, since somebody had gone to the trouble of writing it in letters so big." Later on, a young man who is spending the first time in his life outside institutions or reformatories reads a truck name phonetically and assumes it is in great pain. The message reads, "HERTZ." When Dwayne Hoover walks into his Pontiac agency on Monday morning to find palm trees growing in the showroom floor, he is mystified, having forgotten the special promotion of "Hawaiian Week"; but when his cousin tells him that " 'Them bubbles is halfway up to the *Cathedral* now. . . . The way they're coming, they'll be up to *Moby Dick* in a week or two,' " he understands perfectly—their tourist-attraction cave is being damaged by pollution. Vonnegut himself enters the novel wearing a P.O.W. bracelet for "WO1 Jon Sparks / 3-19-71," which the young man just released from prison cannot comprehend:

Wayne would assume that it belonged to a woman who loved somebody named WO1 Jon Sparks, and that the woman and WO1 had become engaged or married or something important on March 19th, 1971.

Wayne would mouth the unusual first name tentatively. "Woo-ee?" He would say. "Woe-ee? Woe-eye? Woy?"

IX. CONVENTIONS: THE IMAGINATIVE QUALITIES

"The Barringafner of Bagnialdo. He's a guy who each day decides what's valuable. One day it's land, one day it's clothes, etc., so that everybody is wealthy some time or another."

—Interview, Miami Herald, 1/24/71

Trout sat back and thought about the conversation [that trucks carry names because their owners like the "sound" of it]. He shaped it into a story, which he never got around to writing until he was an old, old man. It was about a planet where the language kept turning into pure music, because the creatures there were so enchanted by sounds. Words became musical notes. Sentences became melodies. They were useless as conveyors of information, because nobody knew or cared what the meanings of words were anymore.

What else is sacred? Oh, Romeo and Juliet, **for instance. And all music is.**

—**Preface,** Breakfast of Champions

X. "SOMETIMES I WONDER ABOUT THE CREATOR OF THE UNIVERSE" (Breakfast of Champions)

Two-thirds of the way through his novel, Kurt Vonnegut, Jr., enters the scene—real and in person. He discusses himself and the role of novelists. He comments on the story, and has more of it take place before his (and our) eyes. Annoyed by a bartender, he distracts him by making the phone ring. He plays other tricks like another writer who toyed with the same device: Mark Twain.

From the start of *Breakfast of Champions*, Vonnegut has made reference to himself: his childhood in Indianapolis, his mother's suicide, and his father's last unhappy years as he became old and infirm. These concerns are repeated in the novel's ending, but not in the version that Vonnegut first sent to his publisher. This is how it read in manuscript:

"A question, Mr. Trout?"

He cleared his throat again, and he at last took his Creator seriously. He had one question, and he was as defenseless as an infant when he blurted it out: "Why would anyone want to create an animal as unhappy as I am?"

"To share with you my astonishment at life, Mr. Trout," I said, "and to give you my diseases."

———————

And I am now in that wing of the Midland County Hospital which houses the mentally disturbed. Dwayne Hoover is my friend.

I am unsurprised. I always knew that sooner or later I would write myself into a loony bin. The big trick now is to write myself out again.

In a phone call during August 1973, Vonnegut explained just why he changed the ending. It was a last-minute affair. He had been working on *Breakfast of Champions* in New York for most of 1972, resurrecting and revising the manuscript he'd called back in 1970. As the book approached its final stages, his publishers had messengers carry manuscript segments from Vonnegut's home to their offices on Third Avenue and return with galley proofs. One day, as Vonnegut describes it, two young people from Dell's production department came back to his home with his final typewritten pages. "We don't like the ending," one of them confessed; throughout the process they had been completing their own early reading of Vonnegut's new novel, and were dissatisfied with the book's resolution. Something was lacking, which they could not explain but which Vonnegut suspected he might be able to find.

The young messengers were sensing something in Vonnegut's writing that he himself as a creative writing instructor at the University of Iowa had caught so many times in his students' work: the veering away from something very central to the fiction, "like suddenly dismissing something very important with a flippancy and letting it go at that." Responding to his early readers' objections, Vonnegut turned back to the manuscript and followed their encouragement "to close with the enemy, as they say in bayonet fighting," and to bring the novel to its proper conclusion.

The actual ending of *Breakfast of Champions* goes like this:

"Arise, Mr. Trout, you are free, you are free.*"*

He arose shamblingly.

I might have shaken his hand, but his right hand was injured, so our hands remained dangling at our sides.

"Bon voyage," I said. I disappeared.

I somersaulted lazily and pleasantly through the void, which is my hiding place when I dematerialize. Trout's cries to me faded as the distance between us increased.

His voice was my father's voice. I heard my father—and I saw my mother in the void. My mother stayed far, far away, because she had left me a legacy of suicide.

A small hand mirror floated by. It was a leak with a mother-of-pearl handle and frame. I captured it easily, held it up to my own right eye, which looked like this:

Here is what Kilgore Trout cried out to me in my father's voice: "Make me young, make me young, make me young!"

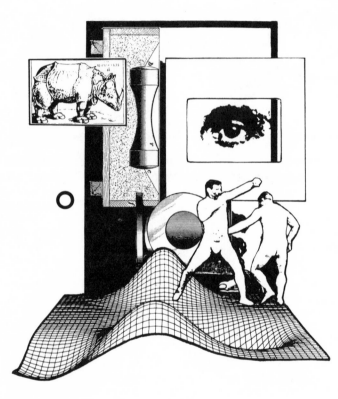

Chapter Eight

Clarence Major's fiction stands in high relief because he has pitted it against two traditions: that of conventional realistic fiction, and that of the commercially received black fiction which has been restricted to the form of social realism. "Black American fictionists have been primarily concerned with subjects involving the racial plight of black people," Major wrote in his regular column for *American Poetry Review* (#3, 1976). The form for this subject matter, Major continued, has been "naturalistic and realistic or deterministic," while in terms of literary techniques "black writers have not ventured often from norms established by the main population of white European and white American authors." Among black authors Major admires Ishmael Reed, Alice Walker, and Charles Wright. Of Wright he states, "His language has the power to suddenly illuminate the dullest moment. He is more interested in impression than in meaning, in *process* than in conclusion." Although he and his colleagues have abandoned the traditional forms of black American writing, Major feels that their revolution is part of the change in black consciousness, for "in order to create art, whether representational or not, one must give one's self to the process of being an entity and not an identity."

By focusing on language, Major has found a way to treat a recognizable subject matter without having it turn into a stereotyped notion of the documentary world. He creates the flavor and tone of everyday black speech not by mimicking dialect, but by using his syntax to suggest the rhythm of the spoken word. He is less interested in external characters than in the imaginations he creates for them, which we are never allowed to forget are projections of the author's own mind. In his novels, the fictional experience is often suspended on images rather than dependent upon narrative drive. First published as a poet, Major has worked to eliminate the distinction between poetry and fiction, taking poetry's lyrical freedom—and especially its freedom from having to offer an organized, linear representation of experience—as an index of what fiction could do with the same basic materials: words.

After an early childhood in Atlanta, growing up in Chicago (with especially memorable summers spent among Georgia relatives), informal study at Chicago's Art Institute, some time as a steelworker in Omaha, an apprenticeship in the Sixties as editor of the little magazine *Coercion*, and work as a researcher on news media coverage of civil disturbances in Milwaukee and Detroit, Clarence Major settled in New York to teach at Sarah Lawrence College and Brooklyn College. At the latter school he met Jonathan Baumbach, co-founder of the Fiction Collective, whose ranks Major joined in 1975. In addition to publishing Major's third novel, *Reflex and Bone Structure*, the Collective featured Major's work in its anthology, *Statements* (New York: George Braziller, 1975), alongside fiction by Ronald Sukenick, Steve Katz, Walter Abish, Russell Banks, Ishmael Reed, Raymond Federman, and Jonathan Baumbach. Prefacing this volume, Sukenick told how their collective work demonstrated "a sophisticated awareness of the formal options and techniques available today to those fiction writers who know their business. And it is precisely this freedom, this destandardization, this educated individualism that is so different about such fiction."

   Sukenick's analysis of what makes the Fiction Collective's work different from the novels of commercial publishers reflects Clarence Major's own achievement in redirecting the tradition of fiction by black American writers: "While it often ignores old forms, dispenses with plot, characterization, and verisimilitude, blurs the distinctions between prose and poetry, between fiction and autobiography or history, makes use of collage, employs new means of narrative order and even redefines the relation of print to page, it communicates the sense of an exploration to discover new forms that better suit the individual artist."

CLARENCE MAJOR

**My present life is a Sunday morning cartoon.
In it, I see Miss Hand and her Five Daughters
rubbing my back and the backs of my legs.
Nat King Cole provides the music and the words.
It's 1949.**

*

1. *"Can you start now?"* [*says the druggist*]. *He smelt of Noxzema.*
2. *And that was the way the boss came: like a burning cigarette.*
3. *Thursday always told us it was cause of TV that slavery finally came to an end. She might have something there, I think.*
4. *What is a lynch town, Moses? asked Gal.* / *A place where fragile connoisseurs of joy reside in the comfort of one another's rationalization.*
5. *As time took up space just happening. . . .*

*

   In the fiction of Clarence Major there is a strong lyricism. He has written five collections of poetry, but only in his novels does that lyricism strike against and then work with the more objective, discursive, "real" aspects of life which one finds in narrative modes.

   "I see our poems, social and political, as scientific new music: these constructs are solar concerts to the infinite tacit incantations of our elegance, as we are, as we long to be." Major wrote this in the introduction to *The New Black Poetry* (New York: International Publishers, 1969), a collection which represented a newly responsible art, sometimes even street poetry, which traded on just the opposite effect: using the studied lyricism of poetry as a context for the startling introduction of simple and harsh realities. But in either Major's poetry or his fiction, the fundamental reality lay in *the words*. In his *Dictionary of Afro-American Slang* (New York: International Publishers, 1970) he wrote that "beneath the novelty or so-called charm of this mode of speech a whole sense of violent unhappiness is in operation." Moreover, "This so-called private vocabulary of black people serves the users as a powerful medium of self-defense against a world demanding participation while at the same time laying a boobytrap-network of rejection and exploitation." Major was the first author to seriously measure this effect, even as he incorporated it into his own creative work.

*

1. **A:** *yes, correct, right.*
2. **Anywhere:** *to possess drugs,* example, *"Are you anywhere?"*
3. **Bad:** *a simple reversal of the white standard, the very best.*

*

Finished with them, I take off on a riverboat, down the Mississippi, looking for work.
On deck they got the Original Dixieland Jazz Band doing "Big Butter and Egg Man."
A guru has the cabin next to mine and everybody who visits
him whimpers something terrible!

Major's genius is his ability to lyricize the physical, to work his imagination upon the bedrock world not usually indulged by poetry. His first novel, *All-Night Visitors* (New York: Olympia Press, 1969), uses sexuality as the vehicle, courting the danger that such an approach tends so easily toward the pornographic (the volume was published in Maurice Girodias's Olympia Press series, and was in fact heavily cut to fit that format, at the publisher's insistence). The argument begins, "This thing that I am, this body—it is me. *I* am it. I am not a concept in your mind, whoever you are! I am *here*, right here, myself, MYSELF, fucking or being driven to the ends of my ability to contain myself in the ectasy of her little red mouth inspires as it works at the knobby head of my weapon, or if I am eating this goat's cheese, the pumpernickel, drinking the beer I have just bought, or whatever I happen to be doing." The lyrical is too often reserved for the subjective or ideal, things already lyrical in themselves. Major roots his work in the deeply physical. As his character in *All-Night Visitors* insists, "I am not *your idea* of anything."

More simply, in *No* (New York: Emerson Hall, 1973) the protagonist announced, "Another thing I'm fast discovering to be mine and mine alone. It's my dick. Though there isn't very much I can do, I can do whatever I want with it." Sexuality is the means of self-definition. Major has commented on the difficulties black authors have in incorporating sex in their works, and how *All-Night Visitors* is a fundamentally "un-Christian" book. An earlier variant of this experience was crime, as he indicates in his collected essays, *The Dark and Feeling* (New York: Third Press, 1974): in Richard Wright's *Native Son,* Bigger Thomas finds that "The crime liberates him (whereas in a white novel, *Sister Carrie* by Theodore Dreiser, the hero's crime ultimately leads him to destruction, inwardly as well as outwardly)." In *All-Night Visitors* Eli Bolton is distraught when his girlfriend leaves; "I'm seriously considering killing Cathy," he admits, "to keep her body here, if nothing else." When it comes, the murder is symbolically accomplished by rape. In *No,* Moses Westby actually kills four children, and then himself, rather than see them suffer more. But murder is hardly preferable—even beyond these deaths, the spokesman of the novel must kill these people "in his head" before he can be free; Moses's actual murder has made little difference. Imaginative action, lyricizing the physical rather than destroying it, is a better option. Against the social realism of a Richard Wright, Major takes an imaginative journey toward the discovery of self, and the scene—instead of the slums of Chicago—is the bed where he's fellated by his girlfriend. "I want to *stay* right here, with her, focused on every protrusion, every cord, abstract circle of myself, of her every 'feeling,' every hurling, every fleshy spit-rich convexity, mentally centered in all the invisible 'constructs' of myself, right here, where she and I now form, perform an orchestra she is constructing in juicy floodtides." Language takes over beyond the action, as he "is percolating, oozing, dribbling at the dick like a river, but a slow river, being tapped by the mysterious rainfalls of Mother, voids, secrets, wet holes of the fleshy world, carried on an expedition to the ends of my psychophysical reality; at the floodgates of emergency, my dark, fleshy Anita, love, a gateway into which I exist, and erupt, enter."

**Stood on deck after dinner watching the clouds form faces
and arms. The Shadow went by giggling to himself.
An Illinois Central ticket fell from his pocket.
Snake Hips picked it up, ran.**

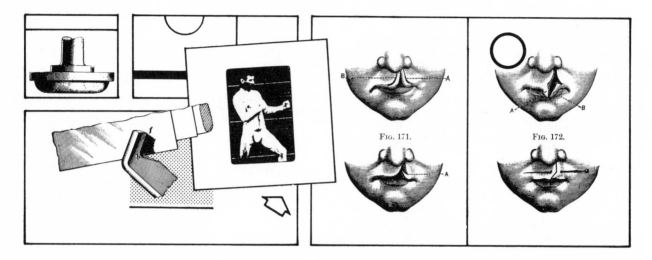

FIG. 171.   FIG. 172.

1.   *As the old man comes toward us, the evil in his encroached face causes him to suddenly blow up with the kind of force behind an earthquake. The vast immodest sound, the liquids of his body, the spermy-substance of his brains shoot out, his eyeballs, rebellious question-marks, hang down suspended on long slimy patheticus strings from his sockets; Eunice's hand, inside mine, tightens; "Oh damn—look at that! That poor man—He's having a heart attack!" The gooey stuff splashes in nearby plates of food, customers jump back in their chairs, an old woman with a bust as big as a bathtub drops her monocle, falls over backwards in her chair, her floor-length gown flying over her head, her broom-stick size legs, juggling frantically for some balance, her rich, pink Playtex girdle is even drenched with the juices from the explosion—I wonder why some of the folks are beginning to hold their noses: then it hits me, the odor of the substance from the waiter's skull smells like shit. He is a lump of slimy flesh and starched garments, on the floor. Eunice is pulling at my sleeve; "Please, let's go, I'm getting sick. I can't eat here." Eunice, even before we reach the street, is gagging.*

2.   *"Hello, Harold," Anita said.*
    He didn't answer but continued to gape at me, as he closed the door. He seemed rapidly reaching a state of derangement. His big wet eyes enlarged. He was breathing with irregular force.
                                    . . . .
    Harold is coming through the door, shit, rasping, without having opened it, the rasping turns into a husky grizzling; Anita and I are on the floor, wrestling playfully; she shifts, sees him first, her wet mouth hangs slightly, corpulent juicy cinnamon.
                                    . . . .
    I get up brush off go up and . . . Harold, this big monster who looks like he'd never sound like a faggot, comes rushing in straight through the wall, with his rod in his hand, flying with a cape attached to his neck, screaming like a girl waylaid wag in a prosaic voice: "Reely now this is rawthuh nasty of you two! Oi weh!"

3. *And if none of this research made sense linguistically nor lingoly, if none of it had any profound bearing on the essence or physical property of the me or the I, then, at least it was great fun and it fed my usually starved ego! All kinds of techniques added to the jigsaw puzzle of my heritage: for instance, according to the Warden, who was never famous for accuracy: on the day my beautiful black mother was born, same date of my birth, 28th of December, but in 1908, 85,000 people were killed by an earthquake in Messina, Sicily; the town was completely wiped out; thirty-two years later, Elizabeth Mamzazi, I call her, left Chicago to vacation in Europe, during April, 1940, and was fucked good and hard, deep and long, on top of a pile of hay under the midday sun, by a swarthy Italian gambler, a member of the notorious Mafia, and I was instantly conceived; however, nine months later ella dropped Eli at the most public hospital in the world, swooped for Mexico, where it is said that she continues to live in her disguise, married to a wealthy landowner. That is just one of the many many versions of how I came about. Mrs. Paulson, descendant from the founder of the school, once told me a brutal, long story of my origin: the gist of which was: my mother, a white girl, was raped in Mississippi by a giant black field nigger, who was burned in kerosene while white men watched and jacked off in the town square; afterwards my mother, under the protective shadow of night, left for Chicago where she lived in hiding, with a German butcher on the near North Side, until she gave birth to me, and gave me to the county.*

4. *. . . your mama's a coal miner with a funky ass-full of coal dust; for drawers she wears overalls, she got fleas in her crack, she stinks like a goat—she's as musty as a skunk—she shits rotten eggs—eats polecat meat—drinks my piss—she sucks the diseased dicks of ole cripples and bums on West Madison Street in Chicago, and for Kotex she uses Brillo Pads . . . your mama is a man! She got a dick bigger 'han the Warden's nose—and that's some job, boy! Your mama—she's got two balls growing under each armpit, and for breakfast she eats ape turds creamed down low in rancid goat piss—drinks cabbage juice of skunk cabbage for coffee—she spreads stinkweed on her bread for butter—she lets the milkman fuck her in the nose, while she lets the grocery boy stick his dick under her eyelids!*

Black slang provides more than just the words for Clarence Major's lyricism. In the case of "playing the dozens," it provides an innovative form as well. The dozens is "a very elaborate game traditionally played by black boys, in which the participants insult each other's relatives, especially their mothers. The object of the game is to test emotional strength. The first person to give in to anger is the loser." In the "Eli" chapter excised from *All-Night Visitors* (later published in *Lotus,* Spring 1972), we find the protagonist first playing with linguistic variations on his mother's name, then playing the dozens with himself as he attempts an imaginative self-definition. The importance is not in what is signified, but *how;* "I saw the work as a kind of drawing done with words," Major reports in *The Dark and Feeling.* Later in the same book he stresses that "All words are lies when they, in any arrangement, pretend to be other than the arrangements they make." Even more fundamentally, Major argues in *The New Black Poets* that "Our language is born of sound clusters, as opposed to Shakespeare's, which derives from the nexus, *sight.*" Playing the dozens would make no sense if the object were the establishment of an objective meaning: first, it would be impossible; second, the attempt would no longer be play. With a novel it is no different. "In a novel the only thing you really have is words," Major told John O'Brien in the latter's *Interviews with Black Writers* (New York: Liveright, 1973). "You begin with words and you end with words. The content exists in your minds. I don't think that it has to be a reflection of anything. It is a reality that has been created inside of a book." Such control makes for a richer vision than is usually found in life. "Moses in *No,* for instance, *is* all the things that happen to him and all the ways that people look at him. . . . I was trying to show all the shifting elements of the so-called self."

*

Texas Shuffle, who sat in with the Band last night,
       this morning, dropped his fiddlecases in the ocean
and did the Lindy all the way to the dining room.
I got off at Freak Lips Harbor.
Boy from Springfield said he'd talk like Satch for me
       for a dime. I gave him a Bird and an introductory note
to the Duke of Ellington.

*

1. *We're in bed watching the late movie. It's 1938. A Slight Case of Murder. Edward G. Robinson and Jane Bryan. I go into the bathroom to pee. Finished, I look at my aging face. Little Caesar. I wink at him in the mirror. He winks back.*
   I'm back in bed. The late late show comes on. It's 1923. The Bright Shawl. Dorothy Gish. Mary Astor. I'm taking Mary Astor home in a yellow taxi. Dorothy Gish is jealous.
2. *To keep my mind off the problems of Cora's death, I watch television. It slushes back and forth before me. In the afternoon TV is dull shit and it lodges you in its dullness; yet it gives you a weird vegetable sort of copout security.*
3. *Canada has to find a way to relax. He sends for Red Garland to play piano. The sunlight comes in through the window showing thousands of kiwis on the wallpaper pecking in New Zealand sand. Stan Getz follows Red. With a funky ballad. The tenor sax is an act of love. Canada closes his eyes. He is back in 1938 listening to Ella sing, "A tisket, A-tasket."*

*

Clarence Major's third novel, *Reflex and Bone Structure* (New York: Fiction Collective, 1975), is a double-edged treatment of the imagination's power. The characters live almost fully in their minds, where the stimulus of a television show, movie, or jazz album is as effective in altering their reality as any outside event. Moreover, the author of the fiction keeps these characters suspended in his own imagination; he refuses to let them "come alive" and "walk off the page," since by doing that the artistic point of their creation would be lost as they melt into the abstractions of what Gilbert Sorrentino calls "the world we already know." The true interest of the novel is the author, and the point is his reaction, his reflex to the bone structure of the novel.

The center of interest for both author and characters is Cora Hull, a Greenwich Village actress. She is trying to find herself—in her profession, in her relationships, and in her own womanhood. Trying to find themselves within her are her lovers: Canada, Dale, and the author. The author's own intentions are complicated by those of Canada, Dale, and Cora herself; all happen simultaneously, often in contradiction to each other, while late-night movies and jazz records compete for their share of the action. Time and space are filled with an infinity of stimuli and responses, until the author's task is to chart this ballet of the human imagination. Scenes are replayed from different angles, highlighting different interests, portraying a coexisting different reality.

At the very start of the story we learn that Cora and Dale, meeting in secret, have been killed by a bomb planted in a suitcase. "I'm a detective trying to solve a murder," the author tells us. "No, not quite a murder. It's a life. Who hired me? I can't face the question." His novel is organized partly like a mystery novel, partly like a crossword puzzle, as he gathers the bits and pieces of his own emotions into the spatial reality of Cora's life and death.

*

1. *And my being alone so much reinforces the tendency to skin-dive beneath the surface. Not that I find solutions. I should ideally strike a balance between the surface and the lower depths. I can do the low stuff very effectively. I need practice on the surface where Cora, Canada and Dale hang out.*
2. *Cora is away being interviewed by Cecil B. De Mille. I'm here, on the bed, thinking about my future. I want to blur the distinctions between it and the past. I'll make up everything from now on. If I want a commercial airline to crash with Cora and Dale on it doing it in the dark, I'll do that. Or have them go down at sea in a steamer caught in a violent typhoon near Iceland, or in an exploration vessel off the West Indies. I'll do anything I like. I'm extending reality, not retelling it.*
3. *I am standing behind Cora. She is wearing a thin black nightgown. The backs of her legs are lovely. I love her. The word standing allows me to watch like this. The word nightgown is what she is wearing. The nightgown itself is in her drawer with her panties. The word Cora is wearing the word nightgown. I watch the sentence: The backs of her legs are lovely.*
4. *Get to this: Cora isn't based on anybody.*
Dale isn't anything.
Canada is just something I'm busy making up.
I am only an act of my own imagination. I cannot even hear my own voice the way they hear it. I got the "Bullfrog Blues."
Cora does the "Charleston Rag."
Dale sings "Hello, Dolly."
Canada covers the waterfront.

*

Elements of Cora's life, and of the author's infatuation with his creation Cora, crowd the book. Tree frogs, salamanders, and other animals from her Southern past appear in her Greenwich Village apartment; Boris Karloff, Peter Lorre, and other figures from her persistent late-night movies smile at her from mirrors. The television screen itself reflects her vicarious participation in the imaginative life it portrays. Clarence Major has admired the same technique in Jonathan Baumbach's *Reruns.* Reviewing it for *American Poetry Review* (#6, 1975), Major described how movie-star images have a heavy influence on the character's life: "He sometimes confuses himself with these two-dimensional figures. Jack's companion, the sniper, shoots a movie star directly off the screen. Things happening on the screen are also taking place in the theatre." We meet film characters on the same conditions as anybody else in the novel: all are equally made up, and chart the true imaginative life of the mind. Impulses and intentions are given the same credibility as acts. "No moment can be claimed as absolutely safe from confusion," Major observes. The truth is that "life does not progress and that the realness of fictional life is an invention of language," since that pure act of the imagination is the only way a writer can be equal to the possibilities of life. Therefore Major, Baumbach, and others create life in their books rather than trying to record it. As the disclaimer to *Reflex and Bone Structure* warns, "This book is an extension of, not duplication of reality. The characters and events are happening for the first time."

*

1. *In* All Night Visitors, *Major's protagonist, Eli Bolton, finds the world on its own terms too unreal, and hence he plays the dozens with himself as he searches out a meaning. Instead of a social examination, Eli undertakes an imaginative study of his origin and existence—not as a rejected orphan and hassled young man, but instead through the mystery of the vagina and the spirit of his erect penis. He rhapsodizes while being fellated by his girlfriend, where the imaginative becomes total freedom and Eli can be "like a nightmare patriarch responsible to no one but myself." There is a lot of sex in this novel, and rightly so, Major argues. "Here was a man," he tells John O'Brien, "who could express himself only in this one natural way because he had absolutely nothing else." But once equipped with a potent and expressive imagination, Eli has access to the real, revealing the truth not in simple reportage but in full visions. . . .*

—Jerome Klinkowitz, Oyez *(1973)*

2. *Clarence Major chooses a modular approach for his second novel,* No, *with two voices passing the action back and forth, and a whole new metaphor for the black experience. The narrator observes of himself and his wife, "I have the trustworthy feeling that Oni and I are definitely on the way down, over, and out! Which, of course, implies that we were at one time in my opinion up from somewhere. Up from slavery?" Major tries instead the metaphor of prison; penal psychology and the image of life imprisonment hold his work together. That and a carefully controlled manner of running parts of the action backward—a scene begins with the penultimate moment, a jump back to the moment just before, then to a sequence of events just before* that, *until by the end of the chapter narrative time has backtracked to the very beginning, when we are suddenly confronted with the end. This dramatic method is played against the quiet counterpoint of Major's two voices, following the action "as time took up space just happening."*

—Jerome Klinkowitz, North American Review *(1973)*

*

There is much critical resistance to writing like this by black authors. In January 1974 Clarence Major led a group of writers complaining to the *New York Times Book Review* about its aesthetically discriminatory notice of Toni Morrison's *Sula.* "For a long time," Major said, "white readers and critics have tried to dictate what black writing *should* be." As a consultant on Afro-American literature at Cazenovia College, Major had to wonder if the course should be Black Excellence in American Literature or Excellence in Black American Literature. The issue as he saw it was the failure to judge a writer in relation to his own personal sense of reality. "Among the black novelists themselves there is so much diversity that *no single* Black Aesthetic or formula or fixed method for looking at their work can be employed," Major argues. "You might do well to employ instead a fresh open mind."

"People who want to write sociology should not write a novel." Major draws the quote from Ralph Ellison. Using race as the dominant critical concern disallows a literary appreciation of works by black authors, and in the meantime fosters a style of very limited social realism. But Major, as we shall see, is not socially irresponsible. He drew criticism for publishing his poetry anthology and black slang dictionary with International Publishers, where they shared the list heavy with titles on Marxism, Cuban revolution, and other political concerns. But as he argues in *The Dark and Feeling,* in an essay titled "Formula or Freedom," "The novel *not* deliberately aimed at bringing about human freedom for black people has liberated as many minds as has the propaganda tract, if not more. . . . A work that takes long root in its author's experience—race being a part of that experience—not only makes sense anywhere in any language but also is likely either to raise hell or lower heaven."

*

Found my way to the Ida B. Wells Youth Center.
Girl named Ella said I have to wait to see Mister B.
Everybody else was out to lunch.

In the waiting room got into a conversation with a horse thief
from Jump Back. Told him:
My past life is a Saturday morning cartoon.
In it, I'm jumping Rock Island freight cars, skipping Peoria
with Leadbelly; running from the man, trying
to prove my innocence. Accused of being complex to handle.
Meanwhile, Zoot, Sassy, Getz, Prez, Cootie, everybody
gives me a hand.

1. *Now, more than ever I realized that Anita was truly a relic of my past. I was also wise to her now: she believed religiously in the values of the White Knight Ajax cleaner Kraft Foods Wildcat and Impala cars, the existential reality of Aerowax and the divinity of jet-age plastic Sperry Rand Frank Sinatra George Burns Maxwell House coffee Jack Benny and Texaco gasoline; she thought the Hully Gully was a game invented by Jewish kids in Israel, that who Stagger Lee shot was his mama, that a Blood was an Indian and that C.C. Rider was a civil service technician.*

2. *I do know this, though, I felt, there, for the first time, in that ring, for those few moments, that I was no longer a victim. I was my own person and I could actually decide whether or not I wanted to go on living—I could play with the question. . . . I felt that, if I could touch the bull's head, and survive such a feat, life, from this perhaps unworthy moment, would be invested with essence. In other words I had to give meaning to it and it had to contain courage. . . . He was bleeding and sweating and half dead but I touched his head and in a strange and beautiful way that single act became for me a living symbol of my own human freedom.*

*

Clarence Major has described just how his strange and terrible novel works. "In *No* the 'spirit' of the narrator's 'head' is meant to function both as a 'scheme' (plot) and as central force, both as conveyor of the 'story' and a screening device for the development of the work as an entity. The main concept involves demonstrating the plight of Moses Westby's tragic imprisoned birth and growth and ultimately how he transcends this penal system." He has defied the white-imposed "traditions" of black literature to develop a brilliant lyricism in new forms of fiction; but his art inevitably turns back to the basic social and personal concerns which must remain at the heart of any literary experience. "I am exploiting a range of taboos, fears, cultural limitations, and social traits," he advises, "springing from attitudes concerning a wide range of human experience, sexual, racial, historical, national and personal." There is no purging of these problems in simple reflection. Major's art eschews this manner for the long-run gains, which he cashed in when his lyrical aesthetic returns to life to clarify it with a vision not possible among the mundane concerns of any other method.

*

Finally, Mister B comes in. Asks about my future.
All I can say is, I can do the Cow Cow Boogie on the ocean
and hold my own in a chase chorus among the best!
Fine, says Mister B, you start seven in the morning!

—Clarence Major, "The Syncopated Cakewalk" **(1974)**

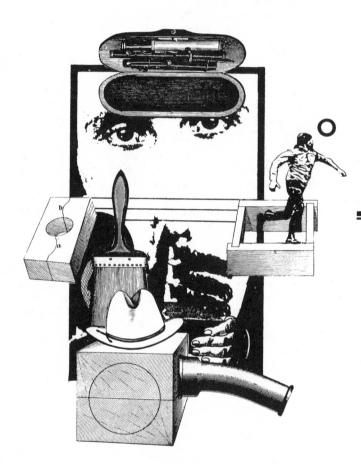

Chapter Nine

Steve Katz made his debut as a character in contemporary American fiction four months before the publication of his own first novel. Near the end of Ronald Sukenick's *Up,* when the author is gathering together his imaginary characters and real-life friends to celebrate the completion of his novel, we're introduced to "Steve Katz, here briefly on a special guest appearance from his own novel with a team of his tumbling mild-nosed Egyptian spotted rabbits, take a bow Steve." At the time, Katz was finishing *The Exagggerations of Peter Prince* and promising to include Sukenick as a character there; Sukenick subsequently appears as a distraction, with Katz complaining, "That's why I haven't got Peter Prince from Italy to Egypt yet. I'm waiting just where he told me for Sukenick to put me in his novel, here on the street corner with the busted lamp. I can take some patience, because if he ever shows up at all he's usually late. And it's probably some little insignificant thing he's going to have me do," Katz continues, "a little trip to Long Island, or a conversation with one of those characters of his who always wears tinted contact lenses." Sukenick, of course, remains as a character in his own novels, and subsequently becomes one as well in *The Book of Daniel* by E. L. Doctorow, Sukenick's former editor—as Professor Sukenick, director of Daniel's thesis.

Their simple agreement to include each other as characters, back in 1968 when they were publishing their first novels, suggests the common goals which Katz and Sukenick share in fiction. The artifice of their books is self-apparent; their fictions take place in a recognizable world, but important parts of that world are the authors themselves, who are the first to remind us that no one can tell just where the historical self ends and the imaginative self begins. They are playfully aware of their act of creation and share the joy of it with their readers, who can easily catch the small jokes which the authors poke at each other and at the conditions under which they write. Their fictive acts are artificial but not phony. As Sukenick says in Raymond Federman's *Surfiction* (Chicago: Swallow Press, 1975), "It seems as pointless to call the creative powers of the mind 'fraudulent' as it would to call the procreative powers of the body such." Together, they have restored artifice (and not mere representation) to its proper place as fiction's primary achievement.

Katz shares Sukenick's interest in the energy of the imagination which fiction redirects into life. Like the other SuperFictionists, Katz writes about a recognizable world; but his goal is to make it "resonate" with the sound and energetic power of his words. Of all his colleagues, Katz is the closest to being a jazz musician with language, using his gift for sound and circumstance to create dazzling improvisations upon the most unlikely subjects. His short paragraphs, published in such little magazines as *Seems* and *Center,* are (like those of Clarence Major and Michael Stephens) examples of pure writing, with no real subject matter at all. His longer stories, which have appeared in such larger-circulation journals as *American Review, New Directions,* and *Epoch,* are distinguished by the very ridiculousness of their subjects: the mundane practicing of cannibalism, the changing of skin with a girlfriend, or the strange experience of receiving a mysterious package of human wrists. These latter fictions, part of a longer work in progress titled *Moving Parts,* are similar in intent to Donald Barthelme's "Porcupines at the University." The point is that the writer takes a situation so absurd that it could never exist in the real world, and uses it as an excuse for his verbal, syntactic, and situational riffs—exactly like a jazz musician taking the bare structures of familiar melodies and using them to create a wholly new and supremely artificial work. The one representational subject Katz does return to is sex. Like Clarence Major's *All-Night Visitors,* Katz's pseudonymous novel *Posh* was published in a series of ostensible pornography. But just as with Major's effort, pornography as a form is simply an excuse for more improvisations with circumstance, all the more noteworthy in a genre usually distinguished by little stylistic art. Major's and Katz's writing is exuberantly sexual even when its theme is far removed from sex; when theme and technique coincide, the results are doubly dynamic.

Katz's writing will play with anything: sex when he can get it, bizarre examples of human conduct when he can find them, or any interesting facet of life which allows free exercise of the human imagination. Like Sukenick, who is fascinated by the work of Carlos Castaneda, Katz has become a friend and admirer of the Sioux shaman Henry Crow Dog. Speaking of his own work, Katz insists that there are "magical connections beyond our ability even to predict or even to describe"; in his writing he is able to reach "an uncontrollable and mysterious resonance that sometimes illuminates." The impetus may be nothing more substantial than the coincidental appearance of the number "43" in Katz's life, so pervasive that it would seem to form a pattern or code—yet indecipherable beyond the magic of his story.

In his presentation of the unpublished "43" at New York's Tin Palace on February 7, 1976, Katz talked about the possibilities of "system" in words similar to those of Walter Abish and Ronald Sukenick on the same subject. "The potential for mystery is everywhere, and infinite," Katz insisted, "and the world of events cannot be circumscribed by a predetermined order no matter how complex and involuted a system of psychology, physics, religion, or occultation is applied." The need is for an *alternative view,* such as Sukenick ascribes to the sorcerer; as Katz says, "Unless we insist on a position of observation and understanding outside the system, unless we use it rather than let it use us, we become victims of the dogma of that system." As a SuperFictionist, Katz reminds us that the conventions of life are merely that, arbitrary assumptions never meant as an absolute or end in themselves. As a writer, he uses those conventions not as a representational base, but simply as the bone structure for his improvisations. His fiction is largely play. But through the energy released by that play, Katz's readers get a sense of what life—beyond all the mysteries we can never penetrate—may be like.

STEVE KATZ

I. KATZ IN THE VALLEY OF DECISION

Tape

Enough! Katz, you're making this all up. It doesn't make a bit of sense. It's not a promising beginning. Why can't you follow the instructions? You can't write whatever you want: Peter Prince Peter Prince Peter Prince. Where's the story? How are you going to catch us up in it and write a novel so the reader won't be able to put it down, he's so involved. He'll put the book down right now and say, "Who cares?" without even a placemark. What will your friends say? They'll say, "Katz, cut it out, you're making it all up. You're fucking around with boredom in our heads." A reader wants to know what's going on. What's going on? Peter Prince, for instance, why write about Peter Prince? Every day of the summer more interesting people than he swim at Jones beach, they eat hot dogs, the ball parks are full of them, they smear each other with newsprint in the subways, roll up their shirtsleeves and sit on the doorstoop, they lean from windows, they're honking at intersections on the cloverleafs, on the East Side Highway, they wait at the counters of the supermarket with their Kool-Aid and their instant rice. Boatloads cruise around the island and they meet each other, friendships depositing and eroding. It's difficult, Katz, to answer this question— Why Peter Prince?—when the wind itself is full of shapeless, hopeful folk blown about like empty plastic sacks, who could be born in a book. Born in a book at a profit to humanity.

Tape ends

This the third page of hardcover fiction published by Steve Katz. The quickest exhaustion of conventional fiction on record. For the two and a half previous pages his protagonist had been strangling his soon-to-be-estranged wife's cats. " 'Cats up your ass,' " he tells her. So much for verisimilitude, the fourth wall of drama, a slice of life.

Tape

You see I'm sick of those passages in our work that refer however suavely to how the work is being made or how it should be made although in a broader sense I still deal with self-referential condominiums the former seems to me at this point like nothing more than another dull literary convention to be purged, like the fat that has to be lifted off the chicken soup before you heat it up again (did I get that from Bellow, Roth or Malamud—I hope from I. B. Singer) I find it hard any more accepting those passages in Ronnie's books and in Gil Sorrentino's, though they both manage to move through it with astounding energy OUT from four to zip is too thickly embroiled in that argument with himself to keep me at that level of pleasure at that momentum I felt down to 4

Sorrentino is real slick at it but the process wears me down in his work I don't feel the necessity the efficacy the inclination to validate some dreams anymore it's that process I find too conventional in my own work peter prince the dream is not the thing so we don't have to justify it but it's the energy that generates the dream that needs to be manifested in the stories we are prone to tell that's why I'm not willing at this point to suspend the suspension of disbelief if we don't have that ain't nobody at all gonna knock on the door and our words won't resonate into their lives which is what the real difference between fiction and exposition is— RESONANCE—echoes of the soundings.

Tape ends

Katz keeps his resonance through three novels: *The Exagggerations of Peter Prince* (New York: Holt, Rinehart & Winston, 1968), *Posh* (New York: Grove Press, 1971, under the pseudonym "Stephanie Gatos"), and *Saw* (New York: Knopf, 1973). His shorter fiction was collected in *Creamy and Delicious* (New York: Random House, 1971); uncollected pieces appear in *Fiction, Paris Review, Epoch, Chicago Review, American Review,* and *New Directions.* He may still suspend disbelief, but he won't allow the story to take itself that seriously. According to Ronald Sukenick, Katz "writes like a seal with the ball continually about to fall off its nose." Just when we think it's about to fall, Katz incorporates the wobble into his act.

Tape

What's the matter. Where's the trouble? What's the problem? Where's the fire? Who's the culprit? What's the reason? Was it easy? Where's the money? When is Wednesday? Who you dating? Can he have it? Do you know him? Did you touch it? Is it poison? Does it hurt? What's the meaning? What's the trouble? What's the problem? What's up Doc? Where's the contest? Are you angry? Is he happy? Did you touch it? What's the answer? What's the hurry? Was it painful? Are you touching? What's the reason? Is he singing? Were you running? Did he grow? Did she answer? Who's the culprit? What's the address? Is it money? Was he angry? Is she waiting? Is it colder? Did he take it? Does it hurt? Was it poison? Where's the honey? Are you running? Who's the boss here? Is he starving? Did you

touch him? Was he up here? Is he down there? What's the matter? What's the trouble? Does it tickle? Is it empty? Does he have one? Did you touch it? Where's the fire? Are you staring? Are you nervous? Is it tender? Is it tricky? Are you happy? What's the matter? Is it over?

Tape ends

Perhaps Katz is unwilling to suspend the suspension of disbelief because his M.A. thesis (since burned) was on Coleridge.

II. KATZ WRITING

Among the self-referential condominiums in Katz's first novel, *The Exagggerations of Peter Prince,* we find worries that his book is being written in an air-conditioned carrel under fluorescent light ("the best books so far have been written by natural light, or long ago maybe by candle, oil or kerosene, and recently, incandescent; but fluorescent?"), reservations about its ability to capture everything ("sometimes it's so hard to tell what has really happened. It's impossible to know. That's why I want to develop multiple possibilities simultaneously"), and irresolute revisions (several scenes are crossed out but printed in nevertheless legible form). But even as he was to claim in his letter six years later, the moments resonate. Don't forget that seal and the ball.

Tape

This was such a great idea when I got it that I leaped out of my seat and zipped around my study like a house on fire. "That's it," I shouted. "You've got it. A Genius touch." I kissed my knuckles, my shoulders, my desk. I had a lot of glee and in my eyes was sparkle. . . . I thumped on my chest. Alas. Here I am X-ing it out like a lady tweezing gray hairs. Mutability. If I had an instant I could call my own I'd lean on something and ponder that.

[splice]

Here, I guess, is a good place to pick up a discussion I dismissed hastily earlier: fluorescence. In my fluorescence is a luminescent emission that is caused by the flow of energy into the emitting body . . . this emission ceasing abruptly when the exciting energy is shut off . . . and the light is out, in the blink of an eye, and who's to know? ME. I know it. And don't think it doesn't twist this book. The result is that of a stroboscopic effect, a very disturbing factor, which causes similar disturbances in my book. The light here, you see, isn't just on all the time, but it's switching on and off at a rate of sixty times per second because those electrodes in that fluorescent tube are constantly alternating their charges with this alternating current, and the fluorescent light with that quick-die technique I just described goes on at that rate. . . . Don't think that this book isn't influenced by the fact that sixty times each second it gets dark in here, making over the period of years it takes to write a book,

no matter how small each instant, an appreciable amount of darkness. This condition of intermittent darkness explains then some of the empty avenues in this book, gaps like highway right-of-ways through the timber, like missing teeth, transitions that are unreadable because you can't see them, all the more easily explained now under the heading of Stroboscopic Blind-Spots.

[splice]

"We just thought at that moment, you know, at the climax of the novel, when the truth of something is finally revealed to Peter Prince, you know, all novels have that moment when everything comes together, and a revelation is at hand. Well we thought at that moment if Peter Prince could mention our product, just say its name, and maybe recite a little testimonial poem, a few of its qualities, you know—it would be a really significant moment for our product."

Tape ends

III. KATZ TRIUMPHANT (PART ONE)

Your first book, *The Exagggerations of Peter Prince,* is an enormous success and lifts you out of the doldrums. You go to Turkey with your kids in a Land Rover and you camp by the Black Sea where you write a book of stories called *Creamy and Delicious* which is received in New York City with all its enthusiasm for monkeyshines and shenanigans. Your children bring back Turkish habits. After a brief rest period something comes into your mind which you call LEROY [*Saw*]. . . . With a final, bruising effort, you finish the book—*Leroy: Starring The Astronaut.* Then you pass out. Your publisher believes it will be an astounding success, and he gives you a big advance with which you buy an island in the Bay of Northumberland and learn to fly a plane. What a bestseller that book becomes. You circle our troubled city in a new twin-engine Aero-Commander you purchase with the royalties. You are flying with your editor, your two children, and the gypsy governess. Everyone asks to see the parking lot that once was Madison Square Garden. You spot a young man through your bombsight sitting on the curb, reading about The Astronaut at an interesting pace. On him you release a shower of soft monographs pressed off the frosty lips of all the women you have loved to date, November 18, 1970. His delight pleases the planeload.

"All this becomes possible," you tell your kids, "because your father discovers The Astronaut and puts him in LEROY."

"Huzzah," shouts the editor.

IV. KATZ IN MAGIC

Tape

"Did you know that turtles don't breast-feed their young? They flat refuse to."

"That's news to me," Beulah said, humoring her husband. She was enough of a zoologist to have that fact down pat already.

"So there is no such thing," he went on, "as good old-fashioned turtle's milk."

"I'll be darned."

"And the old expression, 'chomp down on the turtle's tit,' makes no sense at all."

Tape ends

Katz's fiction is different, even from that of other "different" innovationists. Sukenick describes his work as "the best contemporary example of improvisational style," and "the closest thing to Rabelais since Rabelais." The best way Sukenick can characterize it is that "As abstraction frees fiction from the representational and the need to imitate some version of reality other than its own, so improvisation liberates it from any a priori order and allows it to discover new sequences and interconnections in the flow of experience."

Katz's work is in a close sense magical, drawing comparisons between one mundane thing and another—but in a totally startling way which makes the old-fashioned but never-ceasing-to-be-amazing *flash of insight*. "Outside something present in the midafternoon suburban silence loomed as a bulldozer does during a coffee break over a slum clearance project." This from his pseudonymous "pornographic" novel, *Posh*. Or, a bit more extravagantly, from *Creamy and Delicious:* "They plugged in their IBM beauty till it puckered up and started to blink like an army division looking for its contact lenses in an olympic-sized chlorinated pool."

One fictionist who sometimes equals Katz's similes is Richard Brautigan. His offhand metaphors in *Trout Fishing in America* have the same outrageous quality: "the grass turned a flat-tire brown in the summer and stayed that way until the rain, like a mechanic, began in the late autumn," or "the trout would wait there like airplane tickets for us to come." But Katz enlarges these metaphors until they make the entire story. In "Parcel of Wrists" (*Epoch,* Autumn 1973) he begins with the bland explosion, "In this morning's mail I received a parcel postmarked from Irondale, Tennessee. It was wrapped in heavy brown paper with an oily surface, like thick butcher paper. The box was of even dimensions, 2 feet high, 2 feet deep, 3 feet long, and it was packed from top to bottom with human wrists."

Tape

The wrists were clean and odorless. They had been prepared so neatly, without a trace of torn flesh, that it occurred to me they might never have been attached to hand or forearm. I held one for a moment in the palm of my hand, a small one that might have belonged to a child or a frail girl. It seemed to flex itself there slightly, perhaps in reaction to the warmth of my hand, as if the person to whom the wrist might belong were just beginning to wake up. I put the wrist back in the box, closed it up, and went downstairs to the luncheonette to get some breakfast and mull over the strange detour my life had taken as a result of my opening the morning mail.

Tape ends

For a while the wrists are forgotten, as the protagonist gets involved in other inventions. But later, after they've been planted in forty-three pots (a magic number for this magic writer), the wrists flourish as plants and then bear interesting fruit—lips, eyes—and one even becomes "a tree whose limbs are weighed down with a crop of human legs, like bunches of bananas." They kick the author.

Tape

"I really can't understand how my writing is published. You know it's very different."

[sitting with Clarence Major and the author at The Cookery on University Place one June morning in 1974]

"My first novel was published because, leaving a party, an editor said he'd publish my book if I put on his overshoes. It's kind of been like that."

[splice]

It was a bright clear sunny New York day, a rare one. I headed up 23rd Street. How to describe this rush of energy? . . . Something passed over the sun. A dim, distant honking sound echoed above the din of the city. I looked up. It wasn't clouds. Great chevrons of geese were crossing the sky. They were gathering like a storm and darkening the sun. No one had ever seen so many geese at once, and never in the New York City sky.
   . . . .

It was like a solar eclipse as the great packs of geese gathered above the city. Lights went on. Goose-shit fell everywhere, the streets so slick with it I had to skate up 23rd Street. People hid in doorways, or brought out umbrellas and tried to keep going. . . .

Suddenly the geese all settled around me. Huge Canada Geese, little Brant Geese and Barnacle Geese. Snow Geese. Blue Geese. . . . I continued up 23rd Street, followed by the huge contingent of geese. I moved forward, propelled by their honking. Each time I turned around they stopped and settled down, and watched me, as if I were supposed to say something. . . . I led them up Seventh Avenue. It was, I'm sure, the first parade of its kind in the history of New York City. That was probably why we weren't hassled about a permit. It was 11:54 A.M. All traffic and commerce was halted on the avenue. As far as the eye could see down the avenue my retinue of geese stretched in an endless waddle. I led them without strutting. At least a thousand geese kept themselves at all times between me and the police.

At 1:17 P.M. we were at 86th Street. That was when we crossed the park. I didn't know it, but we were headed for Gracie Mansion. . . . The mayor heard of our coming long before we arrived. He was already in flight

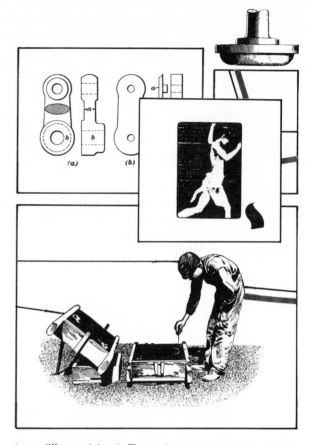

to a different island. The palace guards gave up immediately when they saw our disciplined multitudes. We went in through the windows. We went in through the chimneys, through the drainpipes, through the doors. We occupied every room. We surrounded the grounds. The numbers that wouldn't fit I dispatched through the air to City Hall. It was 3:43 P.M. We had the city under our control.
   . . . .

My geese . . . were now running the city. I had no reason to hang around. If you want to see them you will have to go to their offices in City Hall or visit them on the grounds of Gracie Mansion. I recommend them to you. They are honest, and mild, and willing to listen.

Tape ends

Katz's geese come from a story called "Female Skin" (*New Directions* #30, 1975). His acts are performed "in the skin of Wendy Appel," and it all begins with a detachment similar to "Parcel of Wrists": "I made the first incision at 7:15 A.M. It was an important step. I touched the point in lightly just under the left armpit and slowly pulled the blade down along her side. The knife moved bloodlessly. My system was to accomplish the separation with one continuous lateral cut, dividing her skin in two halves, front and back. That was better than a bilateral division along the axis of her symmetry because it would make for the least disfigurement when the skin had to be replaced and would permit easier disguising of the adjustments and stretching necessary to fit that small skin over my relatively large frame."

"Female Skin" and "Parcel of Wrists" are parts of a yet-to-be-written novel called *Moving Parts.* The key to these pieces, as Sukenick states, is that they are not abstract but *improvisational.* Abstract implies reference—some "thing" from which the piece is "abstracted." Katz's stories are something else, the quality of music, riffs and jams. The ideas are great, first for their imaginative craziness, then for what the artist does with them (the double feature of a jazz original, a bizarre melody [think of Thelonious Monk] and then improvisation upon *that*—as opposed to taking solos on an old standard, the difference between "Straight No Chaser" and "Groovin' High"). In *Saw,* the heroine Eileen makes love with a sphere: "The sphere keeps rubbing her while he makes gentle philosophy. She begins to feel sexy. Perhaps the sphere is just handing her a line, she thinks, and wants only to get her into bed. She feels a pleasant tingling all over her skin. It can't just be a sphere of philosophy that makes her feel this way. The doubts and troubles she has fetched up from deep within are slowly displaced by a round, rising dreamlike motion in herself. 'You . . . you touch me like . . . like this,' she says."

◁O

V. KATZ IN THE TWENTIETH CENTURY

Tape

Ah, the twentieth century hustles by like a centipede, how I love it, how we all behave in it as if it were the twenty-first.

Tape ends

VI. KATZ IN LOVE

Kurt Vonnegut, Jr., has discussed the problems of sex in a novel. "There's a mechanical reason for avoiding adult sexual love in a book," he told an interviewer in the *Meanjin Quarterly* (Autumn 1971). "The minute you introduce that element the reader's not going to want to hear anything more about the factory system or what it's like to be a parachutist. He's going to want to hear about the guy getting the girl and this is a terrible distraction unless you're really going to deal flat out with the sexual theme."

The way Katz handles sex is another indication of how the basis of his work is not representation or abstraction, but improvisation. Here we go.

Tape

She mosied back into the booth and waited. They had agreed not to open the hole through which he poked his, and over which she slipped hers, until they were sure who was there. . . .

O sweat smudges of body heat. Linda Lawrence panted over the protrusion, licked it, lifted her skirts and scissored it. She was so happy she kicked off her shoes and danced on the toilet lid. "Yipe. Yipe." It grew and grew, like a fleshy inflatable telescope, like an expanding water tower, an extendable smokestack. As she palmed it it grew and she lipped it and warmed it and breathed, "Ohhhhh, happy." It was thick around as a weightlifter's bicep, and long as a thigh and a half, and it was growing. She couldn't imagine it. The partition cracked and splintered. . . . From the toilet seat she leaped astraddle and grabbed hold as she used to grab hold of the mane of her mare, Gooper, when she rode it bareback through the pillowy hills, and she slid back and forth on the tough length of it in a delirious delicious lubricious rhythm. Out of her mouth rushed her high, stuttering love noise. It was still growing. She stood up and ran back and forth on it barefoot, like tepid lava underfoot. . . .

She had to bring the swollen thing down. . . . She opened her pocketbook and looked in there for something that would help. Nothing but some writing equipment, sunglasses, her smokes, her lighter, lip pomade, hankies, and a slim paperback by Saul Bellow. . . . The desperate Linda Lawrence pulled out the paperback and began to tear pages from it, slapping them onto the sticky extension as fast as she could and covering it completely with the printed page. Even if she couldn't shrink it she would disguise it, and then maybe slip away.

Tape ends

The pornographic *Posh* is written almost entirely in this manner. Even apart from the purely sexual improvisations, Katz takes the opportunity of every happening to exploit his material. Just as a gifted jazz soloist uses upbeats, codas, and especially transitions between choruses to extend his virtuosity, so too does Katz take advantage of even the least likely development in his narrative, such as when his heroine finds herself fellating a stranger on a bus as she runs away from home: "She caught it in midflight and began to caress it for him with her fingertips, working her body down in the seat so she could eventually get her mouth over the tip of his cock before he broadcast his jissom and soiled her clothes. And it would be more nourishing to swallow it now that she was on her own and short of funds."

VII. KATZ IN TRIUMPH

Tape

The same quality I love in your other work that is the quality of the last gasp I mean all your work sounds like the last gasp the longest last gasp on record giving one that anxious feeling that you'd better hang on to these lines while they're wailing what's wonderful being that in every sentence is implied that well there's nothing more to say after this and yet there's always something more to say and it's always of the same quality of sneaky desperation you write on the edge of a precipice leaning against the wind (ain't that heroic!)

Tape ends

Critically (self-reflectively), Katz speaks a line similar to one by Ronald Sukenick. "You know it's been my feeling for a long time that the novel is a dead form already, an issue of the past," he writes in *Peter Prince.* "Our century and mentality hasn't the patience for it, what with the film and TV and tape recorders and transistors and who knows what else." In the modern world, it is difficult being a novelist. But not a fictive artist. "It's more necessary than ever before these days to shape one's life into a work of art." It is even a respectable theology, a very popular one too (e.g., Sam Keen, *Telling Your Story, To a Dancing God,* and so forth).

Katz's fiction is written this way, and this is how it should be read. "We have to learn to think about a novel as a concrete structure rather than an allegory, existing in the realm of experience rather than of discursive meaning and available to multiple interpretation or none, depending on how you feel about it," writes Sukenick, "—like the way that girl pressed against you in the subway. Novels are experiences to respond to, not problems to figure out, and it would be interesting if criticism could begin to expand its stock of responses to the experience of fiction."

The final gasp before the next gasp: that was Steve Katz's response to the experience of Raymond Federman's fiction. About his own fiction, some words on a home-made picture postcard from Haiti: "As they say in Creole, Lò ou Kraché â lè, li tôbé sou nê ou—or, When you spit in the air / the spit falls on your nose."

Tape

Thanks for the SAW paragraph and however you snuck me into your disruptions. What you are, Klinkowitz, is a smuggler, running the real stuff over the boundaries.

[splice]

The only revolution can be a breakthrough to what's real.

End of tape

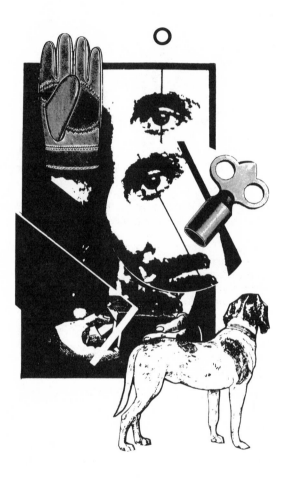

Chapter Ten

It's late November 1974, and the long table at The Big Stein, a neighborhood bar dropped into the center of Milwaukee's downtown, has been taken over by a group of writers from the Coordinating Council of Literary Magazines, meeting down the street at the Plankinton Hotel. Raymond Federman and Ronald Sukenick are huddled at the end, off by themselves, debating whether Federman's *Take It Or Leave It* should be submitted to the Fiction Collective. At the head of the table sits Ishmael Reed, holding court behind a phalanx of empty Blatz bottles, giving a patriotic speech which could have been born on Milwaukee's working-class South Side—which is, after all, only a stone's throw across the dingy industrial valley lying at the end of Plankinton Avenue.

"If anything is going to happen," Reed asserts, "it's going to happen *here.*" He means in the United States, which a few other writers had just been faulting for its racism, imperialism, and other shortcomings. "All the energy, all the enthusiasm, all the imagination are right here in America," he continues. "The other day Allen Ginsberg said America is a lost cause; but his family has only been here since 1903. What right does he have to give up so easily?" Lorenzo Thomas interrupts to remind Reed of what Thomas believes is their common heritage: as slaves kidnapped by foreign enemies, never allowed to make the new country their own. "Now wait a minute," Reed objects; "My family goes back to Virginia in the 1600's, as free men. This is my culture, and I want to have a part in making it work for us."

If there are problems in the culture, Reed sees them as caused by Europe, not by America. He feels that true American cultural expression has been limited by colonial oppression—most specifically by the standards first set by British and Continental literature, and then maintained by East Coast publishers, critics, and academicians. His evidence is the predominance of European forms, to the exclusion (or at least second-rating) of such native American products as the cowboy novel, the detective story, and the comic strip. He agrees with Kurt Vonnegut, Jr., that America's unique contributions have been its jazz musicians and popular comedians, and, like Vonnegut, Reed is eager to incorporate these achievements into his own art. Although as a black author he feels particularly embattled, he sees original black writing as one element among many in indigenous American art. His second novel, *Yellow Back Radio Broke-Down,* combines them all, as an abstract expressionist black cowboy mystery novel filled with an ample supply of vaudeville, radio, and TV comedy. While traditional novels sometimes differ little from their predecessors of nineteenth-century England, Reed's work could only take place (and be understandably read) in a world of jet planes, electronic media, and post-atomic sensibilities.

"The Neo Hoo Doo Aesthetic" is Reed's term for his own fictional plan. It expresses his allegiance both to an indigenous art form and to the supra-representational goals of that art. Although his materials are taken from the familiar world of past and present America, Reed's art is—like the conjuror's—metaphysical in purpose, capturing an essence rather than rendering a photograph, presenting alternative realities with the same persuasive account that has been a model for Ronald Sukenick and Steve Katz as well. His novels are often an amalgamation of American life and culture, but there are few direct relationships. As Clarence Major wrote of Reed's third novel in *Black Creation* (Fall 1972), "A good novel does not contain characters *based on* anybody: the people in *Mumbo Jumbo* are the fixtures of *its* terrain; they are *in* and *of* their own world." Exactly like a conjuror, who brings life to self-created things, "Ishmael Reed gives them the space of his mind in which to breathe."

ISHMAEL REED

Ishmael Reed was born in Chattanooga, Tennessee, on February 22, 1938. Chattanooga built a monument to every Confederate soldier killed in the Civil War, so Ishmael Reed spent his early years bumping into stone. He grew up in Buffalo, New York, where "polack" is scribbled on the bust of Chopin in Humboldt Park.

Ishmael Reed attended the University of Buffalo and left after receiving rude phone calls from an anti-Gnostic bursar. At twenty he was stranded in North Platte, Nebraska. Buffalo Bill once had a drink there. He has taught American fiction at the University of California at Berkeley, and the University of Washington at Seattle.

He startled the scientific community by making his home in New York City [in the Sixties]. Ishmael Reed has been buffaloed by many aspects of American society, which makes him uniquely qualified to write about the West.

—Author's note,
Yellow Back Radio Broke-Down

Ishmael Reed

The Free-Lance Pallbearers (New York: Doubleday, 1967)

Yellow Back Radio Broke-Down (New York: Doubleday, 1969)

Mumbo Jumbo (New York: Doubleday, 1973)

The Last Days of Louisiana Red (New York: Random House, 1974)

Flight to Canada (New York: Random House, 1976)

19 Necromancers from Now (New York: Doubleday, 1970)

"The Neo Hoo Doo Manifesto," *Conjure* (Amherst: University of Massachusetts Press, 1972)

"Introduction, I," *Yardbird Reader #1* (1972)

"Interview with Ishmael Reed," *Interviews with Black Writers,* by John O'Brien (New York: Liveright, 1973)

The New Fiction: Interviews with Innovative American Writers, edited by Joe David Bellamy (Urbana: University of Illinois Press, 1974)

SAM never forgot the advice of this woman whose face looked like five miles of unpaved road.

—The Free-Lance Pallbearers

In the distance large birds with buzzard coupons could be seen lining up for mess.

—Yellow Back Radio Broke-Down

Outside it began to rain on the rooftops of the Hat and Boot store, the Feed store. Their tops, reflecting the heaven's disturbance, went on and off like blue tubes.

—Yellow Back Radio Broke-Down

The cowpokes were pretending to be in a dentist's office of the mind. They had their heads buried in magazines.

—Yellow Back Radio Broke-Down

Taking his threat seriously, many are wearing Cab Calloway for President buttons.

—Mumbo Jumbo

One day, early in 1971, a few of us living in Northern California were comparing notes concerning the treatment of Afro-American artists by callous publishers, editors and others. It was decided that we are treated as commodities; mute dictaphones recording someone's often ludicrous political and social notions—slaves, standing on an auction block as our proportions and talents are discussed. . . . The genius of the slavemaster was to deny our individuality; therefore we were seen as cargo, easily manipulated and bartered. Over 100 years later the slavemaster is assisted by black "Patrollers" who desire to give "Virginia Play" to the fugitive or runaway aesthetic. We will seek to put an end to this foolishness by supplying an alternative. Our motto: "Once a work of art has crossed the border there are few chances of getting it back."

—Yardbird Reader #1

Easterhood looked real simple, like a Bunny Berrigan adaptation of a Jelly Roll Morton hit.

—The Last Days of Louisiana Red

"Why, yessuh! Mr. Swille. I loves it here. Good something to eat when you wonts it. Color TV. Milk pail fulla toddy. Some whiskey and a little nookie from time to time. We gets whipped with a velvet whip, and there's free dental care and always a fiddler case your feets get restless."

—Flight to Canada

After all, in this country art is what White people do. All other people are "propagandists." One can see this in the methodology used by certain White and Black critics in investigating Black literature. Form, Technique, Symbolism, Imagery are rarely investigated with the same care as Argument, and even here, the Argument must be one that appeals to the critics' prejudices. Novels that don't have the right "message" are cast aside as "pretentious," for it is assumed that the native who goes the way of art is "uppity." He loses his seat in Congress, or is dethroned as Heavyweight Champion of the World. . . . In [Robert] Bone's case, for example, the categories he uses—Amalgamation, Open Revolt, Separatism, or Back-to-Africa—are not literary categories, but essentially political ones.

—19 Necromancers from Now

JOHN O'BRIEN: Much of the interest in black literature in the last few years has not really been in such things as poetry and fiction. The nonfiction by black writers has received the most attention.

ISHMAEL REED: This is very true. When somebody like Peter Prescott [book review editor of Newsweek] **comes out and says the most interesting writing from blacks are the autobiographies of Malcolm X and Eldridge Cleaver, it's like saying the most interesting white literature is Richard Nixon's Six Crises and Dwight Eisenhower's** Stories I Tell My Friends. **I think it stems from the old ancient Christian notion that heathens don't have souls. If you don't have souls, how can you possibly possess an imagination or be able to write poetry or deal in ambiguity?**

—Interviews with Black Writers

It's awful admirable dat I'm even able to take my conjure lessons through the mail under the Mojo Retraining Act.

—The Free-Lance Pallbearers

Why, I wanted to become the first bacteriological warfare expert of the race.

—The Free-Lance Pallbearers

Fannie Mae was curled up on the sofa watching the Art Linkletter show where a life supply of pigeons had been awarded to four cripples and some parents of children with harelip.

—The Free-Lance Pallbearers

I was to learn that White authors, as well as Afro-American authors, are neglected by the American university. Before I arrived at Berkeley, there was no room in the curriculum for detective novels or Western fiction, even though some of the best contributions to American literature occur in these genres. At another major university, the library did not carry books by William Burroughs, who at least manages to get it up beyond the common, simple, routine narratives that critics become so thrilled about.

I found that some of the students who didn't understand the language of Chester Himes or Charles Wright were equally at a loss when it came to Horace McCoy or Damon Runyon.

—19 Necromancers from Now

Under her armpit she carries the Christmas issue of the Reader's Digest *(stars, snow and reindeer on a blue cover). The lead article is "Should Dolphins Go Steady—33 Parents Reply."*

—The Free-Lance Pallbearers

I agree with yooz Skinny, another cowpoke said. I'm going to take my roll and gallop on out of here. If he wants someone to herd them cattle he ought to see about importing Eskimos or something they would fit right into this weird irrational discontinuous landscape—cows herded by dogsled over sand, nobody'd know the difference, strung out as the townsfolk are.

—Yellow Back Radio Broke-Down

Man, pass me another whiskey. This place is really getting eerie, never seed no town like this; all the planks holding up the buildings seem to lean, like tilt over, and there's a disproportionate amount of shadows in reference to the sun we get—it's like a pen and ink drawing by Edvard Munch or one of them Expressionist fellows.

—Yellow Back Radio Broke-Down

Cinnamon was over in the corner, congratulating Maxwell Kasavubu on his startling thesis, now being circulated in literary and political circles, that Richard Wright's Bigger Thomas wasn't executed at all but had been smuggled out of prison at the 11th hour and would soon return.

—The Last Days of Louisiana Red

I did research for *Yellow Back Radio* in the Bancroft Library, which is one of the centers of Western Americana. And another critic, L. E. Sissman, who's in love with the old world, said that my book didn't approach what Emily Brontë had done. This is the kind of confusion and ignorance that you have prevailing in the American critical establishment. A man comparing my work—I grew up in Buffalo, New York, an American town—comparing it with a woman writer of nineteenth-century England who was involved with different problems and a different culture.

—*Interviews with Black Writers*

Because of the reception of *Pallbearers* people thought it was esoteric. But there's nothing esoteric about the book when you look at it; it's just a different way of viewing things. I've watched television all my life and I think my way of editing, the speed I bring to my books, the way the plot moves, is based upon some of the television shows and cartoons I've seen, the way they edit. Look at a late movie that was made in 1947—people become bored because there was a slower tempo in those times. But now you can get a nineteenth-century five-hundred-page book in a hundred and fifty pages.

—*Interviews with Black Writers*

He was a blond. He lay in the bed, tossing and turning. His room. What was that odor? The pungent odor of middle-class perfume making the air misty. He didn't feel right. His hair. What on earth was the matter with his hair? It was long and was covering the pillow. The pillows? They had a flower print and were pink. Pink? He rose in his bed and his breasts jiggled. BREASTS? THE BREASTS?? He looked back into the mirror next to the bed and his mouth made a black hollow hole of horror. "O MY GOD. MY GOD." He was a woman. You know what he said next, don't you, reader? He's from New York and so . . . you guessed it! "Kafka. Pure Kafka," he said. . . . Someone was now in the room; a dark foreboding shadow crept to the foot of the bed. A giant colored man—an Olmec-headed giant wearing a chauffeur's cap. Max started to really scream this time. "Please, Ms. Dalton, you will wake the whole house," the figure says.

—The Last Days of Louisiana Red

(Before Sather Gate, University of California at Berkeley, Fish and Andy stand. They are wearing pink robes, sandals and have shaved their heads. Andy Brown keeps his derby. They are shaking tambourines and soliciting.)
Kingfish: *Karmels! Karmels!*
. . . .

Kingfish: *Remember the time we took over the Black studies programs up here, Andy?*
Andy: *Yeah, I remembers. We bopped the buswa nigger who was running it, and he had a big hickey on his head. Then we took over.*
Kingfish: *Those was the days, Andy, the sixties. They took us off television and the radio and gave us freedom to roam the world, unchecked, hustling like we never hustled before.*

—The Last Days of Louisiana Red

You can always get the tip-off that they are trying to use black literature to make some kind of thesis when they begin their surveys with Richard Wright. They all begin with Richard Wright. That's like beginning a survey of white American literature with Norman Mailer instead of with Cooper, Brown, or Hawthorne. That's how you can see that they haven't done careful research on the field. They use it for rather dubious ends. And they never mention Richard Wright's later work, like *The Outsider* and the things he wrote in Europe. They take *Native Son,* for obvious reasons. They use black literature to make a political statement. These people are socialists. And blacks do the same thing.

—The New Fiction

My narrative technique involves having a kind of duo that one associates with the vaudeville stage. There's the straight man and the clown, the jokester. Like Laurel and Hardy. And there's a formula for it: one guy is a straight, sophisticated, intelligent, intellectual dude and the other guy keeps breaking into dialect or slang, and slapstick or burlesque. That's what happens in *Free-Lance Pallbearers.* That's what I attempted to do. I was reading a lot of Mack Sennett and Bert Williams' scripts about that time, and burlesque, and listening to comedy routines.

—Interviews with Black Writers

There were more people performing a Neo Hoo Doo sacred dance, the Boogaloo, at Woodstock than chanting Hare Krishna . . . Hare Hare!

—The Neo Hoo Doo Manifesto

She returned to the television where SAM was making an announcement from the low-down nasty room.

"Slurp, slurp. Dis is the boss, folks. SAM. Slurp. Now I'm not gonna get all flowery like the fella what preceded me, quotin' all them fellas what wore laurels and nightgowns. I'm gonna give you people the straight dope. Now dere's rumors goin' round here that the Chinamens 'bout to run away wit all our fine suburban women. I know that all who loves SAM HIMSELF and ME all in one realize that your man would never tolerate no little dwarfs wit pocket-knives slashing our women's discotheque pants, hip boots, miniskirts or none of them otha fashions that me and Mlle. Pandy Matzabald thunk up for um to wear. Slurp, slurp. . . . Now one more ting before I get back to the low-down nasty room where Mlle. Pandy Matzabald can go down-town on me. To the creeps on the steps of Sproul Hall at Berkeley. KEEP IT UP YOU FREE-LOADEN COMMUNISTS TAFFYPANTS SISSIES. I GOT MY EYES ON YOU AND YOUR MINISTRATORS HAVE PASSED ON YOUR NAMES TO ME. JUST KEEP IT UP AND MY SCREWS WILL CLAMP DOWN ON YOU SO HARD PUNKS DAT YOU'LL WISH THAT YOU WAS DEAD. DON'T FORGET NOTHIN' ESCAPES MY EYES SINCE I GOT THESE HERE BINOCULARS WITH THE FORTY BOOKS OF GREEN STAMPS.

—The Free-Lance Pallbearers

The Free-Lance Pallbearers actually started out as a political satire on Newark. It was going to be a naturalistic, journalistic, political novel. But as it went through draft after draft, the style I thought was mine came back and I developed it. While writing Pallbearers I was reading Kenneth Patchen's The Journal of Albion Moonlight and Charles Wright's The Wig, which is one of the most underrated novels written by a black person in this century. And I was reading a lot of poetry. I learned what poetry is by writing it, and I wanted to bring these techniques to so-called prose. All these things influenced the first book.

—Interviews with Black Writers

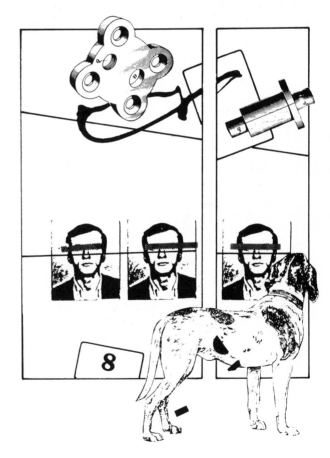

Drag even went and got a mail order bride and it wasn't a week before the Loop Garoo Kid had her running through the mountains in the nude, had done offed her mind and she was screaming foul nasty things like "make that mojo trigger my snatch one mo time" and mumbling some bad nigger words—you know how they move up and down the line like hard magic beads out riffing all the language in the syntax.

—Yellow Back Radio Broke-Down

Folks. There here is the story of the Loop Garoo Kid. A cowboy so bad he made a working posse of spells phone in sick. A bullwacker so unfeeling he left a print of winged mice on hides of crawling women. A desperado so ornery he made the Pope cry and the most powerful of cattlemen shed his head to the Executioner's swine.

—Yellow Back Radio Broke-Down

Think of all the vehemence and nasty remarks . . . like William Buckley, that Christian fanatic, saying that Bach is worth more than all the Black Studies programs in the world. He sees the conflict as being between the barbarians and the Christians. And, you know, I'm glad I'm on the side of the barbarians. So this is what we want: to sabotage history. They won't know whether we're serious or whether we are writing fiction. They made their own fiction, just like we make our own. But they can't tell whether our fictions are the real thing or whether they're merely fictional. Always keep them guessing. That'll bug them, probably drive them up the walls. What it comes down to is that you let the social realists go after the flatfoots out there on the beat and we'll go after the Pope and see which action causes a revolution. We are mystical detectives about to make an arrest.

—*Interviews with Black Writers*

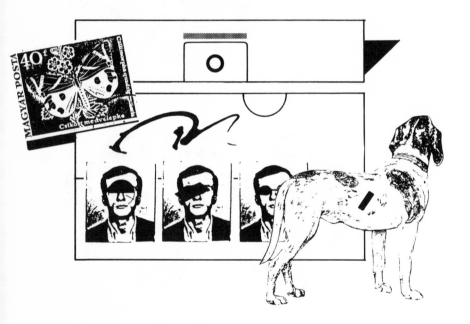

"[*Ezra Pound*] *hardly ever spent time in this 'half-savage country,' " Quickskill observed. "His mind was always some place else. That was his problem, his mind was away somewhere in a feudal tower. Eliot, too. The Fisher King. That's Arthurian. How can anybody capture the spirit of this 'half-savage country' if they don't stay here? Poetry is knowing. . . . They hated America. Eliot hated St. Louis. How can someone hate St. Louis? How the fuck can someone hate St. Louis? I mean, W. C. Handy; the Jefferson Arc. They were royalists."*

—Flight to Canada

What the American Arthurians couldn't win on the battlefield will now be fought out on the poetry field. . . . Raised by Mammies, the South is dandyish, foppish, pimpish; its writers are Scott, Poe, Wilde, Tennyson; its assassin left behind a trunk in which was found: "clothes in fine silk velvets; silks, ermine and crimson; and also hats, caps, plumes, boots, shoes, etc."

—Flight to Canada

The trouble with you Loop is that you're too abstract, the part time autocrat monarchist and guru finally said. Crazy dada nigger that's what you are. You are given to fantasy and are off in matters of detail. Far out esoteric bullshit is where you're at. Why in those suffering books that I write about my old neighborhood and how hard it was every gumdrop machine is in place while your work is a blur and a doodle. I'll bet you can't create the difference between a German and a redskin.

What's your beef with me Bo Shmo [leader of the Neo-Social Realist Gang], what if I write circuses? No one says a novel has to be one thing. It can be anything it wants to be, a vaudeville show, the six o'clock news, the mumblings of wild men saddled by demons.

—Yellow Back Radio Broke-Down

The reason that Hoo Doo isn't given the credit it deserves in influencing American Culture is because the students of that culture both "overground" and "underground" are uptight closet Jeho-vah revisionists. They would assert the American and East Indian and Chinese thing before they would the Black thing. Their spiritual leaders Ezra Pound and T. S. Eliot hated Africa and "Darkies." In Theodore Roszak's book *The Making of a Counter Culture* there is barely any mention of the Black influence on this culture even though its members dress like Blacks walk like Blacks, gesture like Blacks wear Afros and indulge in Black music and dance (Neo Hoo Doo).

—The Neo Hoo Doo Manifesto

The Afro-American artist is similar to the Necromancer (a word whose etymology is revealing in itself!). He is a conjuror who works JuJu upon his oppressors; a witch doctor who frees his fellow victims from psychic attack launched by the demons of the outer and inner world.

—19 Necromancers from Now

Loop seems to be scatting arbitrarily, using forms of this and adding his own. He's blowing like that celebrated musician Charles Yardbird Parker—improvising as he goes along. He's throwing clusters of demon chords at you and you don't know the changes, do you Mr. Drag?

—Yellow Back Radio Broke-Down

To some if you owned your own mind you were indeed sick but when you possessed an Atonist [proto-Christian] mind you were healthy. A mind which sought to interpret the world by using a single loa. Somewhat like filling a milk bottle with an ocean.

—Mumbo Jumbo

The Atonists got rid of their spirit 1000s of years ago with Him. The flesh is next. Plastic will soon prevail over flesh and bones. Death will have taken over.

—Mumbo Jumbo

The philosophy of slavery—the philosophy of inferiority in which the slave's plight was compared to that of fellow slaves: the ancient Hebrews. The philosophy of slavery has been handed down through the ages and has appeared under different names. Moochism, for example.

—The Last Days of Louisiana Red

I see my books as amulets, and in ancient African cultures words were considered in this way. Words were considered to have magical meanings and were considered to be charms. I think that what's happening in American writing now is that the people who interpret American literature have an old-world orientation, old-world meaning Europe and the eastern United States.

—Interviews with Black Writers

Whereas at the center of Christianity lies the graveyard the organ-drone and the cross, the center of Neo Hoo Doo is the drum and ankh and the Dance. So Fine, Barefootin, Heard It through the Grapevine are all Neo Hoo Doos. . . . Neo Hoo Doo never turns down pork. In fact Neo Hoo Doo is the Bar-B-Que of Amerika. . . . Jeho-vah was the successful law and order candidate in the mythological relay of the 4th century A.D. Jeho-vah is the God of punishment. The H-Bomb is a typical Jeho-vah "miracle." Jeho-vah is why we are in Vietnam. He told Moses to go out and "subdue" the world.

—The Neo Hoo Doo Manifesto

They are the moochers who cooperate with their "oppression," for they have the mentality of the prey who thinks his destruction at the fangs of the killer is the natural order of things and colludes with his own death. The Workers [of the Solid Gumbo Works] exist to tell the "prey" that they were meant to bring down killers three times their size, using the old morality as their guide: Voodoo, Confucianism, the ancient Egyptian inner duties, using the technique of camouflage, independent camouflages like the leopard shark, ruler of the seas for five million years.

—The Last Days of Louisiana Red

And the worst betrayal of all was Raven Quickskill, my trusted bookkeeper. Fooled around with my books, so that every time I'd buy a new slave he'd destroy the invoices and I'd have no record of purchase; he was also writing passes and forging freedom papers. We gave him Literacy, the most powerful thing in the pre-technological pre-post-rational age, and what does he do with it? Uses it like that old Voodoo—that old stuff the slaves mumble about. Fetishism and grisly rites, only he doesn't need anything but a pen he had shaped out of cock feathers and chicken claws.

—Flight to Canada

Story-telling precedes "the novel," which Frye and others say is a very recent and arbitrary form. I consider myself a fetish maker.

—*Interviews with Black Writers*

I look for the essential elements. I look for those qualities which distinguish the character from other people, and everybody has that essence. I attempt to abstract those qualities just like someone making a doll in West or East Africa. This may appear grotesque or distorted but this is the best way one captures that principle. When I say I am working on a "hoodoo" aesthetic I know I'm serious and I know what I'm talking about and this falls in line with that. They have in Voodoo a thing they call the gros-bon-ange, and the gros-bon-ange is that which separates from the person after death. It carries all of his essential elements, the qualities which make him unique from other individuals. And this is what I try to do. I'm not interested in rendering a photograph of a person. I'm interested in capturing his soul and putting it in a cauldron or a novel.

—Interviews with Black Writers

Chapter Eleven

Ronald Sukenick describes how he met Jonathan Baumbach, whose career has shown a strange affinity with his own. They were born in New York, a year apart. Both attended graduate school in the Sixties, and each had his doctoral dissertation on modern American literature published by the New York University Press, Baumbach's just two years before Sukenick's. Finding that Baumbach had then published a first novel just a few years before his own, Sukenick sought him out at a party to find out what was going to happen next. "I've just finished another novel," Baumbach confessed, "called *What Comes Next.*"

Baumbach and Sukenick emerged out of the same spawning ground for innovative fiction—American universities in the Sixties, where younger academics, not wishing to follow the tedious paths of their elders, fashioned a lifestyle and fictional approach to that life which would carry them into an entirely new literature. In 1974 they met again, this time to work together in the Fiction Collective. Baumbach and colleague Peter Spielberg had founded the Collective as an alternative to commercial publishing, which, even on the rare occasions when it published innovative fiction, lacked the means and the desire to market it to the proper readership. Sukenick became the Collective's West Coast coordinator and published his next novel, *98.6,* with the group in 1975.

Although not explicitly a fictional "school," the publishing conditions which led to the Collective's formation describe a major development in the history of American fiction. In earlier decades commercial publishing could profitably release a healthy list of novels and story collections—all styles, by known and unknown authors, which could each sell as few as 2,000 copies to a year's worth of bookstore browsers and still show a profit. But economic conditions in the Sixties changed these facts. Mass marketing became the key; 100,000 books by a single author were easier to produce, stock, and sell than 2,000 books by each of fifty writers. Independent bookstores were giving way to national chains, and those chains practiced the economy of unit-buying, which meant that pre-publication decisions by a very few people would determine the readership tastes (or at least availability for taste) of millions. Very soon the fiction published became a product that would sell like other mass market commodities. Under such conditions it became questionable whether innovators such as Fitzgerald, Hemingway, and Faulkner would have been able to start careers in fiction. *The Great Gatsby,* after all, sold fewer than 7,000 copies in its first edition; it waited fifty years to become a mass market item—and only then on the coattails of a popular film.

Members of the Fiction Collective include Baumbach, Sukenick, Federman, Katz, Abish, Reed, Major, Russell Banks, and a dozen others. All have done novels with commercial houses; Baumbach himself published early work with the impressive firms of Random House, Harper and Row, and Holt, Rinehart and Winston. But all these writers saw their works badly distributed, poorly advertised, and taken off the shelves (and out of print), sometimes within six months. What success they did have was due to a special readership, word-of-mouth reputation, thoughtful reviews (albeit a year after publication) in literary quarterlies, sales in specially selected bookstores located in college or counterculture neighborhoods, and association with works by similar writers. The Fiction Collective was formed to publish and sell novels under just these conditions. Their paperback series are sold by subscription and are advertised together; all books are kept in print for the life of the Collective. The members evaluate and edit each other's works, but since the author is his own prime financial backer, there are no economic interests dictating the form of the writing. Small editions are printed, to show a profit at merely 1,500 copies. After a year of successful publication, the Collective received grants from the New York State Council on the Arts to underwrite part of each author's expenses until the books re-earned the investment.

Jonathan Baumbach's fiction has shown a strong development within the Fiction Collective. His work has moved steadily toward a self-awareness of fiction's techniques, especially to contain the heightened imaginative effect he draws from fantasy and dream. As critic and Collectivist, Baumbach is in the ideal position for a self-reflective author. As Sukenick observed in his preface to the Collective's anthology, *Statements,* their organization is primarily for writers "who know their business"—who understand the full potential of their fictive art, and who wish to control all aspects of production so that their art comes through in its full imaginative force.

JONATHAN BAUMBACH

I. A PLOT TOWARD THE PROGRESS OF INNOVATION

I'm not just using the dream in the traditional sense, in the psychological sense where it's an almost compacted parable, with special symbols. I'm just trying to find another way of getting at reality. I mean, my sense is that the conventional novel, for me, anyway, is on its way to a dead end. And I'm trying to get at the way things are in a way that no one has ever seen them before.

—Interview with John Graham,
The Writer's Voice **(New York: William Morrow, 1973)**

If the conventional novel is in trouble, Jonathan Baumbach is uniquely equipped to know. He did his doctoral dissertation on a group of modern novelists who for the most part follow traditions: Saul Bellow, Ralph Ellison, Bernard Malamud, Wright Morris, Flannery O'Connor, J. D. Salinger, William Styron, Edward Lewis Wallant, and Robert Penn Warren—the result was published as *Landscape of Nightmare: Studies in the Contemporary American Novel* (New York: New York University Press, 1965). That same year Baumbach published his own first novel, *A Man to Conjure With* (New York: Random House, 1965). Since then he's done other critical anthologies (*Moderns and Contemporaries* [$New York: Random House, 1968], *Writers as Teachers/Teachers as Writers* [New York: Holt, Rinehart & Winston, 1970]), plus two novels which carry him toward the innovations he claims fiction needs: *What Comes Next* (New York: Harper & Row, 1968) and *Reruns* (New York: Fiction Collective, 1974). Recent stories in *Esquire, Oyez,*

Partisan Review, and *Fiction* have placed him in the company of our most serious experimentalists. In 1976 the Fiction Collective published Baumbach's assemblage of baby stories, *Babble.* The very fact that his progress toward this style has been a studied, conservative, step-by-step process makes his work one of the best indexes to fiction in our time. As he prefaces *Landscape of Nightmare,* novels must endure "as works of the imagination, as works that preserve the possibility of consciousness. As works of art." Studying the fiction of the Fifties and Sixties, writing the fiction of the Sixties and Seventies, Jonathan Baumbach keeps track, amid the changing conditions of our lives, of just how that may be done.

*

Essentially, I teach pretty much the way I go about writing a novel, leaving things open within limited bounds of control for as long as I can stand it.

—Writers as Teachers/Teachers as Writers

A Man to Conjure With, Baumbach's first novel, is for the most part a conventional work. It is a synthesis of various trends in the modern novel, much as *Landscape of Nightmare* brought the criticism of this genre up to date with a summary of American developments through the mid-Sixties. There is experimentation, but within traditional bounds; there is nothing unrealistic in the book except the character's dreams, which are clearly identified as such. The book's structure bears a resemblance to Styron's *Lie Down in Darkness,* which Baumbach described in his own critical study as being "Ibsenic: he must move backward and forward in time simultaneously; he must delay revelation of the past so that each discovery further illuminates our understanding of the present, the final discovery, the lifting of the veil, illuminating all." Baumbach's variation is to delay revelations of the present until the past has come together in a collage which then makes the final chronological act understandable, and enlightening. His protagonist, Peter Becker, is the man to conjure with, who spends most of his time finding persons to conjure with him about the past. "It's as if all the details will add up to a picture of himself," Baumbach told John Graham. "And then, he can look at himself as he was. He has the idea, perhaps, that the man he was at twenty is still somewhere there, all the potentiality that was there at twenty and forgotten and lost. To look at himself at twenty is to come back there and start again, to recoup what he's lost. An analogy is Gatsby's obsession."

*

He made the bed but forgot the top sheet, lying in a wad in a corner under the bed. A big man, he crowded the place with his misery, bumping his head against a low-hanging pipe, discovering the bump hours later. He swept one half of the room and left the dirt neatly piled in the other. The radio blared all day. Peter raged at the thoughtlessness of his neighbors and planned, against the scruples of a lifetime of cop hating, to call the police until he discovered that it was his own radio, which he had turned on in the morning, that was making all the noise.

Moving backward and forward in time, it is the quality of Peter's life which is gradually defined. Deserting his job as a proofreader, he is "not so much fired. . . as somehow forgotten." In the next job he finds, he is similarly dissociated. "A woman he had never seen before waved at him. He smiled back at her. 'Taxi, taxi,' she called as he passed her, and Peter looked around, surprised that there was no cab in sight. For a moment, abstracted, he had forgotten that he was driving one. He was sometimes haunted, sometimes forgetful." He visits his brother, the record player plays "Saturday Night Is the Loneliest Night of the Week," and Peter keeps his hold on reality by thinking it is Tuesday morning. Every detail, past and present, contributes to the cumulative character of Peter Becker.

Much of the action takes place in Peter's dreams, and his character is defined by them. "Dozing, he saw himself falling from the window, arms outstretched like a diver, somersaulting now onto his back, floating—what peace!—landing on the sidewalk like a feather, without a scratch. It struck him suddenly—why hadn't he seen it before?—that he was indestructible." This during a time when Peter is adrift in New York, unable to rejoin his former wife and reconnect his former lives. "His secret. He lifted his head from the pillow, amazed at himself. A hork honked, thunder cracked in the cave of his skull. Rain fell at the entrance; it washed his face, cooled his heat." Then drifting back into sleep: "Lying on the sidewalk, he remembered voices from the past, old faces (his mother and father, Herbie, Rachel, his son Phil), a familiar world. They hugged and kissed one another and he told them what he had discovered about himself, that he was indestructible. No one seemed surprised. Then, in a buzz of voices, in a circle of attention, his eyes closed, and he fell asleep and forgot."

"His wisdom," Baumbach says of D. H. Lawrence in *Moderns and Contemporaries,* "which is considerable, is in the texture of the writing, in the insights of the language, in his profound revelation of the 'passionate secret places' which are the heart and matter of our lives." As a teacher Baumbach makes this caution against the apparent clarity of Lawrence's thesis, as if the answer would be there. Given the conventionality of *A Man to Conjure With,* it is a good test to apply there as well. Peter's dreams are well marked, but their point is not their bizarre events. Instead, it is the quality of experience told through dream-like language. Baumbach's interest in the psychological, first stated in *Landscape of Nightmare,* is more properly a concern with liberated workings of the imagination, not with clinical abnormality. He is not interested in a character's curious behavior except for the way it reveals itself in language; and even then *the way,* the manner, the form, is the important thing. "Novels, like poems," he argues, "are made of words, and to deny the importance of language to the final achievement of a novel (as have some of Dreiser's defenders) is to under-value the weapons of prose." From his own novel: "Their devils made love, their angels in private terror." Or, "They danced on nerve endings to the music of silence. There was nothing to say." The roots of Baumbach's most extravagant inventions in fiction are no more complicated than this.

*

The most Dostoevskian of Malamud's novels, The Assistant **is about an ambivalent saint, a man who in seeking expiation for a crime succeeds only in increasing and intensifying the burden of his guilt. The hero Frank Alpine is congenitally and circumstantially unable to translate his good intentions into moral acts.**
. . . .

This is the essential paradox of Frank's existence; he means to do good, yet he compulsively continues to do harm.

—Landscape of Nightmare

Baumbach's *A Man to Conjure With* achieves the same quality as Malamud's novel, which Baumbach has called "one of the most concentrated and powerful works of fiction to come out of America since the Second World War." Peter Becker is well-intentioned but with a gift for screwing up. Any single incident seems innocent enough, but the effect of *A Man to Conjure With* is that an entire life has been formed from such inconsequence. Just at the point when Peter's life hits us with its cumulative effect, events suddenly turn. His son Phil comes to join him in the city; he and Lois may remarry; "It had started at lunch, this manic sense of his that everything, everything under the sun he wanted, was possible." In euphoria he races down Broadway with his son. But as he makes his way down the block, things become too good. It becomes the quality of one of Peter's dreams:

It gave him a marvelous lift to run with total freedom, the rain a blessing, birds singing to him as he ran. He had never, his legs like springs, moved so quickly in his life. At forty, he may have been—no way of knowing for sure—the fastest man in the world. He flew by his son at the corner, who seemed merely a shadow as he passed him, an imprint on the landscape. It was then he felt something snap, a weight of metal cracking into him—or was it the storm?—lifting him, turning him over and over. And still he raced. Until it was too dark for him to go any farther. He saw the face of lightning. The rains fell.

"Don't crowd him," a voice was saying. "Give him air, for God's sake."

He was lying on something hard, a blur of faces hanging over him, though he saw Lois and Phil clearly, their arms around each other. Wherever he looked, they were there.

His arm was leaking and he waited for Lois to bandage it.

"Stand back," someone yelled. Sirens going off from all parts of the world. A woman was crying.

"Don't worry," Peter said, raising his arm, without the effort of lifting it, to show them that he was all right.
"Look at that," the crowd was saying. "Look at that arm."
"You see," he said, "nothing to worry about. I'm all right."
The boy smiled. The rain. Lois bent to kiss him.
"The truth is," he said, "I can't be killed." They all embraced. He had never felt so much love.
"Listen to me," he said. "Phil, Lois—it's the truth. It's impossible to kill me."
He wondered after all—the weather making communication difficult—if they had understood what he was saying. When he closed his eyes he saw that the storm had passed over, the sky now like the inside of a shell. It was all right. As no one before or maybe ever again, he was flying. What more could he want? He wanted. He was, it was true, never satisfied.

II. INTO THE DREAM

To live in this world, to live consciously in this world in which madness daily passes for sanity is a kind of madness in itself.

—Landscape of Nightmare

"I've stopped leaving the house except for food and sometimes—when the strain gets too great—for air," says Christopher Steiner in Baumbach's second novel, *What Comes Next.* The jacket blurb describes Steiner as "a college student in the process of flipping out entirely." There is no direct provocation for his madness, only the general tone of the world. "Too much violence in the street. Sex, bombing, suffocation, rape. Too much madness. I have what I need—books, a chess set, slide rule, TV, a bathroom, a mirror, windows, a phone. Nothing. I need nothing. It is a final equity." On the one hand, Steiner's world is more comfortable than Peter Becker's—the smooth, prosperous, comfortable Sixties. But the Sixties are erupting into the violence of 1967 and 1968. "The more euphemistic and sterile the surface of life becomes," Baumbach observes in *Landscape of Nightmare,* "the more the primordial forces erupt into meaningless violence." Through headlines and fantasized incidents, violence erupts on every page; it is what comes next, until the experience of Christopher Steiner's life becomes one of dream-like nightmare.

The dreams are indistinguishable from life. Baumbach has naturalistic justification for this technological development, since in Christopher's times things actually happen in the street which were heretofore sequestered in Peter Becker's dreams. As a result, the action is intentionally confused. All we know for sure is that Christopher is taking a tutorial in history from Curtis Parks, who is in turn having an affair with a student, Rosemary Byrd. Christopher spies on them both, and has some contact with Rosemary—but from moment to moment we cannot be sure what is real. There are fantasies inside fantasies, and so the decompression we feel coming out of one nightmare (the experience of Peter's dream in *A Man to Conjure With*) may be only an entrance into another, less startling dream. Which is where the important action is located. "The book is very much about the contemporary scene experienced internally through a rather seismographic twenty-one-year-old," Baumbach reported to John Graham. "Though most people have felt that he is mad and he's certainly mad by conventional standards, it seems to me that his madness is relative sanity. Given any number of public madnesses . . . I don't have to enumerate them." Or as Baumbach said of another work in the *New York Times Book Review,* there is such a thing as "the insane precision of a dream." *What Comes Next* moves closer to establishing it as Baumbach's principal method.

*

The world Antonioni celebrates is damned hard to live in.

—Jonathan Baumbach in Man and the Movies,
edited by W. R. Robinson (Baton Rouge:
Louisiana State University Press, 1967)

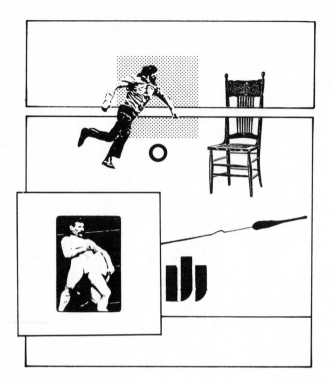

"The thing was to do with your life the kind of thing you did best. To fulfill in some sense your role, your calling. The titans of history, tyrants and saints, presidents and assassins, were, in fulfilling their destinies, enacting the deepest needs of self. . . . The sin was not to do what you were meant to do." Steiner receives this tutorial from the historian Curtis Parks. But the history made manifest in *What Comes Next*—domestic violence, criminal warfare—makes such choices impossible for the young student. Even a walk to the elevated train makes sense for him only in the twists and turns of nightmare:

I run the three blocks to the elevated, hearing the train in the distance, thinking I can make it if I hurry.

There are several planes flying directly overhead, bombers, a squadron of eagles. I feel their shadow across my back as I run. People move out of my way. An ambulance siren somewhere. The sound of big guns in the distance. The shelling recurs at fifteen-second intervals. Craters in the ground. . . .The street on fire.

A dying man hands me a revolver. I go up the gray iron steps, thinking of Rosemary's breasts (someday she will hear of me), gunning her enemy as they rise, two steps at a time, until, leg-weary, teetering, floating, I reach the top of the station. As I make my move, I hear the last train rumbling in. Knowing if I can get through in time there is hope. I take off like an astronaut, the countdown still ticking in his head, taking off. Fight fire with fire, my orders say. Fighting weariness, fears, doubts ("The Battle Hymn of the Republic" on the sound track), telling myself there's no more to go this time, no more, no more, no more, I go up the final flight of stairs. It is three steps at a time this time, the final flight. There is no more to go after this.

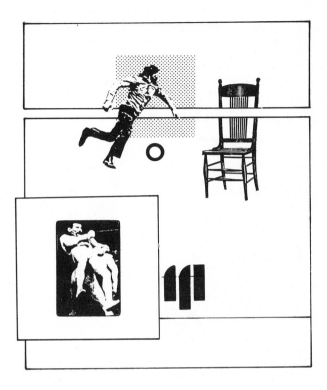

III. GOING TO THE MOVIES

Dreambook is a very hard book to describe. The frame or structure of the book is a rational man. A scientist, though he's an editor of books, is separated from his wife, his family. He's living in a residential hotel room, and he finds a manuscript in the bottom drawer—notebooks. The manuscripts are clearly written by someone wholly unlike him—someone with apparently no superego at all. And he presents the book to us rather grudgingly edited; and he is finally taken over by the book as he takes it over. So, the main body of the book, that is, the interior book, "the dreambook," is the life of a man through certain kinds of dream reality. That is, the succession of episodes in his life, as perceived through what might be real dreams or what might be invented dreams.

—The Writer's Voice

In the old days, before Bergman (Ingmar) and the new wave and the art houses in the provinces, going to the movies was a form of slumming, an obsessive return to the fantasy world—lost, one feared irreparably—of our childhood.

—Man and the Movies

135

Separated at the present from my third wife, Molly, to whom I am not legally married, unable to get a divorce from my second wife to whom I am still on the books husband, the father of four children (perhaps five), the son of at least two parents, Jewish on my mother's side, Italian Irish lapsed Catholic on my father's, American, student, sometime soldier, comedian, filmmaker, revenger, driven in conflicting directions by dream-haunted ambition, I am here without wife or woman (no pleasant place to be), your guide and reporter, a hostage to the habits of rerunning the dead past in the cause of waking from the dream.

—Reruns

Dreambook was never published. It was ready for publication in 1971, at about the time when anything other than realistic fiction began having a hard time with commercial houses. As a result, Baumbach became a founding member of and spokesman for the Fiction Collective, a group of writers who would henceforth publish their own works. *Reruns* was in the first group of novels issued by the Collective in October 1974.

A logical third step for its author, *Reruns* contains no realistic action at all. At the beginning the fantasies are obvious: a lost child seeks aid at a strange house and is greeted, " 'I bid you *well*-come,' a creepy guy in a black cape says in a heavy indecipherable continental accent." Soon after, "Dinner is served in a large steel pot. My host lifts the cover with a wave of his cane. Inside is a child's head with a serpent coming out of its mouth."

A self-admitted "second version" of the same story is enacted. Then the protagonist himself becomes a character in similar bizarre incidents, reminiscent of Peter Becker's dreams and Christopher Steiner's psychotic visions. In one episode we find that "The nuptial bed was crowded that night, packed to the wall. No one wanted to be left out. It was a rousing celebration as I recall. A platoon of Negro National Guard crashed the party at midnight, calling everyone 'Motherfucker.' They were embraced like members of the family." Later on the protagonist meets a young boy; they exchange stories, the protagonist's about his latest adventures, the boy's about "sitting down to dinner in a house of monsters where they were eating a child's head." These are common fantasies. They are reruns.

"Letting dreams happen in an intuitive way and relying on my own notion of process is a way of not letting consciousness get in my way," Baumbach said to John Graham. Consciousness, not leaving it open (as he counseled in *Writers as Teachers/Teachers as Writers*), can detract from the verbal experience and place too much emphasis on the logic of the action itself. As a film critic, contributing "Going to the Movies" as a regular feature in *Partisan Review,* Baumbach argues for the appreciation of visual image in a film; this is more important than the story line or thesis. Sight is the medium of film, expressed through visual forms. In fiction it's the words, and the best way to keep attention on them is to frame experience in the non-realistic but reportable form of dreams. Or movies, as we knew them when we were children.

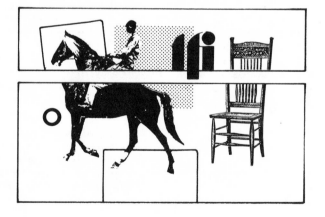

IV. INNOVATIVE FICTION

I have just killed my first woman. It has been that kind of day. Slower than the New York subway system on a slow hot summer Sunday morning.

My first shots took out the red-rimmed headlights of a fiftyish alcoholic, a former winner of the Prix de Rome. I was testing my sights when he staggered into range as if looking for someone to dispel the myth of his immortality.

When I woke up this morning I thought I would have a breakfast of cereal and fresh fruit and just oil my gun. The fruit had gone rotten overnight. That shouldn't have happened.

On the Today show, Barbara Walters was interviewing the first dog ever to publish a cook book. "That dog earns more money than you," my wife said. It was after that that I thought I'd look out the window to see if there was anything to shoot.

—*"Birthday Gifts"*
(Oyez Review, *Winter 1973*)

*

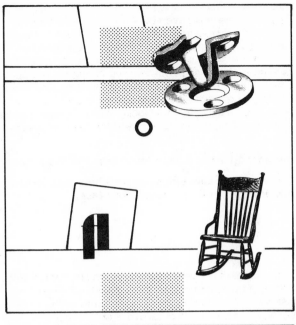

An emergency session with my therapist, Roper. He refuses to believe my nightmares have a corresponding manifest reality. "The beast within you, which is in all of us, walks only in your dreams," he says in the voice of authority.

I ask him to explain the fresh mud on my boots each morning.

—"The Curse"
(Fiction, #1, 1974)

*

"Wipe my drool," he says, "and I'll tell you a story." It is the most words in sequential order I have heard him speak. I pretend not to be astounded so as not to upset his equilibrium, wipe his drool with a yellowing handkerchief.

For an infant, he tells an excellent story. I won't recapitulate it all for you here, but will try to limit myself to the high points. The central figure, not unexpectedly, is a baby.

—*"Drool"*
(Partisan Review, *Winter 1972,*
collected in Babble)

137

Baumbach's first published short fiction, appearing only since 1970, moves a step beyond even the innovations of *Reruns*. There is not even the excuse of the dream to lend "credibility" to the story. But there is no danger that the story might distract from artful invention, since its happenings are very far from real. In these cases the action *can* follow logically without any danger of being confused with history. If anything, the very fact of logic operating inexorably within the affairs of lunacy reinforces the artificiality of the entire business. In the baby's story, the protagonist must "scour the city for someone who will change his diaper without asking in return an excess of gratitude. He leaves a notice in the Personals column of an underground newspaper. 'Groovy baby, Capricorn, interested in meaning of life, seeks mature couple for intimate exchange.' " Still further on, "The baby is followed by a detective disguised as another baby, a deception that fools no one. The detective's outfit is transparently unauthentic, out of style, unlived in. The point of his gun in fact sticks out from under his diaper. He drools to excess."

*

His second story is less fresh than the first, though of greater technical sophistication.

The robot is after him again, this time disguised as a soda vending machine. "You can't have any coke," the robot says, "until you wash your face."

> —**"The Baby's Second Story"** Esquire, **March 1974, collected in** Babble

The baby-hero is totally conventional in all aspects, except that he is a baby. Baumbach's intervention with the traditions of fiction has thrown them into sharper relief, reminding us that they are merely conventions, but also showing just how potent conventions are when the author uses them with a sense of self-conscious power. The baby can be a scholar (like his dad), a detective, a soldier, a knight, or the super-hero "Pagina Man." As the latter, he disposes of his crib toys and becomes a battler against evil. "Pagina Man is not afraid of anything or, which is almost the same thing, acts as if he's not. . . . He is a force for good, although like everyone else he sometimes wakes in a bad mood." He still sleeps in a diaper—to avoid accidents. The baby can become a movie hero; he becomes a little boy. "Got you," cries his playmate; "The baby holds his side, staggers drunkenly, spins almost completely around, and, as seen in movies, collapses in feathery slow-motion to where the ground like some dream of waking awaits his rest." Again most conventionally, the boy is—like his parents—a prisoner of time. As he grows in his childhood, they miss having a baby around the house. But their moments alone are interrupted by a succession of cowboys, masked bandits, and maturing super-heroes:

> He leaps from the chair, falling comically. "I'll tell you why I don't have to knock," he says, thrusting his sword into an imaginary assailant. "I don't have to knock because this is a story I'm making up."
> He rushes out, not bothering to close the door, closing it with a bang as an afterthought, some dim injunction interrupting the flow of his escape. Return, one suspects, is imminent.
> "You'll have to hurry," I'm told.
> There's always something in this life to move you on more quickly than you mean to go.
> Secret gray hairs appear. Like the baby, I am no longer who I was. Who will he be, I wonder, when he returns?
> In the meanwhile, we conduct out business as if we had an existence independent of his story.

Reporting the baby's stories has allowed Baumbach to exercise his talents as a literary critic right within his innovative fiction, as he charts "the further adventures of the only infant hero in American literature."

Jonathan Baumbach's experience as a critic has suited him for his progress in advancing innovations in American fiction—but the position is not unique, nor does it disqualify him as a serious literary artist. Most serious fictionists today have academic credentials, with doctorates in the following fields: philosophy (William H. Gass), sociology (Jerzy Kosinski), medicine-psychiatry (Walker Percy), French (Raymond Federman), and English (Ronald

Sukenick). Others, including LeRoi Jones, Donald Barthelme, Leonard Michaels, Steve Katz, and James Park Sloan, have close associations with the workings of universities (and not merely as writers in residence).

Sukenick described and defended the phenomenon in 1972: "American fiction, as was inevitable, has passed from its autodidact stage to an educated one equivalent to that of writers in Europe, South America, Japan and just about everywhere else on earth besides Antarctica. That implies schools exist and writers go to them and beyond that to the large range of possibilities that we call Culture. You can quote me on this in fact I'm beginning to wish I were making a copy. In other words, only in America could it be considered unusual that novelists actually have ideas and can think. In fact, it *is* a revolution here, but that doesn't make us academic—on the contrary."

With the Fiction Collective, Baumbach has combined another role with that of novelist. Just as a critical awareness of contemporary fiction moved his own work forward, so the role of publisher will enrich the possibilities for fiction. Only with complete control over its own creation can the novel develop in line with the other arts—no painter must submit his design to a commercial medium before seeing his work finished. Now fiction needn't either, and the chances for infant heroes in American literature—and everything else—are that much better.

Chapter Twelve

The Coordinating Council of Literary Magazines administers a grant from the National Endowment for the Humanities. It brings supporting funds to little magazine publishers, and it also brings the little magazine people together. Although headquartered in New York, several times a year it convenes in such places as Boulder, Louisville, New Orleans, Cincinnati, Phoenix, and Milwaukee for committee sessions, conferences, and readings. It gives poets and fiction writers the chance to meet like their commercial counterparts in New York, creating a forum for people like Russell Banks, whose antics might otherwise be restricted to the taverns of Northwood Narrows, New Hampshire.

Banks sits in the bar with Montanan Jim Welch (whose *Winter in the Blood* occupies the front-page review of the week's *New York Times Book Review*), adopted Californian Ron Sukenick, Frenchman Raymond Federman, and voodoo master Ishmael Reed. Texan Lorenzo Thomas has been arguing for the influence of black music, black art, and black lifestyles on the dominant white culture. Banks, for no real reason other than whimsy, objects. Thomas, for no real reason, announces, "I had a white grandmother." "So did I!" beams Banks, "Do you think we're related?" The waitress interrupts for last call, and Banks tells her he wants a "homer," a final bottle of Blatz to accompany him back to the Council's hotel; Milwaukee's contrary liquor law shouldn't apply, he claims, because a "homer" belongs to contemporary New Hampshire folklore. Ishmael Reed announces a party in his room, with some rare New Orleans music that novelist Al Young has taped for him. Banks accepts the invitation, and the evening rolls out like the crazily jumbled plot line of Russell Banks fiction.

An afternoon later Banks and Federman are scheduled to co-chair a panel on innovative fiction in the little magazines. Lined up across the stage, Banks and his colleagues look distressingly like a Senate hearing or a doctors' conference on cancer, until the meeting begins. Banks and Federman rise and talk at the same time; random phrases like "the death of the novel" and "the artist's imperative to seize the means" tumble back and forth amid the audience's confused mutterings. They finish together, take their seats, and are replaced by the four-person panel, which rises in concert and begins talking all at once. After a minute, the show settles down to more rational order. But the point has been won: a partly suspicious and hostile audience has been disarmed by something worse than they imagined might happen, and the playful disruptiveness of the new fiction has been dramatized to all.

Fiction writers such as Banks, Federman, and Sukenick have established themselves as revolutionaries even within such seemingly friendly groups as the CCLM. Their efforts, however, have improved the life of fiction, taking over methods previously used for the survival of poets: conferences, readings, subsidized support, and regular rituals of dinner, drinks, and guerrilla theatre. The fiction being written by these authors is no longer a solitary affair; a community of their peers is now usually at hand, and increased support and readership for their magazines has made the process of writing in this style uniquely alive. Banks, who for several years edited and published *Lillabulero,* has made a life of this world, writing with a quiet sense of laughter and impish playfulness which could never exist without the regular communication of an audience receptive to his fictional tricks.

RUSSELL BANKS

Russell Banks's SuperFiction

Family Life (New York: Avon, 1974). A comic novel which includes: *half a dozen grisly murders!
*several rapes! (for all kinds of sexual interests)
*a palace coup!
*hunting accidents!
*drunken debauches!
*world tours!
*orgies!
*laughter!
  and
The Lonely Search for Love!

Searching for Survivors (New York: Fiction Collective, 1974). 14 Stories by Russell Banks.

Snow (Hanover, N.H.: Granite Publications, 1974). Meditations of a Cautious Man in Winter.

"The Writer's Situation," *New American Review* #9 (April 1970)

> **"Dear Jerry,**
>   **Thanks for your good long letter of the 9th. I'm going to try to answer some, if not all, of your questions here. . . ."**

There is alive and well in America today a kind of prose writing that allows men to communicate with other men in such a way that both will be astonished by what is said about the world they live in.

For novelists (even those who spend their whole lives writing and rewriting a Bildungsroman), the traditional way of confronting the amoral, nonhuman, self-seeking alternatives in their lives has been allegory. Almost all novelists today are allegorists.

"The writer as guerrilla?" Certainly. The only effective didact is the invisible one, he who can teach his reader how, as Barthelme has it, "to invent his own life." To be invisible one needs to be something of a guerrilla, a green fish swimming in a green sea of language. It's the difference between the writers of the bourgeois social-realist novel of the last 100 years and the novelists who precede and follow them.

They played "The Ballad of the Green Man" on the jukebox over and over, all night long, until dawn, when Horse hallucinated and thought the jukebox was a bear and attacked it with his hatchet. He made a beautiful robe of the skin and wore it proudly for the rest of his days.

Their leader, named Horse, was wearing a jukebox. The others were dressed in the usual flashy, slightly tacky, Indian costumes.

He was still wearing his jukebox, and one of the warriors punched E-5, a Buffy Sainte-Marie tune, and the group formed a small circle and started to dance.

The Indians headed south to New Mexico; the Pilgrims headed north to the Empire State Building, the prime shrine in the religious life of every believer in the Empire State. At one time or another during their lifetimes, most true believers managed to make it to the great, stone spire, to worship there in awed silence, perhaps even to join in the traditional penny-dropping ceremony afterward.

Thus he was the definitive guerrilla, a person with absolutely no past.

Clearly, it was important to him that he not be recognized. I was almost ashamed for having succeeded where evidently everyone else—probably for the entire five year period since his death was first announced—had failed. What a stroke of genius, though, to hole up at the Plaza! *Naturally* no one would recognize him here, where every guest looks like a celebrity, where everyone has a face that can't help but look slightly familiar. In such a gathering, no one would bother trying to identify exactly the face of Che Guevara. . . .

One says, Ah, so that's *what happened!* As if he had not been there. *What has* happened, however, has been his life, or a portion of it. "Reenactment," I believe, was Charles Olson's word for fiction—what fiction ought to *be,* not *do.* As an act, reenactment is available to the writer only insofar as he was not there in the first place, was elsewhere. Was enacting. Thus each new work, each reenactment, exists (ideally) as the base for whatever in the writer's life will follow. The risk is ancient. It's the risk all men have run whenever they have tried to use talk as a way of getting closer to the truth of the matter—the risk that they will lie to themselves and to others.

Another reason why many of the new fiction writers also write poetry is that the poets of the last 25 years have managed to get themselves into the twentieth century more effectively than the prose writers, so instead of looking to Mailer, Malamud, Bellow, Updike et al. as models, we find more to admire in the hearts and minds and works of Olson, Creeley, Merwin, Ashbery, Ammons, etc. These poets seem to know that something other than disillusionment happened in the first half of the twentieth century, something that deeply affects our relation to language.

[1949 Hudson]
Shaped more or less like an Indian burial mound from the Upper Mississippi Valley, whether stilled or in motion, the vehicle expressed permanence and stability, blocky, arrogant pacts with eternity.

[New Hampshire air]
I had forgotten its clarity, the way it handles the light—gently, but with crispness and efficiency. I had forgotten the way a man, if he can get himself up high enough, can see through the air that fills the valley between him and a single tree or chimney or gable which is actually miles away from him, making the man feel like a hawk floating thousands of feet above the earth's surface, looping lazily in a cloudless sky, hour after hour, while tiny creatures huddle in warm, dark niches below and wait in terror for him to grow weary of the hunt and drift away. . . .

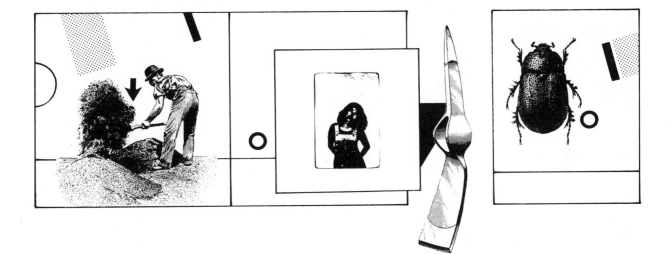

One has found oneself in the middle of a historical episode that does not allow one the innocence of moral or metaphysical certitude, and as a consequence, each individual act of consciousness is a redefinition of the nature, worth, and meaning of one's existence. Any writer who would do more than merely divert himself and his reader must therefore swear a new allegiance—he must commit himself to a continuous, on-going discovery of self. He must forswear his old allegiance to storytelling and commit his voice, not to tell the "truth," but to reveal in his work the conditions that permit continued existence.

There, in total silence, he would make love to her, shoving himself again and again against her quick, twisting body, bringing her rapidly through to the other side of her intent with relentless, soundless thrusts. Then driving himself through, too, his body blossoming out from its still center, spreading, turning from tree to flower, to cloud, to motionless, shapeless pool of water in darkness and silence. And oh, the clarity that would follow.

They went back down the near side of the ditch, crossed the new railbed and climbed slowly back up the embankment to the road. Gerry went around to the car and got into the driver's seat, Reed slid into the passenger's seat. As the car pulled into the whizzing traffic of the freeway, Reed looked out the open window at the torn, muddy plain below. It looked like a place where a war had been lost.

What's my "thing on royalty"? Maybe proletarian American fascination with an image that defines Family in an archetypal way. One of the difficulties of being American is that we are stuck in a kind of historical and cultural cul-de-sac and end up describing our secular, democratic, materialistic lives with religious, monarchic, idealistic images. Thus Che Guevara becomes an image we used to describe Oedipal conflicts. We seem to get at our psychological realities in the most inappropriate ways—if we have a historical continuity, that's probably it. Describing ignominious defeat in Southeast Asia as "victory with honor." I suppose it makes us an interesting people (to anthropologists of the future or other space-people), which is one of the reasons why I'm proud to be an American.

One speaks here as a constantly shifting locus of his own experience, a writer and a man moving briefly across his life and the lives of others. The struggle is to make this movement somehow coherent and just. And as one, in Creeley's words, to whom it's been given to write, there seems no possibility for coherence or justice, except by permitting their brief movement to articulate itself. As the turns in a dance create the fact of the dance, and the fact of the dance establishes its meaning, a wife, children, friends, a place are sought out as occasions for articulation. For one to speak further would be to speak of a dream that had no dreamer, a dance with no dancer. The alternative is silence.

. . . son of Sigmund the Camera, son of Sabu the Dwarf, son of Egress the Obvious, son of Dread the Courteous, son of Norman the Shopper, son of Grendel the Theorist, son of Warren the Fist-faced, son of Arthur the Direct Vision, son of Ray the Innovative, son of Ralph the Meatpacker, son of William the Roadbreaker, son of Harry the Hat . . . and so on. . . .

While making his morning toilet, Egress the Hearty thought aloud (so as to better remember his thought): Reality unperceived is simply form without content. . . .

*

The king reasoned with himself thusly: The meanings of most things lie in the descriptions of them. . . . Explanations, the good ones, are always reenactments. . . . The man with the greatest access to reality is the man possessing the most comprehensive mode of perception. . . . And that man will end up, not merely wise and useful, but also sated, glutted with meaning. . . .

*

The meanings of most things, of passions, certainly, lie wholly in their enactments or in analytical description, i.e., reenactments of those things. The point of human life, when it comes right down to it, is simply to provide content for the otherwise empty forms of reality. The basic difficulty of human life is knowing when a particular form has been fulfilled, or perceived, experienced— knowing when an experience has become redundant.

As soon as Rex graduated from Sarasota High, we got married. It was the summer of 1950 and the second half of the twentieth century had just begun. How were we to know that war with the Orientals would break out and, within a year, with me pregnant, would separate us?

Rex went to Texas as an Air Force cadet and earned his wings in record time. I closed up our little apartment, put our wedding gifts and furniture in storage, and went to live with my mother and father. Three weeks after Rex had left Texas for Korea, I gave birth to our first son, Rex, Jr., whom Rex in his letters instructed me to call "Bif," the name by which he had been known when he played fullback for Sarasota High.

Hunter was born, a healthy, bright child, serious and intense from birth, just as Bif had been boisterous and cheerfully gregarious from birth. Hunter's personality brought out another side of Rex, a side I hadn't seen before. With his second son, Rex was somber, morbid almost, encouraging in the boy, and thus in himself, activities that were solitary, physically strenuous, and somewhat dangerous—such as hunting and deep-sea fishing, rock-climbing, scuba diving. Was this a result of his war experiences, things he wouldn't talk about, even to me? I wondered helplessly.

*

"What else are you going to do with a boy named Hunter?" Rex would tease me whenever I asked him why, for example, he was encouraging his son to hunt alligators in the swamps with Negroes.
"But he's only a boy," I would plead.
"A boy's only a small man," he would explain to me.

One continues to write, then, in order to avoid silence.
One binds himself (or has somebody else do it for him)
to his writing as to a mast whenever, drifting too close
to silence, he hears its siren song.

EPILOGUE: THE FICTION OF LIFE

SuperFiction does not represent reality. It does not re-create reality. Unlike the best of previous fiction, its achievement is measured not by how nicely it casts an illusion, by how well it organizes the impossibilities of life into a neatly probable structure, or by how convincingly it creates characters—recognizable from our daily lives—who walk off the page and into our vicariously lived daily existence.

Instead, it creates a whole life of its own, with all the characteristics of life presented not as an abstraction of something else, as a second-hand reality, but as life itself: with all the energy, playfulness, exuberance, and joy we associate with the best times of living, here under the control of a master creator, the fictionist. It's the difference between watching the neighbors and making your own fun.

Conventional fiction almost always limits itself to a mimetic situation: a dramatization of something which could be played out in the real-life living rooms, kitchens, and bedrooms of our lives. But the human imagination inhabits a much larger sphere, which the SuperFictionists have taken for their own. It begins with the spark of life itself: that game-ish impulse that things might grow into something else, that things just might be made different from what they are. Human activities exist to be recorded by the historians and sociologists; the *energy* is the stuff of true fiction, whether it be in parody, imaginative extension, or simply in the delight of life.

Here is an early example of Super-Fiction, some of the first written by the leader of the field, Donald Barthelme.

It's from a small magazine called *Mother*, which back in 1963 was published in Northfield, Minnesota.

The right of imaginative self-reflection is the *donnée* for which the SuperFictionists have fought. But once won, the further struggle for it is—as Steve Katz has said—just another dull literary convention.

The real issue is having aesthetic freedom for fiction, which is what makes it SuperFiction; the only test is to see what the SuperFictionist does with it.

For one thing, he can have a great deal of fun.

DONALD BARTHELME, SPEAKING FOR THE BOBBSEY TWINS:

Then

ASTONISHMENT, surprise and disappointment were so great for a few seconds after the discovery that the best part of the party—the ice cream—was gone, that no one knew what to say. Then Flossie burst out with:

Then the feast began, and such a feast it was! Mrs. Bobbsey, knowing how easily the delicate stomachs of children can be upset, had wisely selected the foods and sweets, and she saw to it that no one ate too much, though she was gently suggestive about it instead of ordering.

Then a chair would be taken away, so as always to have one less than the number of players, and the game went on. It was great fun, scrambling to see who would get a seat, and not be left without one, and finally there was but one chair left, while Grace Lavine and John Blake marched about.

Then Freddie, anxious as to what would become of Snap if he fought a snake, looked back. He saw a strange sight.

"Then don't you come any nearer if you don't want to get wet," said Bert. "This hose might sprinkle you by accident, the same as it did when Freddie had it," he added.

Then came all sorts of games, from tag and jumping rope, to blind-man's bluff and hide-and-seek. Snap was made to do a number of tricks, much to the amusement of the teachers and children. Danny Rugg, and some of the older boys, got up a small baseball game, and then Danny, with one or two chums, went off in a deeper part of the woods. Bert heard one of the boys ask another if he had any matches.

Then she thought she saw something long and black wiggling toward her, and, with a little exclamation of fright, she, too, turned to follow the others. But, as she did so, she saw their dog Snap come running up the hill, barking and wagging his tail. He seemed to have lost the children for a moment and to be telling them how glad he was that he had found them again.

"Then I'm surely going to be one, too," declared Flossie. "I like good things to eat. I hope our minister isn't very hungry, 'cause then there'll be some left for us when we come home from this picnic."

[and so on for a while longer]

CHARLES STEVENSON (AN UNEMPLOYED NEGRO IN 1966), PLAYED BY CHARLES STEVENSON WRIGHT:

So I threw the employment directory out of the window and made up my mind to see The King of Southern-Fried Chicken. I would become a chicken man. It wasn't work in the real sense of the word. The pay was $90 for five and a half days, plus all the chicken you could eat on your day off. Not many young men lasted long with the Fried Chicken King, but I'd stick it out until I could do better. At least, I consoled myself, the feathers were electrified.

For the truly ambitious, time truly flies. One hour later, I was crawling through the streets of Harlem on my hands and knees, wearing a snow-white, full-feathered chicken costume. The costume was very warm. The feathers were electrified to keep people from trying to pluck them out or kicking the wearer in the tail. So effective was the costume that I didn't even have to stop for traffice signals; traffic screeched to a halt for me. And, as I said, the pay was 90 per week. The Deb and I could have a ball! I planned to eat chicken only on my day off and that was free. I also figured that if I cackled hard and didn't quit, I was bound to get a raise. How many people are willing to crawl on their hands and knees, ten hours a day, five and a half days a week? For me that was not difficult: I was dreaming, not of a white Christmas, I was dreaming of becoming part of The Great Society. So I went through the March streets on my hands and knees and cried:

> Cock-a-doodle-doo. Cock-a-doodle-do!
> Eat me. Eat me. All over town.
> Eat me at the King of
> Southern Fried Chicken!

Or, you can use these same imaginative techniques to extend your range of vision beyond the bland actual things into their true imaginative qualities.

This is the Chicken Man scene from Charles Wright's SuperFiction novel, *The Wig*. For 139 pages he's been trying to make it in the Great Society, seeking work as an ad man, a stocks and bonds man, virtually any upward-mobile position. He runs through the whole NYC socio-realistic scene, but gets nowhere until he meets a SuperFictional invention, the King of Fried Chicken.

Or, you can establish an artificial yet credible frame for a set piece of SuperFiction, as Raymond Federman does in "Cyrano of the Regiment" (an excerpt from *Take It or Leave It*). If you don't pay attention, it sounds like an old-fashioned story: a protagonist making money and mirth writing crazy love-letters at five dollars a crack for his army barracks-mates.

But the point isn't this. The point is *THE LETTERS!*

A LOVE LETTER FROM THE CYRANO OF THE REGIMENT:

Fort Bragg, Fayetteville, N.C.
(Let us say), January 15, 1951

My Darling, My Treasure, My Lovely Adorable Juicy Peach, My Dear M******,

You cannot imagine how much I thought of you, last night, under my lonely khaki blankets, alone, in my narrow military bed, surrounded by the heavy oppressive solitude of life in the army. I felt, in me, through my flesh torn by the pain of your absence, a suffering of indefinable nature. The inner emptiness of my soul rang with shrieks and groans: it was as though needles and knives of fire were piercing my body.

Unable to endure this atrocious suffering, I took my private member in my hands, and feeling it palpitating savagely like a lost animal, no a giant fruit rather, an enormous banana which was pulsating there outside my own body, I began to shake it, to handle it, to squeeze it with all the furor of my desire, and suddenly I felt flowing, full blast, Woosh! a delicious juice that I wanted to transmit immediately to your essential organs. Ah! my dearest reservoir, how much I wanted to feel, at that moment, the wild sugars of my fruit flow in you like a torrent. How I wanted to hear them burst inside of you like a gun, like a cannon (a 75 millimeters), no like a volcano, in the deepest parts of you, in your most secret, tender, wild and unexplored regions.

Ah! if only you knew, my golden treasure, how much I missed you, how much we missed each other, last night, when, alone, naked and vibrant under my military blankets, at the most solitary moment of night in North Carolina my eyes closed, I saw the image of your sweet and soft body sneak next to mine inside my bed. Ah! dear feathery chicken, adorable pitless peach of tender flesh, smooth and rosy body of such lovely round contours, velvety like a mushroom without tail, little sugared snail, landscape of my inner dreams, if I could only make you feel, YES, how much I wanted (last night but also every night) to penetrate you, with what endless passion, what a huge desire I wanted to rush towards you beyond the mountains, beyond the valleys, beyond the rivers and the canals from under my khaki blankets of loneliness, then you would have known the dimensions of my love, depth of my pool of pleasure, despair of my trembling hands, sources of my loneliness and frustration. I see in my dreams your voluptuous and greedy hips and your adventurous thighs, hardly ripe, avidly opened to receive, there in that moist furry triangle of yours, the harvest of my nocturnal cultivation.

Ah! do I worry, do I worry to know that you are alone so far away in your little Missouri hicktown. But . . . are you ALONE? Here comes doubt in my head. I fear the thought that, perhaps, at this very moment, some son of a bitch of another guy (AH! do I tremble) is holding you in his tottering SKINNY arms, while my MUSCULAR arms, my PARATROOPER arms, my arms splendidly fortified by thousands and thousands of pushups cannot hold you, and squeeze you tight to make you feel, despite the distance, with what mad power, what furour, what energy, what vitality I would like to grab those lovely contours of yours and squeeze them out of their last drop of love!

Here life is sad without you. But otherwise everything is fine—except for the disgusting grub. If you have a bit of money saved, could you (my darling) be nice to me and send me a billet-doux *(dig it?). I adore you! Madly and passionately with my soul and body. Give your dear mother (but not your father) a BIG kiss for me.*

Your BIG and SAD Carrot, J*** K******

Beyond this Federman supplies a sample answer, from an innocent girl in Kirksville, Missouri, who receives this para-intelligible letter and feels she must reply in kind.

It is of course all made up. Federman has argued for "the kind of fiction that constantly renews our faith in man's imagination and not in man's distorted vision of reality." Why? Because, "consequently, fiction will no longer be regarded as a mirror of life, as a pseudo-realistic document, nor judged on the basis of its social, moral, psychological, metaphysical, commercial value, or whatever, but for what it is and what it does as an art form in its own right" ("Surfiction—A Position"). But he does not have to turn his fictions into discursive essays to do this, nor does he have to keep arguing the point. He simply takes for granted the ground which has been won (in part by the "Surfiction" essay) and moves on with his own SuperFiction.

SECONDARY READING:

—how Kurt Vonnegut, Jr., does this same stuff in his novels: Jerome Klinkowitz, "The Literary Career of Kurt Vonnegut, Jr.," *Modern Fiction Studies,* 19 (Spring 1973), 57–67.

PRIMARY READING:

—*Out,* a novel by Ronald Sukenick (Chicago: Swallow Press, 1139 South Wabash, Chicago, Ill. 60605, 1973, $7.95).

Charles Wright (on handling life)—

"Ours is a perilous voyage. There is the uneasy knowledge that it might be our last; the harbor hasn't been sighted. We could drown. How stupid of us! Why can't we redesign the lifeboats, take a good hard look at our male and female relationship? Perhaps redefine sin, morality, and corruption for our time on this earth?"

—Absolutely Nothing to Get Alarmed About

Anna Balakian (speaking about Anaïs Nin's SuperFiction, Collages)—

"It is the simple story of a blind man whose only knowledge of reality came to him from the descriptions that his daughter made of it. When miraculously his blindness is cured, he discovers how far removed from reality was the image that his daughter had conveyed to him. But, says Anaïs Nin, he did not die of shock. Instead he told his daughter: 'It is true that the world you described does not exist, but as you built that imagine so carefully in my mind and I can still see it so vividly, we can now set about to build it just as you made me see it.' "

—The Anaïs Nin Reader

Ronald Sukenick (on Carlos Castaneda)—

"Part of this cultural turnabout is the discovery that all accounts of our experience, all versions of 'reality,' are of the nature of fiction. . . . 'For a sorcerer,' says Don Juan in Journey to Ixtlan, *'reality, or the world we all know, is only a description.'*

"This is the key statement in all of Don Juan's teachings, and is also crucial, I believe, for our particular cultural moment. The secret of the sorcerer's power, it follows, is to know that reality is imagined, and, as if it were a work of art, to apply the full force of the imagination to it. . . .

"All art deconditions us so that we may respond more fully to experience, 'to the perceptual solicitations of a world outside the descriptions we have learned to call reality,' as Castaneda put it. . . . What Don Juan is trying to teach Castaneda is not the primacy of one description over another, but the possibility of different description. . . .

". . . one might say that the power of a sorcerer is the power of the feeling he can invest in his description so it is felt as a persuasive account of the world."

—The Village Voice

Twelve representative SuperFictionists give us twelve facets of the new SuperFiction, which is as richly varied as any earlier form of fiction—more, in fact, since it grants so much more power to the individual, idiosyncratic imagination:

GILBERT SORRENTINO————————a comic, exuberant sense of himself in the work, with the author creating it as it goes along, all without illusion; an emphasis upon the sentences as he writes them, not upon the projected and dramatized action of his narrative.

RONALD SUKENICK————————extending the difference between news and fiction; fiction becomes the creation of reality through an imaginative response to the world; good writing becomes the measure of a persuasive account of this separate or alternative reality.

HUNTER S. THOMPSON————————the self at the center of experience, affecting that experience, even making up the experience as a way of getting closer to the truth; creation of his own personal reality as a myth.

MICHAEL STEPHENS————————pure lyricism as fiction.

WALTER ABISH————————language as its own subject; expansion and contraction of the work by adding and subtracting letters; an exercise in human communication, about how (rather than merely what) things are said.

DONALD BARTHELME————————fun and play with his materials, the advantage not seized by the French New Novelists; constructions made of the rejected and discarded elements of our culture, in a way which makes us less alienated from them.

KURT VONNEGUT, JR.————————demonstrating the arbitrary nature of reality, and allowing a graceful way of living within it.

CLARENCE MAJOR————————that reality exists in the play of language, that stimuli such as television, films, and music influence reality as much as other experienced events; the vitality of self-creation through the artist's language.

STEVE KATZ————————improvisation, like a jazz musician, with words and situations, beyond any intellectual meaning.

ISHMAEL REED————————the Neo Hoo Doo aesthetic as the native American counterpart to the new SuperFiction; conjurism as a mode of new fiction.

JONATHAN BAUMBACH————————exploitation of literary conventions as conventions, in order to revitalize literary form.

RUSSELL BANKS————————a playful disruption of content, to make the reader astonished by a world otherwise taken for granted.

Ronald Sukenick *(to Raymond Federman);*

"Rather than serving as a mirror or redoubling on itself, fiction adds itself to the world, creating a meaningful 'reality' that did not previously exist. Fiction is artifice but not artificial. It seems as pointless to call the creative powers of the mind 'fraudulent' as it would be to call the procreative powers of the body such. What we bring into the world is per se beyond language, and at that point language is of course left behind—but it is the function of creative language to be left behind, to leave itself behind, in just that way. The word is unnecessary once it is spoken, but it has to be spoken. Meaning does not pre-exist creation, and afterward it may be superfluous."

What does fiction then become? What is left once the arbitrary conventions such as character and plot are discarded? Raymond Federman, conversing with Ronald Sukenick in the pages of *Antaeus* (Winter 1976), tells what his new fiction is all about:

The kind of surprise we want in our fiction is not in the action or in the unfolding of events towards an appropriate and predictable ending, but in the language. Every page of the new fiction must be a surprise for the reader. That reader no longer wants to know what will happen next; he wants to be surprised by the linguistic ability of the writer, by the incredible feats of the imagination that are going to pop up unexpectedly on the next page. I think language, as it is written, creates meaning.

The point of this writing is to be in the world, alive.

JEROME KLINKOWITZ, the author (b. 1943), is professor of English at the University of Northern Iowa in Cedar Falls, Iowa, where he also works nightly as a rock and jazz musician. His graduate degrees are from Marquette University and the University of Wisconsin-Madison. He is author of **Literary Disruptions,** co-author of **The Vonnegut Statement** and **Vonnegut in America,** compiler of bibliographies of Donald Barthelme and Kurt Vonnegut, Jr., and co-editor of **Innovative Fiction, Science Fiction/SuperFiction, The Diaries of Willard Motley,** and the literary journals **Fiction International** and **Seems.** His essays have appeared in the **New Republic,** the **Village Voice, Partisan Review,** and in a wide variety of scholarly journals in the United States, Europe, and Australia.

ROY R. BEHRENS, the designer (b. 1946), is visiting assistant professor of art at the University of Wisconsin-Milwaukee. He also holds an appointment in art at the University of Northern Iowa, where he is contributing design editor for the **North American Review.** A former Marine Corps sergeant, Behrens studied with Bauhaus potter Marguerite Wildenhain in California, and received his graduate degree in 1972 from the Rhode Island School of Design. His design credits include work for writers Joseph Langland and Jerzy Kosinski, and art editorship of the science humor magazine the **Worm Runner's Digest.** As a writer, he has published more than twenty-five essays on perception, humor, and art, in journals of science and art.